Mervyn
LeRoy:
Take One

MERVYN LEROY: TAKE ONE

BY

Mervyn LeRoy

As Told to Dick Kleiner

Foreword by Jack L. Warner

HAWTHORN BOOKS, INC.
PUBLISHERS/New York

MERVYN LEROY: TAKE ONE

Copyright © 1974 by Mervyn LeRoy and Dick Kleiner. Copyright under International and Pan-American Copyright Conventions. All rights reserved, including the right to reproduce this book or portions thereof in any form, except for the inclusion of brief quotations in a review. All inquiries should be addressed to Hawthorn Books, Inc., 260 Madison Avenue, New York, New York 10016. This book was manufactured in the United States of America and published simultaneously in Canada by Prentice-Hall of Canada, Limited, 1870 Birchmount Road, Scarborough, Ontario. Library of Congress Catalog Card Number: 73–370.

DESIGN BY S. S. DRATE

First printing, March 1974

Second printing, April 1974

This book is dedicated to
my parents
and to the many wonderful
friends and creators who have
helped me through the years

CONTENTS

FOREWORD

by Jack L. Warner

The trouble with becoming an elder statesman is that you're always expected to say something wise and meaningful. Let me tell you immediately that I have no intention of being either wise or meaningful!

Of all the Hollywood greats, Mervyn LeRoy and I have had the most in common. We both started in vaudeville, and, with both of us, there has been some leftover effect. There is the same kind of sense of humor, although I think his jokes are even worse than mine, and my jokes should not be left in the sun too long!

Mervyn and I go way back, and we're still friends, which must mean something. (I'm not going to guess what it means because, as I've said, I am not about to try to be meaningful.) I will say that, over the years, I guess I have seen Mervyn under every condition and he has always come through nobly. Even when I turned him down and would not let him use Clark Gable in *Little Caesar*, he did not blow up. Of course he has never let me forget that mistake, and I don't blame him. I haven't let myself forget it either.

I think that Mervyn is one of the greatest directors we have had. His abilities are very specific ones. He always had an innate talent for realism. He did not think of the *actors* but the *characters* in his pictures. Mervyn and I were never too introspective when it came to making films. We did not think of anything except trying to make a picture the public would enjoy seeing. That was always my goal, and it was Mervyn's goal, too.

His talent is nothing he has to think about. It's in the marrow of his bones. He feels things. When you are gifted with that ability, then who needs reason? The feeling is sufficient.

Maybe because of that, Mervyn has never had a flop of any consequence. He had a few that were no great Shakespeare, but never an out-and-out failure. He always had his finger on the public pulse, to coin a cliché, and that's the big thing in this business.

Another thing about Mervyn I would like to point out is his great ability—and believe me, it's essential—to get along with a cast. I often visited his sets and found everybody laughing. Mervyn would be telling some corny joke and it looked more like a club meeting than a picture set.

Besides everything else, besides his ability to do an important directorial job with a picture, he is one of the nicest people around. Maybe the word "nice" is old-fashioned. What would they say today? Cool? Groovy? Heavy? I can't keep up with the way the language is changing. I still like "nice." To me it means a person who is always decent and honest and friendly and good and kind and all that.

That's my good friend, Mervyn LeRoy. After you've read this book, I think you will agree with me about him. But I have worked with him for so many years and seen him under so many trying conditions that I think I know better than anybody. He's a great director and a nice guy.

Mervyn
LeRoy:
Take One

1

DOCTOR:

MAKE SURE THE FLAME
IS REAL LOW

An autobiography is, by definition, a man's own story of his life. It has one advantage over other forms of literature and certainly over my own art form, the cinema. That is this: There's nobody who can contradict the author.

This is my book about my life. There is no producer or film cutter or studio boss who can make me change it. For once in my creative life I am about to have the last word. When I say something in the pages that follow, that's the way it was.

I will begin by making a statement that I think sums up much of my life. I started out with two strikes against me, a long shot in any race. When I think back to the things that happened to me in my first six years on this troubled planet, I'm frightened all over again. I don't see how I survived without some sort of deep emotional trauma. It's probably because I was young and didn't know how bad it was. That's one wonderful thing about children: If they don't know any different, they assume their life is normal and average and they have no idea how dreadful it is. It is only later, when they have a basis of comparison, that they understand just how rotten or difficult or unhappy things really were.

I woke up to the truth about myself one gray morning in 1906. I had gone to bed the night before, reasonably content. Not that everything was perfect—I had no mother around, and I knew enough to realize that that was abnormal. But otherwise I was just an ordinary six-year-old boy. My thoughts, if any, were ordinary six-year-old thoughts, centering around such major issues as the tricycle I kept at my father's store, or my dislike of spinach, or my admiration for my strong and cheerful father. Before twenty-four hours had spun past, I would know such terrible tragedy that I would be forced, at that tender age, to take stock of myself and who I was.

The place was San Francisco, where my father's family and my mother's family—the Armers—had lived and worked and made love for three or four generations. The roots were deep; the love for the city strong.

The date was April 18, 1906. I was sound asleep in my bed on the second and top floor of our home at 62 Geary Street. It was a good, solid stone house, my castle and my refuge.

At exactly twelve minutes and thirty-eight seconds past five o'clock, I woke up. I know the time so precisely because it was an historic moment, not just for me but for San Francisco and the world. At that exact moment, the earth rumbled and buildings began to sway and collapse. The great San Francisco earthquake had begun.

I had been through earthquakes before; anybody who lives along the Pacific Coast must experience them. California is earthquake country. Every few months there is a little bounce and we look at each other, smile nervously, and say, "Did you feel that one?" So I knew something about earthquakes, that morning in 1906. This time, however, it was no little bounce.

The first thing I knew, as my eyes opened and my heart skipped a beat, was that I was falling. My bed was falling and I was on top of it. Instinct saved me. I clung to the brass bedpost, and I buried my head beneath my pillow as floor, rug, bed, me, everything collapsed. The noise was terrifying. People who have never been through a major earthquake don't realize that one of the most frightening aspects of the whole affair is that it is so noisy. As the earth shakes and shimmies, everything screams—the twisting boards, the crumbling bricks, the shattering mortar, even the earth itself shrieks out its protest.

I woke up to that scary symphony, to the noise, to the falling, to the combination of all that, set in the blackness of night. You can imagine how frightened I was, how frightened any six-year-old would be. Psychologists say that a child is born with some built-in fears, including the fear of falling and the fear of loud noises. Here was a situation in which both those fears were present, coupled with the sickening sensation of the ground moving.

It has been many years since that terrible morning. Fortunately, the fear is gone and with it the explicit memories of how I felt. I don't remember what I did. I suppose I called out at first, instinctively, for my mother. That would have been the normal thing for a child to do. I'm sure I burst into justifiable tears; that would have been normal, too.

Then, I like to think, reason took over. I knew there was no mother to answer my call. So I yelled, with logic, for my father. I remember he was there, in his nightshirt, calling my name, pulling away boards and stones and overturned furniture, struggling to reach me.

"Mervyn, where are you?"

"Here, Poppa. I'm over here."

He pulled the pillow from my face. "Are you all right?"

I was still crying. There was blood from some scratches on my legs where something had hit me. I took a moment to assess my condition. "I'm all right, Poppa. Are you all right?"

"Yes, thank God."

We clung together in the darkness as the aftershocks rumbled and more things fell down around us. My father gathered me in his arms and fought his way out into the street. He had to push his way past, over, around, through, between piles of debris that fifteen minutes before had been our home, but we eventually got outside. There were our neighbors, and we ran to each other as people do after a catastrophe. We compared experiences and injuries. We looked around us as the first light of dawn shed a faint glow on the awful scene. Most of the houses on the block were down. A few stood. There was no logic to it.

"I have to see how my store is," my father said.

I could understand how he felt. The store—it was called The Fair—was his life. It was the fount from which our comfort flowed, a very successful department store. My father worked there all day and generally long into the evening, six days a week. I think he loved that store. Maybe, next to me, he loved The Fair more than anything in his life.

It was cold. All we had on was what we had been sleeping in. Poppa went back into the wreckage of our house and rummaged around and found two coats—both his—and we put them on and walked the few blocks to where The Fair was located. I think this was the first time I ever saw my father cry. His beloved store was a total ruin—broken, twisted, burning, a pile of nothing.

"My God," Poppa muttered. "My God, it's gone."

I tried to hold his hand, but he pulled away from me and buried his face in both his hands. He sat down on the curb and wept, and I sat next to him, bewildered, and patted him on his broad shoulder.

It was obvious that the store was ruined, beyond repair. By the light of the flames, we could see the merchandise inside going up in smoke. The few things that couldn't burn were smashed or dented. Then I caught sight of my tricycle, my favorite possession of all. I guess that's when I realized the magnitude of the disaster. My tricycle was only some bent metal, the flames licking at its red paint, the spokes misshapen until they looked like charred spaghetti. I knew, finally, that something terrible had taken place.

At that early hour on that dreadful day, fires were sporadic. It was a hit-or-miss phenomenon. On that block, for example, The Fair was the only structure burning, and no one was doing anything about it. It was as though God had pointed a terrible finger at my father and had said, "You will suffer the most." I think I stored that strange picture in my mind because of my father's constant repetition—"My God, my God"—as he sat there on the curb and cried.

The worst was yet to come. The first shock of the great earthquake, we later learned, had been a horizontal motion. Then aftershock followed aftershock, coming from other directions, shaking the city as a cat shakes a mouse. Buildings kept falling, chimneys tumbled, walls collapsed, stately spires disintegrated and crashed to the ground.

My memory is a kaleidoscope of pictures. I have always thought mostly in visual terms and when I recall that morning of April 18, 1906, I see a mental album of tragic pictures.

The horsecar trolley tracks bulged up in the air like some surrealistic painting, silvery curves against the sky. The air was heavy with dust and smoke, gloomy as though the night were reluctant to yield to the day. All electric power had immediately gone off, so there were no lights at all. I recall the image of that dirty brownish color in the air, a kind of atmosphere that years later would be called smog.

The front walls of many of the buildings had dropped off, and you could see the insides of homes. It was almost obscene, a kind of enforced nudity that bared the secrets of buildings. We walked along, my father and I, hand in hand, and I stared in horrified fascination at the insides of houses, the wallpapers, the beds, the chairs, even the bathrooms.

At first the people gathered in groups, comparing tragedies. Then, ten or fifteen minutes later, a second reaction seemed to strike everyone at once. There was a need to protect what little you had left. People scurried back into the wreckage, pawing over rubble to find their possessions. It was a hysterical occupation, because there was no sense to what they dragged out of their shattered homes. I remember seeing a man walking along with three hats on his head, one on top of the other.

That hysteria gripped us, too. We began to run back to the house. It wasn't on fire—later, it would be swept by flames, like that whole part of the city—and my father and I began seeing what we could find. It wasn't easy. The stones that had been our home's façade seemed to be on top of whatever we wanted. They were too heavy for us to budge. I found a few nonessentials but my father had to do most of the work. He dug out clothes and photograph albums and pots and pans and all sorts of odds and ends. We piled it all on the sidewalk, and all along the street other similar piles of junk blossomed as our neighbors did what we were doing.

"Now, Mervyn," my father said, "you stay here and watch our things. I'll be back in a little while."

He was in command of himself again. The depression that had gripped him looking at the ruins of The Fair was gone. He was once again the strong, self-assured Poppa I had always known. He gave me a kiss and ran down the street. I didn't know where he was going. All I knew was that he had told me to stay there and watch our things. So I stayed.

It seemed like hours before he was back. Probably it was no more than forty-five minutes or an hour. It was a long time for a scared little boy. By then, looting had broken out. I could see them, shifty figures darting into stores and houses and coming out with lamps and silver and clothing. I could hear the sound of gunfire; martial law had been declared and looters were being shot. I edged closer to our pile of belongings, determined to defend it with my life. Fortunately, nobody tried to take any of our things.

Then he was back. My father called to me: "Mervyn!" and I looked up. He came down the street, sitting on the top of a horse-drawn wagon, clucking to the horses. He had rented the rig from a friend who had a livery stable. I ran over to him and he pulled me up beside him.

We hugged each other and then Poppa jumped down and I

followed. We piled our stuff on the wagon. It didn't take long. There wasn't much to pile. We began to move away from the house.

The fires were serious now. They had broken out, a half hour or so after the quake, in the Mission District and quickly spread. The city had always had a first-class fire department and nobody had ever worried much about fire in San Francisco. But this was not an ordinary situation, and it was worsened by the fact that the city's fire chief had been killed by a falling chimney at the moment the quake hit, and also by the rupturing of the water mains. So fire after fire was started—mostly when the gas mains broke—and there was no water to put them out. The city began to burn. Many years later, in *Quo Vadis*, I shot the burning of Rome and I drew on my memories of the burning of San Francisco as a grim model.

We were making our way, my father told me, to the Presidio, San Francisco's Army base. He had heard there was a place there for refugees, a place to sleep and food to eat. It took the better part of the day to get there. We would start down a street and find it blocked by a fire or by impassable heaps of debris—fallen houses or trees—across the road. We would have to turn the wagon around and try another route. Time after time, we had to back-track that way. It was slow and terrifying, and I got hungry and thirsty.

We stopped once, I remember, where we found a woman selling water. This was a street that seemed completely undamaged. The water mains were still in service there, and the opportunistic house-wife was peddling cups of water to the homeless who passed her door. I don't remember how much she charged, but my father treated me to a cup and it was delicious.

I remember passing along another street, completely wrecked. There was a man sitting on what had once been his front porch, and he was playing hymns on his violin and crying. I think the violin must have been the only thing he saved from the wreckage.

Because of the martial law that was in effect, there were many soldiers, fully armed, and they gave us hard looks as we drove along.

We passed Jefferson Square, another untouched area, and it was jammed with people who were already camping out on the grass. People were squabbling over choice areas. I remember seeing one man in a long white robe marching up and down and screeching, "The Lord sent it, the Lord sent it." There were tables of food set up, manned by charitable volunteers and Red Cross workers who had come out of nowhere, and we stopped and had some bread and beans, and that was delicious, too.

Finally, after an all-day odyssey, we reached the Presidio. The Army had hastily erected every tent they could find, and the place was run like a military camp. It was a good thing, too, because without that kind of organization, it would have been chaos. As we drove the wagon in, a soldier stopped us and took our names and assigned us to a tent.

We moved our things in. There was nothing but the bare tent, on the bare ground, and some kerosene lanterns. We saw people coming back to their tents carrying supplies. So my father left me to watch over our belongings again while he went looking for the things we would need. He had to stand on one line for cots and another line for blankets. He brought them back to our tent and we set up our beds. Then he went out again and stood on a third line and came back with our food for that night.

The Presidio was to be our home for six months. They came to call it Tent City. At first it was like a game. We were safe there, and that first night we fell into an exhausted sleep when the bugle signaled lamps out. It had been a long day.

By the end of the first week, it wasn't so much fun. The quake had happened on a Wednesday morning. The fires burned unchecked for three days. We could see the smoke easily from the Presidio. More and more homeless straggled in, more and more tents went up, the lines for food were longer every day.

On Sunday it rained. That helped put the fires out, but it also turned Tent City into a quagmire. By that time, we had been issued Army clothing. Of course, I was too small to fit into an Army uniform, so I continued to wear the things my father had found for me the morning of the quake. My shoes were beyond polishing, the mud caked in thick layers. Mud was everywhere and I'm sure I even ate some of it. My clothes, which I wore day after day, became torn and dirty beyond belief. It was next to impossible to wash anything; it was hard enough to wash yourself, much less your clothes.

Then, one day, word spread that a shipment of donated clothing had arrived. We lined up, as usual. (We lined up for everything.) There were new clothes and—miracle!—new shoes. I don't know where they came from, but I later found out much of the money to provide the clothing came from show-business people. I like to think that my new shoes, new trousers, and new shirt came from show folk. I learned, much later, that George M. Cohan sold newspapers on Broadway to raise money, that Sarah Bernhardt gave a benefit, that the big circus donated one night's receipts, that heavyweight champ Jim Jeffries sold oranges and handed over the proceeds to earthquake victims' relief.

Somehow, the new clothes were a turning point for me. The weather cleared, too, and dried out the mud. It was still dirty, of course, but dry dirt isn't nearly as unpleasant as wet dirt. I began to make friends, to play games, to enjoy life. Some makeshift schools were set up and I went to class in a tent. My father left me more and more to find relatives and to begin to look for a job.

The quake had wiped him out. The store was damaged beyond repair. He had insurance, but all the insurance companies went bankrupt. He had no savings to speak of; everything he made had been poured back into the business, to make The Fair bigger and bigger. That was one of the lessons the quake taught me, that you have to put something aside for an earthquaky day.

Because of his absence, I was left on my own much of the time at the Presidio. I was always outgoing, and I guess I had an appealing look—small for my age, blond hair, blue eyes, in clothing that I suppose didn't quite fit. Anyhow, I made friends among the kids and the adults. I would wander around, talking to people and listening to them talk, observing the human condition in that strange environment. It all helped me in later years, because a knowledge of people and how they behave is raw meat for a director.

There was the day I got into trouble. Tent City was run strictly by Army rules and regulations. The adults were supposed to salute the officers, just as though they were enlisted men. I don't imagine that rule applied to children, but one officer apparently decided to have some fun with me. I was running across the field and suddenly this huge man in his huge uniform reached out a huge hand and pulled me to a stop.

"Hey you," he said.

"Yes, sir."

"You didn't salute."

I didn't say anything. I didn't know what to say.

"Do you see these epaulets on my shoulders?"

I said yes, I saw them.

"Have you got any epaulets on your shoulders?"

"No, sir."

"Well, then. You'd better salute."

So I saluted. He gave me a lecture about saluting, and I saluted every epauleted shoulder I met from then on. I suppose it was a big

joke to him, but it frightened me. It was my first brush with authority.

Once in a while, my father would take me with him when he left
the camp. There were long lines everywhere in the city, which
continued to smolder for weeks and months. I was particularly
impressed by the line of people waiting to get on the ferry to escape
to Oakland, which had been barely touched by the quake. On those
trips, I noticed rats were all over. There was a virtual plague of
rats, roaming free, eating the refuse of the disaster. There were
piles of debris, gathered by volunteer workers and then shoveled
onto horse-drawn trucks and taken to the waterfront. From there,
the stuff was put on barges and taken out to sea and dumped. All
the wagons were manned by policemen. Right after the quake, the
wagon owners had begun gouging the public, charging a fortune
for rental (we had been lucky that my father rented his from an
honest friend) until the city's mayor, Eugene Schmitz, had ordered
the police to take over all the wagons.

But the best thing I noticed was that there were signs the city
was stirring back to life. Within a few weeks, new buildings started
to go up. As the skeletons of the old ones tumbled, the bones of the
new ones were set in place. There was never any thought of aban-
doning the city. San Franciscans are notoriously chauvinistic, and
the only thought on the minds of most of us was how soon we
could get back to the business of putting the city together again.

Because of that fierce loyalty, San Franciscans came to hate
Enrico Caruso after the story of what he said became public
knowledge. The great tenor was visiting the city at the time of the
quake, as part of the Metropolitan Opera Company's tour. He and
the other singers were staying at the Palace Hotel on Market Street,
where the first fire started. When the quake awakened him, Caruso
threw open his window, sang a few high notes, packed his valise,
carried it down to the middle of Market Street, and sat on it.

Later that day, he took the first train he could get and left the
city. A reporter was there to get his reaction, and he was quoted as
saying, "This is 'ell of a place. I never come back." When he
reached New York, he told reporters there that he would rather
have Vesuvius than San Francisco.

He never did return to San Francisco. But I doubt that he was
ever invited to return, either. For most of us, there came to be a
kind of pride of having been there that day, of having survived, of
having witnessed our city's agony and then its eventual triumph.
We were like a huge club, the Survivors of the Earthquake of

1906, and we resented anybody who said anything unkind about the city we loved.

The casualties weren't as high as first feared. They were high enough—the official count was 452 killed—but not anywhere near what they were expected to be. Thousands more were injured, of course, ranging from major wounds to the minor cuts and bruises that my father and I suffered.

Casualties, however, cannot be measured exclusively in terms of the dead and the injured. My father is Exhibit A.

The earthquake ruined my beloved Poppa. The Fair was a total loss. The bankruptcy of the insurance company meant that the loss was not reimbursed, not even a penny, nothing. Through the months we were at the Presidio, he was the man I had always known—strong, kind, gentle, commanding—but that was only on the surface. That was for my benefit, to keep me from going to pieces in those harsh and uncomfortable surroundings.

Underneath, however, he was a beaten man. He never could recover from the wounds the quake inflicted on his spirit and his wallet. Afterward, he went to work for the Heinz Pickle Company, driving one of their buggies and selling pickles to stores and restaurants. He made enough to keep us in food, clothing, and shelter, but it was nothing for a man of his drive and character. He had been the boss, now he was one of the many lowly employees. It hurt, and I could tell. He rarely smiled after that. As young as I was, I recognized the change. I did my best to keep him fighting, with my boyish love and enthusiasm, but my best wasn't good enough.

The quake changed many things, from the look of the city to the look of the people who lived in it. What it changed most, however, was the lives of the people themselves.

It was as though we had all been reborn. What went before meant little. For my father, the change was tragic.

For me, however, the change was a positive thing. I was born again. The little tricycle-riding boy was dead. It's possible that I would have become the man I am had there been no earthquake in San Francisco that morning, but I doubt it. The quake set off a chain of events that led, inevitably, to my present career.

My first life, the life before the earthquake of 1906, was more or less a conventional one. To explain a life, anybody's life, you must start with the family. My families—the LeRoys and the Armers— were good, solid stock. They had been in San Francisco for a couple of generations, long enough for them to subjugate their Jewish heritage in favor of San Francisco-ness. I believe that if anybody had asked them about their loyalties, they would have thought of themselves as San Franciscans first, Americans second, Jews third. They were far from the Jewish family you read about in those ethnic novels. My family was assimilated to the point of complete absorption.

Nobody spoke anything but English. They were irregular, at best, in their attendance at religious services and many of them never attended at all. Unlike the storied Jewish family, they were not particularly obsessed with education. Kids went to school, of course, but there was no pressure to go on to college or to be a doctor or a lawyer.

The nonethnic philosophy had reached the point where my mother and my aunt had had some convent education. (There was another lady in our family—a great-aunt, I believe—who had run away, left her husband, and taken up with a policeman named Clancy.)

This was the family I was born into on October 15, 1900. I was then, and forever, an only child. I did have a couple of cousins, Bernice and Edith, who were like sisters to me. Both of them had gone to a Catholic college. Then, too, I always had a talent for getting along with people, for making friends, for being gregarious and outgoing. So, despite the absence of siblings, I was never totally alone.

My arrival, that autumn morning in 1900, was a little out of the ordinary. Over the years, the story has been told and retold so often that it has become a family legend, so I cannot vouch for its authenticity. Legends have a way of becoming distorted, and this one may have been twisted a little, too. The facts, however, are probably true.

I was born on the kitchen table in the house—62 Geary Street— that was my home until the quake wrecked it. My mother was a slight woman and I was very small when I arrived on the scene. The doctor who attended my mother took one look at me and said, according to the legend, that if I was to survive, they would have to take desperate measures. I weighed only two and a half pounds.

"The best thing," the doctor is supposed to have said, "is to put him in a turkey roasting pan, put it in the oven, and keep him there. Make sure the flame is real low, however."

So I started my life in that makeshift incubator and was there for the first few days of my life. I survived, obviously. My adoring parents, grandparents, aunts, and uncles stood around the stove, peeking in the oven door to see if I was done—or alive. Maybe I was the world's first stove-incubator baby.

My mother's greatest passion was vaudeville, which was the only entertainment available in those days. She always had opening-night seats at the vaudeville theater, the Orpheum, and every week when the bill changed, she'd be there. Sometimes my father went with her. But generally she went alone—or with some other man.

She was such a constant member of the Orpheum's audience that she became good friends with the people in the San Francisco theatrical set. There was a man named Fred Butler, the director of the Alcazar, with whom she was particularly friendly. When I was about six months old—out of the oven and healthy by that time— Butler mentioned to my mother that they needed a baby for a show they were doing, *The Squaw Man.* My mother volunteered my services, so my debut was in that production. I was carried on stage as a papoose, every night for a week and two shows on Saturday. Naturally, I can remember nothing of that experience, but I like to think that I enjoyed it. Maybe it helped shape me—everything one does helps—and contributed to the fact that the only career I ever seriously considered was show business.

The business world, as represented by my father and The Fair, held no allure. For me, as a boy, it was always good fun to go to the store. The smells were particularly delicious and memorable— the smell of roasting coffee and the smell of all the fresh materials in the yard-goods section and the smell of the store itself. I enjoyed that, and enjoyed riding up and down the aisles on my tricycle. Naturally, being the boss's son, I was always treated kindly by the employees.

One day, I almost came to a tragic end at the store. As usual, I was racing down the aisles on my tricycle. Suddenly a customer was in my path and I had to swerve to avoid her. The swerving was a mistake. I crashed into a display of cut-glass bowls, and one of them came down right on top of my head. I still have a scar over one eye to remind me of the incident. Blood came pouring down my face and I was terrified. It took a few stitches to close the wound, which also served to close out whatever interest I had in the retail business world. Of such little things are careers determined and, to my young mind, "business" was always associated with being conked on the head by a cut-glass bowl. Not for me a career that encompasses a bloody skull. That was the end of my big business career.

I really had no ambition in those early years. Few children do. I lived from day to day, from sensation to sensation, from experience to experience.

When I was about five years old, I went to bed one night to the cozy pleasure of my mother's goodnight kiss. When I woke up the next morning she was gone.

My parents never told me why they separated, and I never asked. I never found out why it was my mother who had left, instead of my father. Piecing it together in my own mind, I assumed that she had gone away with another man. The other man turned out to be my stepfather, Percy Teeple, who became almost as close to me as my father, after my father's death. At the time, however, I knew nothing of this. I had never suspected anything was wrong between my mother and father. To me, secure in a home I thought was a loving one, both parents had always been there and I operated on the childish assumption that the status quo would persist eternally.

Then, that morning, there was no mother. My father tried to calm me and eventually succeeded. He didn't go to work that day, but stayed with me, talking to me and trying to make me understand that he would never leave me.

"Mervyn," he said, "we have to make it on our own now, just you and me."

"Okay, Poppa," I said, and I held his hand tight. "But where's Momma?"

"She's gone. It's just the two of us now. But you'll see your mother from time to time; in fact, very often."

That's the way it was, from then on. You could say that that was the first of my two broken homes. The other, when the earthquake hit, was a literal one. Two of them before a child has his sixth birthday is a lot to live through.

My mother wasn't gone from the face of the earth, however. We found out, shortly, that she was living in Oakland and still going with Percy Teeple. I would frequently visit them there. My father would come along on some of those visits. Curiously, they remained good friends after that, and my father and Teeple got along well, too. Teeple had been a San Francisco newspaperman, but then he had gone into the travel business. He would go all over, selling hotel reservations, and my mother always went with him. They would be gone for months, or so it seemed to me. I missed them when they were away, because I gradually came to spend a lot of time with them in Oakland.

I adored both of my parents. I would, like the offspring of

divorced parents usually do, plead with them to come back together again. They would just smile and shake their heads and say it was impossible. I guess they had just concluded that they simply couldn't live together, although I cannot remember them ever fighting or yelling at each other before the separation. I had never heard the word then, but I imagine it was simply a case of incompatibility. Later, I would understand exactly what that meant, in my own first marriage.

That's why it was just my father and I who faced the earthquake that morning in 1906. And, after our six months at the Presidio, it was still just Poppa and me. My mother existed for me, but she was someone to visit, like other children go to see their grandparents or a favorite aunt.

Life went on, after the quake. It was, however, an entirely different kind of life. We had never been rich, but we were always comfortable. Now, however, we had to scrounge. Selling pickles was not a very rewarding career, unless you were Mr. Heinz himself. My Poppa was just another salesman and, it developed, not a particularly successful one.

He still went through the motions of his existence. He had always been a great horse race enthusiast and before the quake had been the president of the Emeryville track, the forerunner of Golden Gate Fields. His greatest triumph as a horseman came one day when the usual San Francisco fog was at its thickest. He owned a horse called Salinas, named after the Bay Area town. Salinas was a good horse, but far from great. He had his moment in the sun—or fog—however.

Poppa's trainer had a hand in the proceedings. He saw how the fog had shrouded the track, particularly the backstretch. He told the jockey not to take Salinas to the starting web (this, of course, was long before the automatic starting gate had been invented) but, instead, take him to the half-mile pole. In all that fog, nobody could see him there.

"Listen for the sound of the webbing going up," the trainer said. "When you hear the pack coming, turn Salinas loose and go like hell."

The other horses came around and the jock turned Salinas loose and he went like hell—winning by twenty lengths and setting a record that solemnly went into the record books and stood for many years.

Poppa was completely innocent of the whole sneaky business but he enjoyed the story. For years afterward, he would tell it with great relish.

He used to love to get together with his friends, have a few drinks, tell a few stories. He was always a happy-go-lucky sort of man and, for all I know, a woman-chaser. That all changed with the quake. There was little enough money for food, let alone having a wild time. My father kept up his interest in racehorses, but it was purely from the sidelines. He had no more horses of his own, and rarely, if ever, placed a bet.

I prefer to remember him as he was before the quake. That was a man! Even after my mother left—perhaps more so after she left—he was what a father should be. He loved me very much and, as far as I can remember, never gave me any more punishment than a harsh word. Yet I was always a good, obedient child, and I think that I was a happy child, despite the peculiarity of my parental situation.

There were hints, I suppose, of what I was to become. The interest in vaudeville was always there, due mostly to my mother's fascination with it. I used to do a lot of playacting, in common with most only children, using imaginary playmates in make-up games. There were also two older cousins, Jesse and Blanche Lasky, who were vaudevillians, and that helped kindle my interest in show business.

Until the quake, however, all I was doing was growing up. It was a strange life, I suppose, but what do six-year-olds know?

2

THEODORE ROBERTS:

HOW WOULD YOU
LIKE TO BE
AN ACTOR?

We are all products of many things. Genetically, I inherited a love of show business from my mother and an outgoing personality from my father. Environmentally, the big thing in my life was the earthquake. Had it not been for that, had my father continued at The Fair, I might have grown up and gone into business with him or into some other business venture (despite my collision with the crystal). I would probably have had some outlet for my love of show business, maybe acting in amateur theatricals or, if I made a lot of money, becoming an angel for Broadway plays.

The earthquake changed my path of life before I even knew I had one. Although my father and I always had enough to eat, there was never an extra dime around the house. And there were things I wanted, like every small boy. I can't remember exactly what those things were anymore, but I would guess that they were such items as a new tricycle, or candy bars, or ice cream.

So I decided to earn the money myself. I was twelve or thirteen when I became a newsboy. Selling papers may seem like an unlikely first step in becoming a motion picture director, but a chain of events was set in motion that day when I first peddled the San Francisco papers.

My father actually seemed to approve of the big step I had taken. "Earning your own living is a good thing," he said. "I think everybody should make his own way in this world."

Education didn't mean much to him. I think he admired educated people, but somehow felt that it was too remote and too unattainable for people like him or his family. He had never had much education himself, and it didn't seem to hold him back in any way. I think he would have backed me to the hilt had I come to him and said I wanted to go on to high school and college. But he backed me just as strongly when I didn't.

He really didn't care much about anything anymore. He was a beaten man. He went through the motions of living, but without the flair, without the zest, that had always characterized him before the earthquake. For a while, he took up with a woman—her name was Briley—and she lived with us for a few months, but then she died. Maybe, had she lived, she could have given him back his *joie de vivre*. I tried, but without much success. I kept after him to go out again, to go to the racetrack or the vaudeville shows, anywhere. No, he said, he'd rather stay home. I could see him waste away before my eyes.

When I had had a good day selling papers, I'd take him out for dinner. He had a favorite restaurant, the Black Cat, where you could get a good French dinner, complete with wine, for thirty-five cents. I tried to make those occasions joyous, but it wasn't easy. He sat there, saying little, and my juvenile attempts at festivity were largely futile.

One summer, he sent me away for a couple of weeks to visit some friends who had a place in the country. I was ten—I know that because I still have a couple of postcards I wrote to my father from the country. It was my first taste of things rural, and it would be my last for many years. Judging by the postcards, which my father saved and I eventually found among his things, I had a pretty good time, but I can read between the lines and detect a sense of homesickness. I wrote on July 16, 1910:

Dear Poppa,

    Why don't you write to me? I am feeling fine and having a good time. Everybody feels great. Last night I went horseback riding. It's fun.

                        Your loving son, Mervyn

Then, six days later, I sent this enthusiastic card:

My Dear Poppa,

I got your card. I tell you it is simply fine up here. I went to Auburn twice. I drink milk to get fat, go down to the station every day to get mail. Write soon.

Your son, Mervyn

That was the extent of my countryside experience. I came back to Oakland and San Francisco and, a couple of years later, I was scrapping for my living on the city streets. In those days, newsboys had to battle it out for choice corners. You fought your way up the pecking order and the better you were with your fists, the more advantageous corner you'd get. I wasn't big but I was, as they say, wiry. I sold papers all over, but I was aiming for the corner in front of the Saint Francis Hotel.

I started out, as I remember, at the Key Route Inn, in Oakland. This was where the trains came in, and there was an arcade lined with shops. I did pretty well there, but it wasn't what I really wanted.

I fought my way to a corner in Chinatown. The Chinese restaurant owners were good to me, and would let me come in for a meal once in a while. They taught me to use chopsticks, and I can handle them as well as a knife and fork. I loved Oriental things then, and the love has lingered. One of my great passions—fortunately shared by my wife—is Oriental art, and I'm able to indulge that passion. It dates back, I believe, to my days as a newsboy in Chinatown.

For a while, I sold my papers on the Barbary Coast. It wasn't as tough in my day as it once had been, but it was still pretty rugged. That was part of my education, too, learning the facts of life in an area where they were virtually on the surface. I became a pet of the Barbary Coast prostitutes. I knew them by their first names, and I knew their pimps and customers, too. They would buy papers from me before, after, and sometimes during their business arrangements.

One night a streetwalker gave me some advice that I found exciting then and still think was pretty valuable.

"Mervyn," she said to me, "never chase a girl—it's only good when a girl wants you."

I always remembered that. Later on, when I was in a position to take advantage of girls, as a director and producer, that advice came back to me and I took it. It was sensible.

I sold papers on Fisherman's Wharf, and that, too, was part of my education.

It all helped. A newsboy, if he has his eyes open and his brain working, can see life and that can be better than a college education. Over the years, I often wished I had gone on to a formal education, but I did what I could without it. In some ways, I think, I was better off. College gives youngsters their education on a silver textbook; it's all too easy. When you must teach yourself, everything you learn becomes a treasure you have mined personally, a goal to reach, and, consequently, you value it more highly. I have never stopped reading and learning. I am not a galloping intellectual, but I am able to discuss almost any subject with some knowledge.

Then, too, I have something that sheltered, college-trained kids never have. I saw life in the raw on the streets of San Francisco. I met the cops and the whores and the reporters and the bartenders and the Chinese and the fishermen and the shopkeepers. I knew them all, knew how they thought and how they loved and how they hated. When it came time for me to make motion pictures, I made movies that were real, because I knew at first hand how real people behaved.

Every move I made, in my newsboy career, was directed at one goal—to have the lucrative corner at the Saint Francis Hotel in the morning, and the exciting corner in front of the Alcazar Theater in the evening.

The first was self-explanatory. I wanted to make some money, to help my poor, pickle-peddling Poppa.

My desire to get the Alcazar corner was not as easy to explain. I'm not sure I even understand it myself. I had no plans for my future. It was a day-to-day life, exclusively. My ambition was limited to small things—a good meal, a little fun, a new pair of shoes, and a warm coat for winter. I played games, like every boy does, and perhaps some of those could be interpreted as portents of my future. At ten or so, I made believe I was shooting a movie—Jules Verne's *Twenty Thousand Leagues Under the Sea*. That project occupied my friends and me for many cheerful weeks. But everything in those early days played second to my chief occupation— selling papers.

Yet, always, I found myself drawn to the Alcazar Theater corner, as though some mighty magnet was pulling me. The Alcazar then was the showplace of San Francisco. All the great touring companies played there. The finest actors in America came to the

Alcazar in the biggest contemporary hits and in the classics. I would save for months to get the price of a ticket so I could see the shows. My appetite was insatiable; I didn't care what was playing, nor did I care whether or not I understood the production. All I knew was that I was fascinated by live actors, speaking beautiful words beautifully. I sat there, not moving a muscle, while the play unfolded.

I recognized all the actors and the glorious actresses. They were my heroes, my heroines. The Alcazar stage door became, for me, the doorway to heaven. I had to get that corner for my own.

Eventually, I did get it. Unknowingly, I had taken the next giant step on my accidental route to Hollywood. Trace anyone's life back and you will find a train of accidents, lucky breaks, coincidences. Of course, a person must be able to capitalize on those breaks when they happen, but without those fortunate events there would be no career. Thus it was with me. Without the earthquake, and my father's ruined career, I would not have become a newsboy. That was the first step for me. The second came one evening as I hawked my papers in front of the Alcazar Theater.

I was, I think, fourteen at the time. I was still small for my age. (Even today, I'm small for my age, but then it was more noticeable.) I had been on the corner a few weeks and had gotten to know some of the actors. Among them was the handsome Theodore Roberts, who would later become one of the first silent movie stars.

That evening, he came walking down the street, heading for the stage door.

"Good evening, Mr. Roberts," I said, as he gave me three cents for the paper.

He smiled at me and took the paper and started away, casually glancing at the headlines. Then he turned back to me, almost as an afterthought.

"How would you like to be an actor, young fellow?" he said.

"Me?"

"Yes, you. I'm rehearsing a new play, and there's a part in it for a newsboy."

"I'm a newsboy, but I'm no actor."

"Well, all you'd have to do is be yourself. All you'd have to do is stand there and sell papers, just like you do every day. You know, it might be a good idea to have a real newsboy playing that part."

For a moment or two, I thought he was kidding. Then I could tell he meant it. When he even told me what time I should show up for the rehearsal, I knew he was serious. I jumped at the chance.

When I appeared backstage at the scheduled time, I discovered that it wasn't really a newsboy's part at all. Oh, I had newspapers under my arm, but I didn't have to appear to be selling them. The play was *Barbara Frietchie*, by Clyde Fitch, and it was a Civil War drama, set in the South. I had one line, four words, and I rehearsed them and rehearsed them like no four-word speech has been rehearsed before or since.

I was supposed to be up in a prop tree and hollering down, "The Yankees are coming!"

If I do say so myself, I said that line with fervor. People in the last row of the balcony knew that the Yankees were coming. There was no doubt in anybody's mind. Then came my first experience with the disaster called overconfidence. I think it was the third or fourth night, and by then I was secure in my role. I hadn't even bothered to rehearse that day. Mistake number one.

Casually, carelessly, with what I thought was professional nonchalance, I shinnied up to my position in the tree. And when it came time to deliver my line—I fell out of the tree.

Naturally, everybody laughed. Even the cast laughed, and I could feel myself turning beet red. I ran off the stage and was sneaking out the stage door, convinced that my acting career was at a merciful end, when the stage manager grabbed me.

"Hey, kid," he said, "that was a funny bit. If you can take that fall every night, I'll raise your salary."

I had been hired for three dollars and fifty cents a week. A raise sounded exquisite.

"How much?" I asked, wiping away the last traces of the bloody nose I'd gotten in the tumble.

"Five bucks," he said. "How does that strike you?"

It struck me as great. So I agreed to do it, and for the next few weeks—plays at the Alcazar never ran very long—I fell out of that tree at every performance. I found that the bruises didn't hurt as much as the laughter soothed. I had fallen for the siren song of audience approval. It wasn't much, but it was a beginning.

When *Barbara Frietchie* closed, I went back to selling papers. But the stage bug had bitten, and the itch would never leave me. I cast about for other ways of basking in that warm glow that emanates from an appreciative audience.

Another coincidence gave me my next impetus. One day, roaming about the city, I was walking along when I noticed a car.

Automobiles were still rare enough to be objects of curiosity, so I watched. Even for an auto, this one was behaving strangely. It was full of men and strange pieces of equipment. It drove along slowly and the men seemed to be looking for something.

Then it stopped. The men jumped out. The equipment, I quickly figured out, was a camera on a tripod. Then it dawned on me—they were shooting one of those newfangled things, moving pictures. I had seen a few of them and I had liked them—not as much as vaudeville or plays, of course, but they were fun—so I was intrigued and I watched.

Then I recognized the actor. He was Charlie Chaplin—no mistaking the baggy pants, the moustache, the derby, the cane. He ran up the stoop of a house. The camera was at the bottom of the stoop, on the sidewalk. The director yelled something—I'm not even sure if it was "Action!" or not—and Charlie went into his tramp character. He started down the stoop, stumbled, and fell.

That was all. They piled back into the car, actors and director, camera and tripod, and drove away. Later, I learned that was Chaplin's technique in those old, penny-watching days. He'd "steal" shots because he couldn't afford to build sets or rent places to film in.

I began looking for him, and several times I lucked out, and would watch Charlie Chaplin at work. He fascinated me. I began working up an imitation of him. At first, I did it at home, in front of a mirror. Then I built a make-believe camera out of some old broomsticks and a tin can, and I'd con some friends into playing the movie game with me. They would be the director and the cameraman, and I'd be Charlie Chaplin. We would go out and I'd do all the things I'd seen Charlie do, beginning with that first stunt —falling down a stoop. I got to be pretty good at it, too. At least my friends and my family told me I was, and I came to believe it. Somewhere, I acquired the props—the pants, the cane, the derby hat—and I painted a moustache on my upper lip, which was not yet glandularly equipped to grow one of its own.

I still sold papers, but my heart and my mind were more and more in show business. In those days, amateur contests at local theaters were a big thing. Usually, they were scheduled for Sunday afternoons, as a lure to get bigger crowds. The theater owners knew that if they held an amateur contest, all the young entrants would show up with their private claques—friends and relatives. For me, it was a chance to get more of that lovely feeling—audience approval.

So I put an act together. I called myself The Singing Newsboy. My big song: "'Twas Only an Irishman's Dream." I'd heard it somewhere and I liked it and I thought I could sing it beautifully. The only thing my act lacked was the proper Irish costume.

My grandmother came to my rescue. She found an old pool table somewhere and took the green felt top off it. From that, she fashioned an outfit that looked, to us, like what every Irishman wore. In reality, it was just a green suit, but it was enough. She also found a shillelagh in some store, and that rounded out the costume.

I began entering every amateur contest I could find, dressing up in my pool-tabletop green suit and singing "'Twas Only an Irishman's Dream." I won my share of prizes, too—a second prize (usually three dollars) here and a first prize (five dollars) there. It all helped, because money was important to my father and me.

He was working less and less frequently. I watched as his decline deepened, and then came the day, inevitably, I suppose, when he was bedridden. It didn't last long. I don't know what the doctor wrote down on the death certificate, but to me there was only one possible cause of death: broken heart.

My beloved father was dead. I was fifteen.

I went over to Oakland, then, to live with my mother and Percy, my stepfather. For a while, I went back to school. The only thing that interested me, however, was show business, and the only part of school I enjoyed was the band. I didn't know how to play an instrument, but I lied and told them I was a drummer. They needed a drummer, so they took me. I ad-libbed the drums, as I later found I could ad-lib a lot of things.

Oakland and the Grant School band and my stay with my mother and Percy were temporary. I was too restless to get on with what I now knew was my career. Children who know what they want to do with their lives are always that way—nothing can persuade them to deviate from that goal. I feel sorry for many of today's youths who have no specific dreams, no pot of gold to reach out for and pursue. I was positive that somewhere in the world of show business there was a place for me. I didn't know what that place was, but I knew I had to find it.

So it was back to the streets, to selling newspapers, to the amateur shows. I kept looking, constantly, for something else to do, for other outlets for my restless drive.

I found one outlet in a theater called Ye Liberty Theater in Oakland. It was a small company, professional yet not big time. I tried out and got a part, and then became a semiregular. They did

plays with titles like *Mary Jane's Pa*, items from the current reper-
toire. And they did classics, such as *Tom Sawyer* and *Little Lord
Fauntleroy*. I played all the boy leads—I was Tom Sawyer and I
was Little Lord Fauntleroy.

Once they did a play called *The Midnight Bell*. That was important in my progress, too, because it raised, for the first time, the
issue of sex. There was a girl in the cast—I can't remember her
name and only have a vague memory of what she looked like—but
I came down with a virulent case of The Crush. I had noticed girls
before, but only in a cursory sort of way. Naturally, I had no
experience, so I just looked and stared and daydreamed and night-
dreamed, too. That girl in *The Midnight Bell* was different. She
was attainable and I could tell, from the way our eyes met so often,
that she liked me. I didn't do anything about it—I had no time for
a personal life, I worked too hard, what with selling papers and
doing the play, too—but I filed that away in my mind. It was a
delicious lesson, to learn that the other sex existed and, what's
more, that a member of that soft sex found me worth looking at.

The next serious crush I had—I guess she would have to be
called my first love—was with a girl named Donna Gray. She was a
chorus girl with a company that played in Oakland, called Dillon
and King. They had their own theater in Oakland and did little
musicals. I thought she was maybe the most beautiful girl I had
ever seen and I tried hard to make a date with her. But I was only a
kid and she was a chorus girl, so nothing ever came of it. That, too,
was a valuable lesson—unrequited love is every bit as instructional
as the requited kind. As proof, I submit the fact that I still remember her name, yet I have long since forgotten the names of girls
who did go out with me.

When there wasn't a part for me in the plays at Ye Liberty
Theater, I'd head for the amateur show circuit. Between all of that
and my newspaper business, I kept busy. I really never had the teen-
age life most kids have, but I don't remember being unhappy or
feeling sorry for myself. Show business—the plays and the amateur
shows—was my hobby. Selling newspapers was my education. It
was a full and rounded life.

And there were friends, many friends. San Francisco and Oakland, at that time, were both full of young hopefuls who would
later make names for themselves in show business. It seems as
though all my life I knew Al Jolson. His father had a tailor shop in
Oakland. There were two boys in the family—Harry and Al. Harry
was the one with talent, a singer with a big, expressive voice. He

would often sing at the Bell Theater in Oakland, and I tried to catch his act as often as I could. I was a singer of sorts at the time, too, but I knew I could never equal Harry Jolson. He could entrance an audience, make them happy or sad, just with the emotional way he sang.

When Harry Jolson left Oakland, he and his brother Al decided, for reasons I never did find out, to switch their names. Harry, the singer, became Al Jolson and it was as Al Jolson that he became one of the greatest stars this nation has produced. He remained a friend until he died, and so did his brother Al, or Harry.

Then there was Lou Holtz. Lou and I had something in common. We both stuttered. I imagine it was the earthquake that brought about my stutter. It wasn't a serious thing, but it was occasionally embarrassing. Holtz stuttered, too. The two of us, both ambitious for a show-business career, worked to overcome our speech impediments. We tried talking slowly, talking fast, singing, talking with pebbles in our mouths, everything we could think of or that we had heard about as a possible cure.

We had one gimmick between us. Often, we would get on the telephone and talk to each other. Our reasoning was that the more we talked, maybe the less we would stutter. We had heard that somewhere. So we would call each other and talk for hours. If one of us got the stutters so badly that he couldn't talk anymore, he would knock on the phone with his knuckles. That was a signal to the other one: Hang up, I'll call back when I can speak again.

He conquered his stutter and went on to become one of our greatest dialect comedians. I conquered mine, too. I never did stutter when I sang and very rarely when I was performing on stage. It was only a private problem and it seems now, in retrospect, that it was easy to overcome. But even today, if I am excited or nervous, the stutter comes back.

Another friend at the time was my cousin, Jesse Lasky, and his sister, Blanche. They were the stars of the family. Older than I was, they had been bitten by the show-business bug first and had gone into vaudeville. They had a unique act—they played trumpets, wearing stylized uniforms and marching around the stage. I imagine today people would laugh at them, but there were all kinds of odd acts in vaudeville. I think that the fact that my two cousins were making a go of it helped encourage me to believe that maybe there was a place for me in that glittering world. I kept working.

For a while, in amateur shows, I billed myself as "Mervyn LeRoy, the Boy Tenor of the Generation."

This might be a good time to explain my name, only I can't explain it. I never did find out how or where my parents got the name "Mervyn." Once I asked my mother about it, and she gave me the unsatisfying explanation: "That's simple. Your grandfather's name was Morris."

So it was "Mervyn LeRoy, the Boy Tenor of the Generation" who went around and sang wherever and whenever he could. More and more, there were places to work. San Francisco was booming before World War I. It seems like there were theaters everywhere. There were the curious new nickelodeons and the old established vaudeville palaces and legitimate theaters. They ranged in size from the immense to the very small, and one of the latter group was a source of good fun to me.

It was called Zabelsky's Novelty Theater, and it was run by a little old man named Jake Zabelsky. If Jake Zabelsky were living today, I think he'd be a big man in public relations. He was ahead of his time.

There were still horsecars in those days, and Zabelsky would ride the horsecars. Every few blocks, he'd yell at the driver, in his thick Jewish accent, "Hey, driver, let me know when we get to Zabelsky's Novelty Theater—I hear there's a great show there this week."

During the show at his theater, it was a very common sight to see Jake Zabelsky running up and down the aisles, talking to the customers: "Isn't this a fine show? Be sure to tell all your friends to come down and see it."

I often went to Zabelsky's Novelty Theater, and to all the other theaters in town. The vaudeville houses were important to me as a would-be vaudevillian; I wanted to study all the acts. The plays were important, too; I was absorbing subconsciously much about dramatic construction. And the nickelodeons were vital; I was seeing every moving picture I could, because the new entertainment medium fascinated me. Besides, I was still doing my Chaplin imitation, and I wanted every chance I could get to watch Charlie in action so I could perfect my act.

At the time, my ambition was a modest one. I wasn't looking beyond vaudeville. That was my goal. And yet, all the time I worked in plays, I found myself more intrigued with the production and direction of the plays than I was with performing in them. Very often, I would watch as the director put the play together, and thoughts about how to improve it would come to me. I was still only a teen-ager, so I knew my place was to keep my mouth shut and do what the director told me to do. Still, there were times when I had to force myself to keep from shouting out some bright idea I felt would improve the play. Maybe, in some deep corner of my mind, I was even then planning on becoming a director.

I lived from day to day, from play to play, from amateur show to amateur show. Then came my next big step, although at the time it seemed like just another chance to trot out my Chaplin imitation.

There was an announcement that there would be a contest at the Pantages Theater on Market Street for the best Charlie Chaplin imitation. This was in 1915, and Chaplin was the biggest thing around. So a huge crowd of men and boys in baggy pants, derbies, canes, and moustaches showed up at the Pantages on the day of the contest—close to a thousand of them.

When it was all over, I had won. The prize was ten dollars and, more important, a little silver cup. I still have that cup today, and it stands next to my Oscar.

From the standpoint of my career, the ten dollars and the cup were not nearly as important as the fact that Sid Grauman was in the audience. Afterward, Grauman approached me with a proposition. He was going to have a show at the Pan-Pacific International Exposition, the big world's fair that would open that winter. He offered me a job, doing my Chaplin imitation in front of his show, which was to be called "Chinatown by Night." It struck me strange then, as it does now, that he'd want a Chaplin character in front of a Chinatown show, but I wasn't about to discuss the pros and cons of that. I took the job.

I became part of the exposition, which was the greatest thing to hit the West Coast up to that time. It was proof to the world that San Francisco had come back from disaster and was once again a booming, bustling, healthy city. The exposition was a great success and it was thrilling for a teen-ager to be part of it, with its lofty Tower of Jewels, with the first public exhibition of trick fliers cavorting across the sky, with our own very successful show, "Chinatown by Night." All that year—the exposition ran from February 20 to December 4—I put on my Chaplin outfit every night and paraded up and down. I got ten dollars a week for being the out-front ballyhoo for the inside show.

This was a major step for me, because it meant that I gave up being a newspaper boy. It was with some regret that I said I was quitting, since I had enjoyed peddling papers. Even today, I look back on that experience with pride. Not too many years ago, I was asked by our State Department to entertain King Baudouin of Belgium at my home in Bel Air. When I stood up to speak, I said, "Your Majesty, it's so wonderful to have you here. Little did I think when I sold papers on the streets of San Francisco, that someday I'd have a home fit for a king."

Nowadays, when I go back to San Francisco to visit my cousins, I often go down to the corner in front of the Saint Francis Hotel, where I used to sell papers. There is a man there these days, an elderly man doing what I did as a boy almost sixty years ago. And I'll buy all his papers, his entire stock. He never asks me why, nor do I tell him.

Another stop for me is the cemetery in Oakland where my father is buried. It has been nearly sixty years since he passed away and, of course, he never saw any of the things I did. When he died, I was a newsboy and an occasional performer. I would like to believe that he knows, somehow, that I have made a reasonable success of my life. I am not much of a believer in mysticism and spiritualism, however. So I tell my father, as I stand by his grave, that I made it. I tell him that things worked out pretty well for me. I tell him that the same earthquake that ruined his life started me on my way.

He can't hear me. I guess I'm talking to myself as much or more than I'm talking to him. I'd like him to know, however, that I've never forgotten him. When I needed him, he was there. I believe, too, that I helped him during his last, troubled years.

Poppa didn't even live to see me in vaudeville. He knew that was my goal, but he died before I met Clyde Cooper. It was after the Pan-Pacific Exposition closed that Cooper and I got together. This was to be the next accident that led me to where I am today. We were both on a bill at an amateur show. I sang and Cooper played the piano. Afterward, we talked. We discovered that we were the same age—both sixteen—and had the same dream—vaudeville. I don't remember which one of us suggested that we team up, but the idea struck us both as sensible.

The team of LeRoy and Cooper was born that night.

Suddenly, without really making a conscious decision about it, I was a show-business professional.

Clyde Cooper and I threw ourselves into our new routine with everything we had. We gave ourselves a name—"LeRoy and Cooper, Two Kids and a Piano." We wrote ourselves an act—an opening song, "Hello, Everybody" (which we composed ourselves) and a string of standards and comedy numbers we knew. We designed costumes—little English Eton suits with big collars.

Clyde Cooper came from Hayward, California, where his father ran a hotel. At the time we met, he was going to a military academy but, like mine, his dream was show business. It didn't take much persuasion for him to give up the strict discipline of the military academy for the cheerful, nondisciplined life of vaudeville. Nor did it take much for me to give up my own life, which was pretty haphazard after the exposition closed. This was what I had been wanting.

We broke in our act in little places around Northern California. We played anywhere we could get booked—theaters, bars, wherever. We would have played toilets if they had offered us some money. We played in San Francisco, Oakland, San Jose, Fresno. Clyde played the piano and the two of us would sing.

"Hello, Everybody" was our opener. Then I'd sing a song called "Cohen Owes Me Ninety-seven Dollars" in dialect. Then we would do a bunch of songs, things like "Are You from Dixie?" and "The Missouri Waltz." In between songs, we told alleged jokes, and hoped that somebody would laugh.

Pretty soon, we made it to one of the vaudeville circuits that controlled California show business in those days. It was the Ackerman and Harris Circuit, which booked acts throughout the northern part of the state. We were playing at the Wigwam Theater in Oakland when the manager—I remember his name was Cluxton—came backstage and told us that a man from Ackerman and Harris wanted to see us. We looked at each other. This was it! The big time! We had been discovered!

It meant more regular bookings, and it meant that we didn't have to try to find our own engagements. We were on a bill that toured around, and we had our route for three or four weeks ahead of time.

Then we got bigger, or better, and they began sending us out of state. Our first non-California booking was in Butte, Montana, and after that we played all over the country. We toured for months at a time, living out of our suitcases, seeing nothing but the inside of the theater, a run-down rooming house, and a train.

I still have some souvenirs from those days, reminders of that frantic, frenetic life.

There is a contract for LeRoy and Cooper to play the Regent Theater in Bay City, Michigan—four days, $128.60.

There is a vaudeville route sheet, for a monthlong tour of Montana, Wyoming, and Canada. It lists theaters like The Theatorium in Red Lodge, Montana. The bill consisted of LeRoy and Cooper,

Honeysuckle and Violet (they were an Australian comedy team), Frances Fay (I remember she was a big, fat singer and all she ate were heads of lettuce), and Barth and Barth (an acrobatic act).

There is a postcard. I had them printed up to hand out to my fans (even small-time acts had fans in those days). It shows me in white trousers, a black jacket with a white handkerchief stuck jauntily in the pocket. There is a printed signature, which, at the time, I thought was quite snappy. It says, "Yours vaudevillingly, Mervyn LeRoy."

There is another contract, in which the team of LeRoy and Cooper agree to present their "singing, talking, piano" act at the Mikadow Theater in Manitowoc, Wisconsin—for one night, for seventy dollars. We signed it and so did the owner of the theater, Mrs. Frances Kadow.

We played together, Clyde and I, for more than three years. At the time, I think I considered us a damn good act. In retrospect, I guess we were fair. We had dreams, as all vaudevillians had, of playing the Palace in New York, and those dreams sustained us, but we never made it. We did all right, and I think we kept working steadily for most of those three years plus, but I doubt that we would have ever made the really big time. We did get to play the Pantages Circuit, so we couldn't have been too bad.

We kept trying for that greatest of spots on the bill, next to closing. I still have a letter that shows how we tried and how we complained and how we didn't make it.

The letter is addressed to LeRoy and Cooper, in care of the Park Theater in Brainerd, Minnesota. It is on the letterhead of the Gus Sun Booking Exchange, and it is signed by a Mr. Paul Goudron, the Chicago representative of that organization.

> Dear LeRoy and Cooper:
> Now when I arranged that bill you were on, I had you next to closing and at the last minute the opening act, which was a single, cancelled on me and the single I got to replace I had to put on in your place and put you on opening, but what's the difference, nobody will see you in those small towns anyway.
> Yours very truly,
> Paul Goudron

I don't remember if Clyde and I swallowed that somewhat fishy story or not. Probably not. Probably we wrote Mr. Goudron a nasty letter, saying that we deserved the next-to-closing spot and if we didn't get it on our next bill, we would quit and go somewhere else. We did make next-to-closing a few times and the man was right—in the small towns we generally played, it really didn't make much difference.

The important thing was that we were having a wonderful time. I doubt that there could have been a more exciting existence for a teen-ager. Every day was an adventure, every night an experience.

We would travel by train, arriving generally just in time to rent a room, then go down to the theater and rehearse. It wasn't that we needed to practice our act—that rarely changed, except once in a while we'd put in one lousy joke in place of another lousy joke—but Clyde had to check out the local piano. It never failed to amaze us how so many of the theater pianos were clunky and out-of-tune. Sometimes there would be an orchestra, in the bigger places we played. That meant we'd have to rehearse with them, too. They were usually worse than the pianos.

We'd hang around the theater until show time. We'd do our act, or do it twice if there were two shows that night, and then we'd be free. Usually we would get something to eat at the greasy spoon— there was almost always a greasy spoon around the corner from the theater. If I had a little money, I'd take a girl out, usually a girl who was on the bill. If I did have a date, we'd go to the best place in town. I'd check with the old man at the stage door and ask him for the best place, and we'd head there for a good dinner. Many times, that was the same greasy spoon that was around the corner from the theater.

I was young and single, so why not have fun? I had no responsibilities, except to myself and my approaching manhood. There was no family to support, no needy relatives to send money home to, no goal to save for. So the money came and the money went.

If it didn't go on girls and dinner, it went on clothes. Clyde saved his money; he was that kind of person. But I'd go out and buy the best, most expensive overcoat I could find. We'd need a warm coat, playing Wisconsin and Minnesota and Montana in the winter. But Clyde always tried to make last year's coat hang on for another season. Not me. A new coat each year. New shoes when I wanted them. The best suits and shirts and ties.

It's funny, though, how I economized in other ways. Somehow, I never could see spending money on keeping my good clothes cleaned and pressed. I did it myself. I'd get to my room, in whatever flea bag we found ourselves, and stick my trousers under the mattress. That was a good (cheap) way of pressing them. I'd do my laundry in the bathroom sink, and stick the handkerchiefs on the windowpane to dry.

We generally had a room to ourselves, but once in a while Clyde and I would economize with a double room. If we had a few days in a city, we'd sleep late in the morning. If not, it would be up at the crack of dawn to catch the train to our next stop. When we had some time in a city, particularly a big city, we'd go around to the offices of the music publishers and listen to the new songs. Once in a while, we'd add one of these to our act.

Some of these publishers were very anxious to get us—to get any vaudevillian—to do their songs. They would indulge in a kind of primitive payola to convince us to do them. Once, I remember, one particularly hopeful publisher gave us a new wardrobe trunk if we'd perform his number. At the time, we needed a new wardrobe trunk. I didn't feel corrupted in any way when I sang the song, and it was nice to have a brand-new wardrobe trunk for my nice clothes.

Through those years in vaudeville, Clyde and I met a lot of the all-time greats of the business. Once, when we were on the big time, the Orpheum Circuit, we appeared on the same bill with the great Sarah Bernhardt. We were just kids, so we didn't know who she was, only that she was supposed to be something very special. We watched from the wings as she gave her recitation and, I must confess, I wasn't too impressed by it. It was, I thought, overdone. Even then, I was beginning to be selective and I never did like actors who were overemotional in their performances.

Another time, we were playing in Texas. I think it was San Antonio. The famous magician, Houdini, was on the bill with us. Some years later, I would be the second cameraman on the first movie he ever made, but neither of us had any thought of movies that week in San Antonio.

The climax of his act, which I thought was very exciting, came with a patriotic flourish. After he'd done all his big tricks and illusions, he'd walk down to the front of the stage, break a candle in half, and produce an American flag. Everybody would stand up and cheer and he'd march off to big applause, as the band played a rousing chorus of "The Stars and Stripes Forever."

Around the third day of our week in Texas, I had an idea for a joke we'd pull on Houdini. That was one way we livened up the day-to-day routine that was vaudeville—we'd pull practical jokes on any likely-looking victim. When Houdini wasn't around, Clyde and I sneaked into his dressing room, found his prop candle, and removed the American flag.

That night, he did his act and everything worked to perfection. Clyde and I were watching from the wings, and we couldn't wait for the finish. Right on schedule, he did his last stunt. Then he grabbed the candle, walked down to the front of the stage, and snapped it in half.

Nothing.

He had the strangest expression on his face. He just couldn't believe it. He looked in the candle and he shook it a few times but, of course, there was no flag. He bowed and the audience gave him a big hand anyhow—they didn't know that something was missing. But he knew, and when he caught sight of Clyde and me snickering in the wings, he immediately understood what had gone wrong.

He chased us for two blocks, out the theater and down the street, but we were younger and faster, and he didn't catch us. I think he might have killed us if he'd ever caught up with us.

We worked on the same bill with Jack Benny and Burns and Allen (George and Gracie) at the Great Northern Theater in Chicago. For me, those were the beginnings of two lifelong friendships. Today, I guess I'd say that Jack Benny is my very best friend, and George Burns and I have always been close, too. At the time, Benny and Burns and Allen were among the leading vaudeville acts, and it was an education to watch them in action.

The Great Northern was a unique vaudeville house. They had nine acts on the bill during the day, which stretched from eleven in the morning to six in the evening. Then they had another show at night, from six to midnight, with an entirely different slate of nine acts. One day while we were there, something happened to one of the acts, and Clyde and I had to play both halves of the bill. It was a long day.

There was another theater we played at in Chicago. I forget the name, but I do remember—funny what tricks the memory plays—that it was at the corner of Cottage Grove and Sixty-third Street. That one had a backbreaker of a schedule every Sunday—the acts had to play six shows.

We were there one Sunday and got up in the morning facing those six shows and it just felt like it was going to be too much. So Clyde and I decided not to wear our Eton suits. They weren't the most comfortable clothes in the world, and we felt we could make it through the day a lot easier if we wore ordinary street clothes.

So we went out and did the first show that Sunday in those regular clothes. We took our bows and went back to our dressing room.

"LeRoy and Cooper!"

It was the booming voice of the manager, echoing through the backstage area. We poked our heads out of the dressing-room door.

"We're here."

He came toward us, murder in his eyes.

"Hey, you two. Where are the Buster Browns?"

"The what?"

"The Buster Browns. Those suits with the funny white collars you always wear."

"Those aren't Buster Browns. Those are Eton suits."

"I don't care if they're Buffalo Bills, where are they?"

We explained that we felt we couldn't get through the day wearing them for six shows. He brushed our explanation aside.

"Look, you two. In the picture of your act, which is at this very moment on display in the lobby of this theater, it shows you two in those Buster Brown suits."

"I know," I said, "but for six shows a day—gee, that's too long to wear them. How about, just this one day, we can wear our regular clothes?"

"Look, you two. If you wouldn't wear the Buster Browns in the next show, you're canceled."

We didn't wear them, and we were canceled.

It didn't matter. We always worked. When you're young, small doses of adversity can be turned into adventures. We had our share. I remember once we were stranded in a town called Appleton, Wisconsin, when something went wrong. A booking fell through, or the theater had closed down or burned down or something. Those things happened to everybody on the vaudeville circuits once in a while. It happened to us in Appleton, among other places.

We had never saved any money. I spent all mine and Clyde sent his home. When a booking fell through, it meant we had no money to eat or sleep or, worst of all, to buy railroad tickets so we could get out of town and on to our next booking.

Some vaudeville acts have had real trouble in similar situations —I know of a few cases where men and women have had to resort to taking regular jobs. Fortunately, we didn't have to stoop that low. With our fresh, boyish faces, we were able to get somebody—I think it was the manager of the Appleton Hotel—to advance us enough money to buy our train tickets.

We were stranded a few other times, too. Once I wired my cousins in San Francisco for the money to get out of town, and they came through. I think on another occasion Clyde wired his folks, and they helped, too. I'm sure everybody—the Appleton Hotel manager, my cousins, and Clyde's folks—were promptly repaid. We were always very careful about that. The worst thing that could happen to a vaudeville act was to get the reputation of being deadbeats.

We played the big time—not the Palace, but we did get to the Halsey, in Brooklyn, just across the river—and we played the small time, too. When I say small, I mean very small—the teeny-weeny time. There was one day when we were booked into a town called Mabton, Washington. We got there and went to the theater to see who else was on the bill with us and got the shock of our lives. There was nobody else on the bill—it was just us, just LeRoy and Cooper, Two Kids and a Piano. It was sort of an exhilarating feeling. We thought, for a few heady moments, that we had arrived, that we were S*T*A*R*S. Then we realized that this was Mabton, Washington, and we came back down to earth in a hurry.

"How many pieces in your orchestra?" I asked the theater manager.

"Three," he said, with a grin. "Piano, cover, and stool."

Crisscrossing around the country, we got to play with most of the vaudeville acts of that era. We were all one big, close, and generally happy fraternity. We shared secrets. We made love. We knew all the gossip and the dirt about everybody.

There was a mentalist act that we often played with. She was a girl who billed herself as Princess Wah-Let-Ka, and she dressed like an Indian. At night, after the show, I'd help her make up the answers for the next show's questions. If I ran into her today, I bet I could still do her act with her.

Dave Chasen, who became the owner of that most popular Hollywood restaurant, Chasen's, was in vaudeville in those days, with an act called "The Electrical Wizard." I used to help him select his stooges as they came in the theater; they had to stand there holding a cake of ice, which melted all over them, and they were just there for laughs.

For a few months one year, Dave and I were not-so-friendly rivals. We were both in love with the same girl. Her name was Ruby Myers, and she was part of a song-and-dance act. Neither

Dave nor I wound up with Ruby, but, at the time, it was pretty serious stuff.

There were lots of other girls, of course—more than I can remember, or want to.

There was one girl I liked. She was very beautiful and I knew she liked me. She was the mainstay of a dance act and she had long black hair and sparkling black eyes. Whenever our paths crossed, when her act and our act played on the same bill, we'd get together. She would sit on my lap and we would talk.

The only problem was that she was only five years old. Her name was Rita Cansino, of "The Dancing Cansinos," and when she grew up and became a movie star she changed it to Rita Hayworth. I was seventeen or eighteen at the time, and I'd like to be able to boast about spotting her potential when she was five. Truthfully, however, I didn't. I knew she was a very pretty little girl and a brilliant dancer—for a five-year-old—but I honestly can't say that I was sure she was going to be a big star.

Her father, Eduardo Cansino, liked me, too. Later on, when I was in New York and broke, he helped me out, loaned me some money and got me a few bookings. I never directed Rita in any pictures—she did most of her films at Columbia and I was almost exclusively at Warner Brothers and Metro-Goldwyn-Mayer—but we would often meet at parties and premieres. We would talk about vaudeville days but the one subject we would never discuss would be age. She knew that I knew how old she was—I was, and still am, twelve or thirteen years older—and glamour girls don't like people who know their true age.

We never dated. She was too young, by far, to date in the days when we were in vaudeville together. There were many others, however. We would go out to dinner. We would go to movies. I saw every movie I could, because the new art form fascinated me. More and more, I was interested in movies. I guess, in the back of my mind, the idea of becoming part of the motion picture industry was forming. It was only just that—something in the back of my mind. In the front of my mind, still, was the idea of being a big vaudeville star. Clyde and I continually struggled to get bigger spots in better theaters, or better spots in bigger theaters. We were getting to be veterans, after more than three years of playing around the country, and we felt that we could hold our own with anybody.

We got to be pretty vain about ourselves, too. I remember one day a theater manager came up to us, after our act, and said we would have to cut it down to fifteen minutes.

"That's impossible," I said. "We bow for ten."

When things didn't break for us as we thought they should, we would be temporarily discouraged. We played for all the major vaudeville circuits—Pantages, Gus Sun, Orpheum—and sometimes we felt we were standing still. We never considered quitting, but there were blue days. It wasn't all easy but, in retrospect, most of it was a great deal of fun. Then, too, it was a great primer, although I didn't realize it at the time, for the career I eventually followed. I learned show business from the bottom up. I learned the value of dialogue, the value of music, the value of timing, the value of holding an audience. Vaudeville was the best possible teacher for me at the time.

Then, one day, out of the clear blue Western Union, that phase of my life came to an abrupt end. We were playing somewhere upstate New York—Albany, I believe—and as we came off stage, the theater manager said, "Hey, Cooper, a telegram came for you. I put it in your dressing room."

Telegrams could only mean trouble. Clyde ran to the dressing room, and I was right behind him. He ripped open the yellow envelope, read it, then showed it to me: "YOUR FATHER PASSED AWAY THIS MORNING. PLEASE COME HOME AT ONCE." It was signed "MOTHER."

He did. He went back to Hayward. At first, he said he'd come back and rejoin me as soon as he straightened out his father's affairs. But it wasn't to be. Clyde had to stay in Hayward and run the family hotel. After a while, he began playing piano at night in a San Francisco café, but that was his only show-business experience after our act broke up. We remained good friends, and he lived until 1971.

The ironic thing about the timing of his father's death was that we later learned we had been booked into the Palace in New York the next week.

3

JESSE LASKY:
TAKE THIS OUT
TO THE STUDIO
IN HOLLYWOOD

I didn't know it then, but the death of Clyde Cooper's father meant the death of my vaudeville career. It didn't die all at once; the demise was a slow, lingering, and painful one.

At first, I thought I could make it on my own. First, I proudly proclaimed myself a single act. I got some bookings, but I was starting at the bottom again. LeRoy and Cooper had become a fairly well-established act and the theater owners knew us. We were a known quantity. LeRoy by himself, however, was an unknown quantity. It was a bitter blow to my vanity to have to go back to the dumps and be an opening act again. But I did it, for a few months.

Then a man named George Choos asked me to join one of his acts. He had a group of girl acts, as they were called, but what they were, really, were miniature musical comedies, all in one package. Each one was a comparatively large group for those days, and I became a member of one of them. I sang some songs and told some jokes. It was a comedown for me, but it kept me working.

We were playing Cleveland when Gus Edwards saw me and invited me to join a new act he was putting together. It was called "The Nine Country Kids." In a way, it was like his famous "School Days" troupe, only instead of a bunch of school kids, this was a bunch of kids of different nationalities. I was the Jewish kid. We were all supposed to be on a farm—I don't remember how he maneuvered nine kids of different nationalities onto the same farm —and we each sang a song. My song was called "See Saw," and I still remember the words:

> See saw, see saw,
> See us go up and down.
> Say, kids, don't it feel
> Like an automobile,
> Riding and gliding through old New York town.
> While we see saw, see saw,
> We can't make love anymore.
> We get all our joys
> Just to be girls and boys
> On the old see saw.

Between my single act and my stints with George Choos and Gus Edwards, I guess I lingered around the vaudeville scene for a couple of years after Clyde and I split up. Increasingly, I was becoming disenchanted with the whole vaudeville business. I imagine mostly that was because I was just a small cog in a larger group with Choos and Edwards, rather than being half of a two-person act. It just wasn't as much fun anymore.

When we got to New York—I think this must have been in 1922 or 1923—I quit.

I was broke. Everything I had made I had spent. I picked up some odd jobs here and there—that was when Rita Hayworth's father got me some bookings—but mostly it was a day-to-day scrounging to keep body and soul together.

There was a group in those days called the National Vaudeville Artists, a kind of club for vaudevillians, to which I belonged. They had an office in New York. I had gotten to know the president of NVA, a man named Henry Chesterfield, and I'd hang around the place with the other out-of-work performers. I suppose we were all waiting for lightning to strike. For me, in a way, it did.

One day, a man came in and said he was working for a movie company. They were shooting a film and needed a kid to play the part of a grocery boy. I was twenty-two then, but I still looked like a teen-ager, so he asked me if I'd like to play the part. With nothing better to do, I said sure.

The movie, he told me, as we drove up to Fort Lee, New Jersey, where they were shooting, was to be called *The Perils of Pauline*.

The star was a girl named Pearl White. Then he explained my part. It was very simple.

I was supposed to be delivering a basket of groceries. The set was a two-story, two-family house. All I had to do was climb the stairs, knock on the door of the second-story apartment. A Chinese man would open the door and I would hand him the basket of groceries. That was all there was to it. Very easy.

We got to Fort Lee and everything was as he had described it. When it came time for my bit, they put me in a costume and handed me the basket. The director said, "Action!" and I climbed the stairs and knocked on the door. The Chinese man opened the door. I handed him the basket.

At that point, however, things didn't go according to the script. Suddenly, the Chinese man dropped the basket, picked me up, and threw me over the porch railing. I yelled. I thought I was done for and, as I fell, I kept thinking, "Well, at least there are plenty of witnesses, so that Chinese nut will get what's coming to him."

I wasn't hurt. I landed in a net that I hadn't noticed before. Everybody was laughing. Then they told me that what had happened was what was supposed to have happened. They just hadn't bothered to tell me ahead of time, because then I might not have done it—and they were damned right.

They gave me a few more dollars than we had agreed on for the stunt. I think we had settled on five dollars and they gave me ten. It tided me over for a few days.

During those few days, I did a lot of thinking. Even though my first movie role had been rather traumatic, I found that I had enjoyed the experience. I hadn't enjoyed being tossed over the porch railing, of course, but I had found the movie business exciting. As I'd waited for my scene, that day in Fort Lee, I had watched them making *The Perils of Pauline*, and it was thoroughly intriguing. The idea of motion pictures as a career, that idea that had been slowly growing in the back of my mind, surfaced that day.

The problem was, of course, how to put the dream into motion, how to transfer a vague hope into a definite fact. Then I remembered my cousin, Jesse Lasky.

Jesse, who had preceded me into vaudeville by many years, had long since left the field. Some ten years before, at about the time I was doing plays at the Alcazar, Jesse had entered the motion picture field.

As things turned out, he was one of the pioneers of the movie business. His sister Blanche had married a glove salesman named

Sam Goldfish, and Jesse and Sam had teamed up to make movies. Sam later changed his name to Goldwyn but he was still Goldfish when he helped start a company with the impressive title of The Jesse L. Lasky Feature Play Company. All they had was the title, about twenty thousand dollars they had begged and borrowed, and a third partner. They had once offered my father a third interest, four thousand dollars, but he thought they were crazy.

The other partner was a not-too-successful playwright named Cecil B. DeMille. One of the three suggested that their first film be *The Squaw Man*, which I had appeared in when I was only six months old. Since it dealt with Indians, they decided to shoot it out west. Until then, Fort Lee had been the motion picture capital of America, but *The Squaw Man* was to change all that.

Lasky and Goldfish were staying in New York to handle the business details. DeMille was the artistic head of the new company, and he was to produce. He had picked Flagstaff, Arizona, as the site of the production. DeMille took the train west, accompanied by his leading man, the distinguished Broadway star, Dustin Farnum, and the man who was going to direct the movie, Oscar Apfel. Apfel was better known as a cornetist and orchestra leader; his film credits were limited to a few two-reelers, but nobody had much in the way of previous movie experience in those early days.

If not for a quirk in the weather, Flagstaff might have become the headquarters of the American motion picture industry. When the train carrying DeMille, Farnum, and Apfel chugged into the Flagstaff station, it was snowing and snowing hard. Obviously, DeMille decided, this was no place to shoot a Western. He took one look at all that white stuff piling up and got right back on the train and continued west, to Los Angeles.

Lasky and Goldfish didn't know anything about DeMille's decision, at least not right away. Goldfish was the salesman in the triumvirate, and he was probably the best salesman ever born. I think, if he'd wanted to, he could have sold swimming pools to Eskimos. He managed to sell sixty thousand dollars' worth of advance bookings for *The Squaw Man* at a time when he hadn't heard from DeMille in two weeks. He and my cousin were getting worried. There wasn't a word from out west, until finally there came a telegram: "FLAGSTAFF NO GOOD. HAVE PROCEEDED TO CALIFORNIA. WANT AUTHORITY TO RENT BARN IN HOLLYWOOD FOR SEVENTY-FIVE DOLLARS A MONTH."

Hollywood? Nobody in New York had ever heard of the place. But Lasky and Goldfish were committed, and they figured they had nothing to lose, so they wired DeMille the authorization he had requested.

DeMille, when he got off the train in Los Angeles, had found the sunshine that was lacking in Flagstaff. He and Apfel had ridden all over the Los Angeles basin, looking for someplace to serve as a studio. On a dirt road, running between orange groves and pepper trees, he had found the old, deserted barn that would be ideal. The dirt road, he learned, was called Vine Street. DeMille converted the barn into a studio, turning the barn's stalls into offices and dressing rooms. Outside, he had built a stage, with a big, umbrella-like device over it to control the too-bright California sunshine.

On December 29, 1913, Cecil B. DeMille shot the first foot of Hollywood film.

I was selling newspapers in San Francisco at the time, completely unaware—as was most of America—that something historic was taking place.

There were problems with the picture. DeMille had rented his cameras by the day. Over the course of the filming, he had used several different types of camera. When the finished product was projected, the sprocket holes in the film from the different cameras varied, with the result that the projection was jerky and uneven. Lasky and Goldfish were appalled; it looked like a disaster. But a brilliant film technician in Philadelphia named Sig Lubin saved the day by splicing uniform sprocket holes along the entire film. *The Squaw Man* became a huge, instant hit, and The Jesse L. Lasky Feature Play Company was in business to stay.

It prospered over the decade or so after *The Squaw Man*. On that day when I finally decided to try my hand at movies, it was a huge operation. Its top star, Mary Pickford, was earning a million dollars a year. It was now called Famous Players–Lasky, after a merger with the company headed by Adolph Zukor.

For several days, I mulled over my problem. I knew I was finished with vaudeville. I knew, just as positively, that I wanted to get into the movie business. Still, I couldn't quite get up the nerve to go over to see my cousin, Jesse Lasky. Everything I'd done, up to that point, had been always on my own. The idea of asking a relative for help didn't sit well with my ego. I couldn't help but remember something my father had always said: "Stay away from lawyers and relatives."

There was another problem. What did I want to do in the movie business? Or, to put it more bluntly, what was I equipped to do? The sum of my entire cinema experience was that one day on *The*

Perils of Pauline, and there wasn't much call for a young man getting himself thrown over a porch railing.

So I hesitated. The end of my hesitation coincided neatly with the end of my bankroll.

One day in October—it was the day after my birthday—I took my hat in my hand, tucked my pride in my pocket, and went over to the Fifth Avenue offices of Famous Players–Lasky. It took me a while to work my way up, through channels, from receptionist to secretary to Lasky.

I hadn't seen Jesse in some years. He'd gotten rich in the interim, and with wealth generally comes a commanding manner, and he had that in spades. He was very busy, and didn't have much time for, or interest in, my small talk.

Still, it took me a few minutes to work up my courage to explain my mission. For as long as I could, I procrastinated with chitchat about our mutual relatives, the weather, and any other nonessential conversational topic I could call to mind.

Finally, he broke the ice.

"Mervyn," he said, "it's good to see you, but I'm a busy man. Tell me what's on your mind."

"I want to get into the movie business," I said.

There. It was out in the open. It just seemed to hang there, like some heavy, invisible cloud, while Lasky laughed and toyed with something on his desk. My heart was thumping so loud I was sure he could hear it.

"Everybody wants to get into the movie business," he said. "What makes you think you've got anything to contribute?"

"Well, I can act. I've been in a lot of plays in San Francisco, and you know I've been in vaudeville for about four years."

"Movies are a different thing," he said.

There was a moment of silence. Then, with a sigh, he reached for a pad and a pen and scrawled a note on a piece of paper. Then he folded it up and put it in an envelope and sealed it.

"Here," he said. "Take this out to the studio in Hollywood. They'll give you a job."

I took the envelope and got up and started out, but at the door I turned back.

"Something else?" Jesse said.

"Yeah. I don't have the money for a railroad ticket."

"I thought so."

Jesse took out his wallet and extracted a hefty sheaf of bills, and counted out enough for the ticket.

"I'll pay you back, Jesse," I said, as I pocketed the money.

He looked me in the eye for a moment, then said, "Yes, Mervyn, I believe you will."

Once more, I started for the door. This time, it was Jesse who stopped me.

"One more thing, Mervyn," he said. "From now on, you're strictly on your own. It would help you a lot if you didn't tell anybody that we're related. Okay?"

"Okay."

That was the way I wanted it, too. I didn't want to make it, if I made it, because I was somebody's cousin. I wanted to make it on my own, as I always had. Rise or fall, it would be because I was the person I was.

The next day, I was on the train, bound for Hollywood, California.

A week later, I was in Hollywood. Not only was I in it, but I was a part of it. In those days, the early 1920s, it was quite something to be part of, too.

Over the years, it has become fashionable to make jokes about Hollywood. Some of them were well deserved, I suppose, but most of them were just jealous jokes, sour-grape jokes. When outsiders can't get in anywhere, they protect their egos with that kind of snide humor. In this case, everybody, secretly, wanted to be part of the Hollywood scene. Why not? The most beautiful women, the most handsome men, the most talented musicians, the most capable writers were all working in Hollywood in the 1920s, 1930s, and on into the 1940s.

That was the surface attraction. I found, however, that underneath that glamorous veneer there was something even more thrilling. Hollywood, the movie business, was youthful and full of dreams. Young men and young women with young ideas were the soul of Hollywood. It was, at the time I arrived on the scene, an infant among the arts. New ideas were welcomed with open wallets. New approaches were tried. Almost everything that was done was being done for the very first time anywhere. To be a part of it, even a very small part, was like sailing with Christopher Columbus. I doubt that anywhere else, at any time, have so many young people tried out so many brand-new ideas as in Hollywood in the last days of the silent films and the first days of the talkies.

This was the world I walked into, that day in October, 1923. I didn't consciously think those thoughts—I wasn't given to too much introspection and philosophy at the time. My thoughts were more practical, dealing with the basic necessities of living. I had to get a job and I had to have a place to live—in that order.

I checked my suitcase at the station and went directly to the studio, Famous Players–Lasky, which was still where it was when Cecil B. DeMille found that deserted barn ten years before. There had been some changes. Vine Street was paved now, but there were still orange trees along the sidewalks. The old barn was gone, demolished to make room for the beginnings of a studio. There was a gate, a fence, some low wooden buildings housing offices, and three or four stages. They weren't called sound stages then because, of course, there was no sound then. They weren't soundproofed, either; they didn't need to be because everything was still silent. Besides, there were very few airplanes around to make any annoying noises.

I walked through the gate, showed my envelope from my cousin Jesse to the guard, and he directed me to one of the offices. I found the right person in the employment department and he ripped open the envelope, read the note, and told me to show up the next morning for work.

"Where will I be working?" I had visions of something exotic—assistant director, perhaps, or, at the very least, an actor.

"Wardrobe," he said.

I swallowed my disappointment. Well, what's the difference? Wardrobe today, star or executive tomorrow. It wouldn't take me long to be discovered, to prove my invaluable worth.

Before I left his office, I asked him if he could recommend a place to live, a boardinghouse or a rooming house. He handed me a list—the question was obviously asked of him very often—and I took it with me.

I went to the place on the list that was the nearest. It was Mrs. Grover's Boarding House, on the southeast corner of Sunset Boulevard and Vine Street. Today, there is a high-rise office building there, but then there were private homes on all four corners of that famous intersection. Mrs. Grover gave me a big smile and I felt at home immediately. She was a wonderful old lady. She liked movie people, which is rare among landlords. Generally, they think of anyone associated with the film business as a potential deadbeat or worse. (Often, unfortunately, they are right.) But not Mrs. Grover. She loved us. And we loved her back.

I moved right in, sharing a room with a couple of young men who later became pretty big names as actors—Richard Van Mattimore, who became Richard Arlen, and George O'Brien, who was the son of San Francisco's police chief. Their welcome was warm, and I went to bed that night with the cozy realization that I had a job, a bed to sleep in, and, best of all, some friends.

The next morning, right on schedule, I reported for duty. That morning, however, as so often happened to me over the years, I had a problem of getting through the gate. My boyish appearance, which frequently was my ally, was also often my enemy. The guard wouldn't let me in—"Get out of here, kid, and come back when you're fully grown"—until I persuaded him to check with the man at the employment office.

I wasn't the only one to have such problems. One morning, I walked in just behind Adolph Zukor, one of the studio bosses. I heard an extra turn to him and say, "Hey, shorty, got a match?"

That first morning, it took me just long enough to gain admittance to the lot so that I was a little late my first day on the job. The head of the wardrobe department didn't seem to notice my tardiness, however. He simply explained my duties.

They were shooting a big Civil War picture, *Secret Service*, on the lot. There were hundreds of extras in the blue and gray uniforms of the Confederate and Federal forces, as well as dozens of stars and featured players. Hugh Ford was the director and Robert Warwick the top-rated star. My job was to be one of several people in the wardrobe department who had to check the uniforms out in the morning and in the evening when the day's work was done. Then they had to be folded and tagged and put away neatly. The ones that were finished with had to be stored in mothballs. As the weeks wore on, more and more uniforms were no longer needed, which meant more and more mothballing.

It got so the smell of mothballs permeated everything I wore and became a temporarily permanent part of my being. My approach could be detected long before my appearance because of that pungent odor. At Mrs. Grover's my new friends teased me.

"Here comes Mervyn Mothball," they would say, as I climbed the stairs to our room.

I would hop in the shower right away, and I'd put my clothes on the window ledge, so they would air out. Nothing really helped very much; the mothball aroma persisted.

This was, however, a minor inconvenience. The glow of being in the movie business, no matter how minor a cog, was still burning sufficiently bright that I could overcome the small annoyance of mothballs. I loved being on the studio lot. At my lunch break, I wandered around, becoming acquainted with the place, exploring all the shops, investigating every nook and cranny. I stared at the stars like a tourist. There were plenty of stars on that lot at that time to stare at, too. One day, I passed that handsomest of couples, Douglas Fairbanks and Mary Pickford. I gave them a big smile and a cheerful "Hello," and they smiled back at me and thereby made my week. Then there was Marguerite Clark, a tiny thing with a huge crop of brown, curly hair and big, sparkling eyes. She returned my greeting, too. It all seemed to be one big, friendly club.

I liked the attitude. At that time, Hollywood was as friendly and open as I felt it was. It was that same psychological thing, all of us being part of a very youthful, experimental business. We were all equals in discovery.

We were, however, unequals in the rewards of those early discoveries. One day, as I stood in line for a weekly paycheck, somebody told me that Mary Pickford was making twenty thousand dollars every week. My check totaled twelve dollars and fifty cents.

"Nobody is worth twenty thousands dollars a week," I said.

That was one bit of financial philosophy that stayed with me. Years later, I made a lot of money myself. Of course, I didn't turn it back, but I knew it was ridiculous.

I felt, however, that my own twelve-dollar-and-fifty-cent salary was just as ridiculous, at the other end of the ridiculosity spectrum. As I became acclimated to California living, I was finding it increasingly difficult to make ends meet on that pittance.

I could pay my rent and that meant that I had board and room. But now I was beginning to be part of the social life of my new circle of friends and, no matter how you try to economize, a social life is always expensive. With Arlen and O'Brien and the others, there was something going on every night, every weekend. There were parties and dates and assorted shindigs. We all loved the beach and Arlen had an old, immense Pierce-Arrow and on Sundays we'd all get dates and pile in that huge car and tootle off to the ocean. There was nothing there then, nothing but the sand and the rolling (unpolluted) ocean and the bright blue (smogless) sky. I never went in the water myself—water, I have always maintained, is for fish.

In the 1920s, when I used to go barreling down to the beach in Arlen's Pierce-Arrow, there wasn't a soul there. The reason for it being so unpopulated was simple: The roads were so bad and cars so slow that it took us a couple of hours to make the trip from

Hollywood to the ocean. Today, the same trip, via freeway, is thirty minutes. For us to go to the beach, in the 1920s, was equivalent to a motorist of today driving to San Diego from Los Angeles. It didn't matter to us; we loved the riotous trip almost as much as we loved the beach.

Mrs. Grover would pack a picnic lunch for us and away we'd go, all crammed in the car, singing and laughing and calling out to anybody and everybody along our cheerful route. Dear old Mrs. Grover was our mother figure. If we were a little late with the rent—and somebody was always a little late with the rent—she just shrugged it off.

"Next week, dearie, will be fine," she'd say.

If she thought we looked "a bit peaked," as she put it, she'd whip up something especially rich and nourishing for us. She'd darn socks and sew on buttons. If there was an emergency—a sudden date or an important audition for one of the actors—she and her ironing board were always at the ready.

Her table was plain and simple fare, but it was sufficient to sustain life, which was all that mattered to us at that point. Gourmet food could, and would, come later. Occasionally, for variety's sake, we would dine out—at a grocery store that was at the corner of Vine and Selma—but that was a rare thing. Almost always, we'd all gather around the table in Mrs. Grover's dining room for our evening meal. It was a raucous, delightful group and I'll always have fond memories of those days and dinners.

The group quickly adopted me. They included me in their parties and all their social doings. It was difficult for me to keep up with them financially. Nobody was rich but everybody was richer than I was. I had trouble staying abreast of them on my $12.50 a week. But they would take me along and often underwrite my participation. They liked me, because I was fun, told jokes, was always cheerful. They took me along for laughs.

"Hey, Mothball, come on," somebody would yell up the stairs.

"What's going on?"

"There's a party. Let's go."

And away we'd go.

After a few months, I was bored to distraction with folding and unfolding, tagging and untagging, mothballing and demothballing all those Civil War uniforms. I knew that wasn't what I wanted to do with my life. Whenever I had a free moment, I'd visit the stages and watch them make movies.

There were some excellent directors working at the studio then, men like Cecil and William DeMille, George Fitzmaurice, Jimmy Cruze, Hugh Ford, George Hannaberry. I'd stand at the back of the studio and observe, like a college student auditing a course. I didn't say anything, just watched. To me, then as now, the director seemed to be the center of the artistic universe. He took raw words on paper, he took a bunch of actors, he took lights and cameras and film, and he created something from all those diverse elements. He was like a fine chef creating a masterpiece from many different kinds of ingredients.

I knew, then, that someday I was going to direct.

After that knowledge penetrated my conscious mind, I grew more and more restless in the wardrobe department. Working with mothballs was no great preparation for the job of director. I had to get out.

I went to see Jesse Lasky when he was in town on one of his frequent visits, and asked for a transfer, or promotion, or something. I guess I had a good job record because he talked to somebody and they went along with me. I was given a job in the lab.

This was better. It wasn't the top yet—far from it—but I realized that I had a lot to learn and a long way to go. The lab was a step up—and three dollars and fifty cents more a week.

There were handicaps, of course. In place of wardrobe's mothballs, now I was confronted with the lab's dyes. Remember that this was Hollywood's formative period, and the technique of film was still in its infancy. Everything was shot in the studio, and they tried to get effects by dipping the film in various dyes. For a night scene, the film was plunged into a vat of blue dye. If the scene was supposed to be in bright sunshine, it called for amber dye.

That was my job in the lab, dipping the film into those vats of various-colored dyes. We called them "washes." All day I'd plunge the film into the vats and the film wasn't the only thing to come out tinted—my arms would be, too. I'd come home with blue or amber forearms, sometimes a bit of both. I got used to seeing people look at me with odd expressions on their faces, when they caught sight of me and my colorful arms. My friends at the boardinghouse now greeted me with "Here comes the rainbow."

It was during my stay in the Famous Players–Lasky lab that I had my first Hollywood triumph, however. One day, I happened to overhear a conversation between William DeMille and two of my lab superiors. He was making a movie with Wanda Hawley and Tom Foreman and he was having a problem with one scene. The two were in a rowboat, out on a lake in the moonlight. They were supposed to look at that romantic view—the moonlight shimmering on the water—and fall promptly and madly in love. The problem was that romantic view; nobody had yet managed to capture on film the look of moonlight dancing on water.

I had an idea. That night, I stayed late in the lab. Somewhere, I got a big wooden box about twelve feet square, painted the inside black, and lined it with tar paper. Then I filled it with distilled water from Jesse's office—he only drank distilled water. I got a spotlight and carefully set it up so its light played along the surface of the water in the box. I took one of the studio's Pathé cameras, found a supply of raw film, and shot some five thousand feet of my pseudo-moonlight-on-the-water.

I had directed my first scene in Hollywood.

The next morning, there was hell to pay. The head of the raw film depot wanted me fired for stealing film. I persuaded him to wait until I'd shown William DeMille the footage I'd shot. At first, he was reluctant even to take the time to see it, but finally he agreed.

He loved it. He called me a "genius" and other complimentary things, and he used my footage in the film which, to me, was a lot better than compliments. What was even more exciting, he said that he felt my talents were being wasted in the lab, and that I should be doing something more creative. Naturally, I was delighted to go along with him on that notion.

"I think you should be behind the camera," DeMille said.

"That's what I want," I said.

A few days later, they told me I was being switched from the lab to a job as an assistant cameraman, which brought me a few extra dollars in pay. Gone were my blue arms and amber wrists. Instead, I developed a new assortment of ailments.

The chief function of an assistant cameraman, lofty as that title may sound, was to help move the camera around. In those days, cameras were pretty heavy, and I was pretty light. I think I must have weighed in at somewhere between 115 and 120 pounds around that time, and the camera outweighed me by a hundred pounds or so. Besides, these were on wooden tripods, which were pretty hefty, too.

All I can remember of my days as an assistant cameraman is aching legs and back and arms, and cut and bleeding shoulders from where the tripod dug into my flesh as I lugged it around. All day long, the other assistant cameramen and I would heave that contraption around, at the whim of the director and the chief cameraman. There was, I remember with acute pain, one film we shot on location, on the side of a mountain in the Hollywood hills. For the better part of a week, I was on that mountainside, lifting that terrible machine up and down. I'd go home at night, apply some liniment to my protesting limbs and back, some Mercuro-chrome to my bleeding shoulder, and then sink into bed.

Still, I was happy. Not content, of course; I still wanted more. But, despite my aching little body, this was better than folding uniforms or dipping film in washes. I was able to watch directors at first hand, which was, for me, very exciting. I began to be able to tell which ones were good and which ones weren't. More and more often, I would say to myself that I could do better than they were doing. It was a comforting realization, to know that the goal I had picked out for myself was one I could handle. All that remained was for someone to give me a crack at a film. I knew that I would be able to turn out a solid film. The only thing I didn't have was the chance.

In the meantime, there was living to do.

It was a good life. People who have never been to Hollywood think it's a land of wall-to-wall orgies. I know for a fact that there are more orgies in Rome than there are in Hollywood. We've had our playboys and our playgirls, but basically this is a pretty square town. I found that out early and, since I'm somewhat square my-self, I decided that the social climate agreed with me.

As an assistant cameraman, I was making enough money to be part of the crowd. In some ways, I was still on the periphery, however. There is a pecking order in Hollywood, as there is every other place in the world, and assistant cameramen aren't very high up.

Still, I made friends. One of my best and closest in those days was an all-time Hollywood star, Wallace Reid. He was a truly wonderful person, and he took me under his wing. He was a man who did many different things, and did them all well. One of the first of Reid's extracurricular enterprises in which I participated was his jazz band. Thanks to my boyhood experience with the drums, I sat in with the band often as the drummer. Some of the men—the band was recruited from actors and technicians—were pretty good. Some were only fair. I was in that latter group, but what we may have lacked in skill we made up for with a tremen-dous zest. We were also loud.

Through Reid, and through my boardinghouse buddies, I got to know some of the biggest stars of those silent days. I'd hang around with Hoot Gibson, Betty Compson, Buster Collier, Ward Crane. We'd go tearing around the city—big town was what it was then—heading for some party or some nightclub, waving at the people and blowing the car's horn.

Cars were a tremendous status symbol in Hollywood, even then. The public were big fans of all the silent stars, and they became fans of their cars, too. They recognized people by the cars they were driving. They knew Arlen's Pierce-Arrow and Reid's Macfarlane and all the others. They'd yell at us as we went by—"Hey, Mr. Reid, gimme a lift"—and we'd all wave back at them. I have a feeling they would look at me, perched in the rumble seat (that was usually where I would find an inch) and wonder who I was.

At the time, of course, I was still pretty much a nobody, but I was traveling with the somebodies. There was a kind of ambivalence that went with my semiposition in the crowd. While they treated me as one of them, still I recognized the fact that I was really an outsider. I wasn't a star and, sad to say, I wasn't making a star's salary, either. There were times when I just couldn't afford to do the things they did. There were other times when I understood that I wasn't welcome places, because of my relatively lowly station. For a while, for example, I became Betty Compson's unofficial date. She liked to go to parties alone, and yet she liked to have somebody drive her there and pick her up afterward. So she'd ask me to be her chauffeur. I'd drive her to those swanky parties and I'd be dying to go in, but I knew I couldn't.

I tried to dress like my idols dressed, too. Here again financial considerations made that almost impossible. I dressed well—I've always been a bug on neatness in my clothing—but I couldn't afford the flashy, one-of-a-kind outfits they all wore.

All this made me determined to try harder. It wasn't for the sake of vanity or pride or envy, but simply that I had this great urge to make something of myself. First and foremost, I felt I had a contribution to make to the motion picture industry. I wanted to direct a picture so badly that I would dream about it at night, dream up a situation and direct my actors through it while I slept. In the morning, though, it was back to lugging that brute of a camera around.

My reward for all that expenditure of perspiration and blood came after about six months. I was promoted to second cameraman. Now I had somebody else to do the carrying. My responsibility was loading the camera and making sure it was in focus. The promotion backfired.

On my very first picture, on my very first scene, I did something wrong. I thought I had followed my instructions perfectly, but obviously I hadn't. When the director—it was William DeMille again—screened that first footage I had shot, it was all out of focus.

DeMille watched the shots unfold on the screen as I cringed in my chair. When it was all over, and the lights in the projection room were back on, he turned to me and said, with acid dripping from every syllable, "Congratulations, Mervyn. You've just invented a new kind of focus."

Years later, of course, that type of shot I had accidentally filmed would become a permanent part of Hollywood's techniques. It would be known as "soft focus." Then, however, it was just a horrible mess.

I thought I was finished in the business.

One of the truisms often said of Hollywood is that "you're only as good as your last picture." As I went back to Mrs. Grover's after having ruined the focus on William DeMille's picture, I couldn't help but wonder if my fiasco would mean the end of my Hollywood life.

DeMille's attitude seemed harsh. True, I had spoiled some film. Still it was only my first picture and I felt that I deserved a second chance. I knew, too, that often accidents, such as mine, had turned out to be constructive and had actually benefited the miscreant. There was a well-known incident that had occurred to Cecil B. DeMille only a year or so before. He had shot some close-up footage of an actor with a borrowed light and the result was that the actor's face was only half lit. DeMille liked the effect, which was purely accidental, and had optimistically sent the finished movie off to Sam Goldwyn in New York. Goldwyn took one look at it and wired DeMille: "CECIL YOU HAVE RUINED US. YOU HAVE LIGHTED ONLY HALF THE ACTOR'S FACE AND THE EXHIBITORS WILL PAY ONLY HALF THE PRICE."

DeMille was the kind of man who reacted well in a crisis, and he proved it then. He wired back: "IF YOU AND THE EXHIBITORS DON'T KNOW REMBRANDT LIGHTING IT'S NO FAULT OF MINE."

Goldwyn, no slouch at recognizing a profitable sales ploy, hopped on the "Rembrandt-lighting" gimmick immediately. A few days later, DeMille got this telegram from New York: "CECIL YOU ARE WONDERFUL. EXHIBITORS WILL PAY DOUBLE FOR REMBRANDT LIGHTING."

I felt that if I had been the director of that William DeMille film I had ruined, I would have somehow turned the disaster into a triumph. I would have capitalized on the mistake and told the world—and the exhibitors—about this bold and inventive new kind of focus. I wasn't, however, the director. So, instead of a triumph, it was a disaster—my own personal disaster.

I looked around for something else to do. I was lucky. My friends, the actors at the boardinghouse, told me that Cecil B. DeMille was hiring actors by the hundreds for his coming epic, *The Ten Commandments*. Surely, Cecil would find a place for me in the huge cast, because he knew me. The next morning, I rushed over to the studio, presented myself to DeMille, and was immediately hired.

DeMille—Cecil, not William—had always seemed to like me. As the top director of that era, he had been the magnet that had drawn me to his set as often as I could go. I loved to watch him work. I remember one day his assistant director, Hezi Tate, had tried to throw me off the set. DeMille was way up on a boom camera; he saw what was going on and he called down, "Hey, Mervyn, where are you going?"

"I've been thrown off the set, Mr. DeMille," I called up.

DeMille yelled at Tate, "Hezi, you let Mervyn LeRoy stay on any set of mine as long as he wants to."

Tate was the man who once had replied to a DeMille bawling out by saying, "Yes, God, I'll do it your way."

So I was among friends when I hired on as one of the children of Israel for *The Ten Commandments*. I was excited. This would be a chance to watch DeMille, the greatest epic director of them all since D. W. Griffith, at close range. I'd be able to see an epic take shape from the inside. Everybody in Hollywood was excited about *The Ten Commandments*. The word was out that this was going to be the biggest, gaudiest, and most expensive motion picture yet made.

DeMille was a daring man, and he had a lot of guts. He had to have, when he took his idea to Adolph Zukor in New York. Zukor ran the studio, with Lasky's help, and he was a tough man with a dollar. Until that time, the costliest Hollywood movie had been *The Covered Wagon*, which director James Cruze had made for Lasky, for somewhere under eight hundred thousand dollars. DeMille went to New York and told Zukor he wanted to make a film about the flight of the Israelites from Egypt.

"How much?" That was Zukor's reaction. (DeMille wasn't surprised. Zukor's reaction was always "How much?")

DeMille didn't bat an eye. He just said, with a great display of outward calm, "One million dollars."

Zukor slid down in his chair and DeMille could only see the top of his head. He told me later that at that moment he remembered a classic story about Zukor and his short stature. Zukor was supposed to have been in his office when a society lady came in and said, "Sir, I am accustomed to having gentlemen rise to greet me." Zukor, in an offended tone, answered her: "But, madam, I have risen."

DeMille addressed what little he could see of the film magnate and told him all he was going to do for that million dollars. He explained the story and detailed the spectacle, scene by scene, and —after DeMille had spoken about how much money the picture could make—Zukor and Lasky finally agreed.

So we knew, in Hollywood, that this was going to be something special, the biggest thing the screen had yet seen. I looked forward with tremendous anticipation to being part of it. The experience would be of great help to me forty years later, when I made my own epic, *Quo Vadis*.

I was just one of a crowd—a crowd that would number, before we were finished, some 3,500 people. Almost all my friends were in the mob scene, too, so it was pleasant work.

DeMille had built a small city for his cast and crew in the desert northeast of Los Angeles. It had to be big, because, besides the 3,500 humans involved in the production, there were roughly 3,000 animals in it, too. There were tents for the actors and corrals for the animals. DeMille's own tent was, as befitted the leader of such a monumental expedition, larger and gaudier than all the rest. There were expensive imported (just for the occasion) Oriental rugs on the floor and he had gone out and purchased an antique four-poster bed, with the heads of snakes at the peak of each post, on which he would sleep at night.

No matter what is said about DeMille, there was one phase of movie-making at which he was a master. He knew how to organize a tremendous motion picture better than anyone else. That was the secret of his success with spectacles. Everything was planned and routinized, and the huge machine functioned like an army. It had to.

We were awakened at dawn—I seem to remember that it was 4:30 A.M., or some such dreadful hour—by a bugle blowing reveille. We lined up for breakfast at the mess tents. Then we were divided into groups, which were called by military names—platoons and companies—with assistant directors in charge. They had military titles, too. Lieutenants were in command of platoons, captains in command of companies. These officers gave us our instructions. They, in turn, had gotten their instructions from colonels and generals.

At the pinnacle of this mountain of military officialdom was the commanding general, DeMille himself. It was off limits for any but a select few to approach him directly. If there was any reason you had to consult the director, you had to do it through a strictly-by-channels chain. Among the actors, there were only a handful permitted the luxury of talking to the great man.

Theodore Roberts, the man who had given me my first acting job in San Francisco, was one. He was playing Moses. Others in that rarefied group were James Neill, who played Aaron, and a few others, such as Charles DeRoche, Estelle Taylor (later Mrs. Jack Dempsey), and Julia Faye. But even they found it difficult to get an audience with DeMille.

Once, I remember, Roberts and Neill wanted to see him, but were kept waiting by subordinates outside the command tent for almost an hour. Finally, Roberts grabbed DeMille's assistant director, Hezi Tate, and boomed: "Tell God that Moses and Aaron wish words with him."

The picture dragged on. We struggled through the sand in temperatures well over 100 degrees. I gobbled salt tablets and drank water, but I still lost weight. Yet every day was exhilarating, as I watched DeMille forge a film from that mass of humanity.

It was taking longer than he had anticipated, and that meant it was costing more money. The projected million-dollar budget looked less and less realistic. Zukor, the guardian of the buck, grew so worried he came out to the desert to see for himself what the problem was. He looked incongruous, that pale little man in his city suit out there with all of us tanned-to-a-crisp Israelites in our white robes.

I happened to be near them, when Zukor and DeMille got together. Their handshake was brief and perfunctory. They never were what you could call dear friends.

"Well, Cecil," Zukor said. "The money keeps piling up. What's the story?"

DeMille, hot and tired and nervous to begin with, blew up at that question, which came without the usual preliminaries of socially graceful conversation.

"What do you want me to do?" he bellowed. "Stop shooting now and release it as *The Five Commandments*?"

Zukor, of course, never intended that DeMille stop his filming. He just wanted him to hurry it up and get it done so the expenses would stop.

I learned much about the handling of crowds from my experience on *The Ten Commandments*. There wasn't much else for me to do but learn. My own role was merely that of an extra and, aside from keeping the sand out of my eyes and brushing the flies away from my face, I had no other major responsibilities. So I kept my eyes open and watched the Master, as we all called him, at work.

One of the key scenes in the picture was Moses' descent from Mount Sinai with the sacred tablet. We Israelites were clustered at the base of the mountain as Moses made his way down the slope. It was obviously a scene that was vital to the whole production and had to be just right. What DeMille wanted, he kept reminding us, were expressions of awe and reverence on our faces. We had been working in that heat for weeks and weeks, and it is hard for anybody to look reverential under those conditions. Actually, I guess we looked bored and uncomfortable, instead of awed and reverential. DeMille wasn't happy with what he saw.

He shot it once. Then he called a break, and we tried to find shade somewhere and sank down, exhausted. I saw DeMille talking to Tate, but didn't think much about it. The next thing I knew, the bell in the town church nearby was tolling. It was a new sound out there in the bleak desert and none of us knew what was happening. Then we heard the call for us to gather around DeMille.

He addressed us through his megaphone. His voice was breaking. He choked back sobs. And he told us how one of the members of the cast had died. He had just received the terrible news. The poor man, he said, had left a widow and eight children.

"Now, in his memory," he said, "I ask for two minutes of respectful silence."

We all stood there, silently, our faces mirroring the tragedy we had just heard. There were tears in many eyes. There were awed and reverential expressions on every face.

We had been had. While we stood there for that expression of respect for the departed, the cameras were grinding away. Nobody had died. It was just DeMille's way of getting what he wanted on film. That scene, of the Israelites at the foot of Mount Sinai waiting for Moses to descend, was hailed as one of the most magnificent and spiritual in the entire movie.

After several months, the picture was finished. I went back to Hollywood, back to Mrs. Grover's boardinghouse, and I decided to continue with acting for a while. There was nothing better to do at that point in my life.

I was cast as Gloria Swanson's brother in a film called *Prodigal Daughters*. It was a pretty big part and I think I did a good job in it. Gloria and I became good friends, even though she was one of Hollywood's reigning queens and I was a virtual nobody—just Jesse Lasky's cousin.

There were evenings when Gloria and I walked out of the studio gate together. Crowds would surround her. Nobody, of course, even noticed me. There was something inside me, gnawing at me—I wanted to be noticed, too. I'm not sure why. I have an ego, like everybody else, but it was more than simply that. It was a measure of success, that phenomenon of being noticed. Above all, I wanted to be a success, but also to be very, very good at something and have the world recognize my ability.

Those nights, when I felt the cold taste of the world's nonrecognition, I would go back to my room at Mrs. Grover's and I would be depressed. I wondered if I would ever become somebody. It seemed to me that my time in Hollywood had been wasted. I had gone sideways, instead of up. I was wrong, of course. Everything I had done had been learning, storing things in my head that would be invaluable when my chance finally came. But that's like telling a child, "Look, kid, do what Mommy and Daddy tell you to do, because we know best." It isn't until years later that a child realizes his parents were right all along, and that they actually did know best. At the time, however, the words mean nothing.

If somebody had told me then that everything I had done was great for my future, I would have punched him in the nose. I would have said, "I'm spinning my wheels, I'm doing nothing, I'm wasting my life." To me, at that time, that's what I thought I was doing. I watched people around me move ahead, get discovered, become stars. I felt I was just standing still. I couldn't help but wonder— was I just a vaudevillian, after all?

Those fits of depression seldom lasted long. I have never been the kind of person who stays down in the dumps. I find life too much fun to cry about it.

There was a social life waiting, for one thing. I was a healthy, red-blooded American boy and there were girls to meet and court and make love to. There were flings to be flung. There were wild oats that desperately cried out to be sown, and I've always been one to heed the cry of a desperate wild oat.

On Saturday nights, we would almost always go up to Mrs. Cudahy's house. Don't get the wrong idea about the word "house." It wasn't that kind of place at all. Mrs. Cudahy, of the Cudahy Packing Company Cudahys, was a Los Angeles socialite. She loved movie people, and every Saturday night there would be a party to which the movie colony was invited. Her house was a huge, imposing mansion at the top of Vine Street. There were tables set with mountains of food. There were drinks to be had, even though this was during the darkest days of Prohibition. There were a couple of orchestras placed strategically for dancing. Over all this opulence, Mrs. Cudahy reigned, dressed always in the same costume, like an Egyptian princess.

At the time, I was going with Anne Cudahy, one of Mrs. Cudahy's three daughters, so I was like one of the family for a while, until that alliance broke up. Even afterward, I was welcome at the Cudahys' on Saturday nights and for several years that was part of my weekly ritual.

One big thing that held me back in those days, both socially and I think professionally, was my relationship to Jesse Lasky. There was then, and always has been, a feeling in Hollywood about the relatives of studio bosses. It's a feeling of suspicion, perhaps of envy, certainly of fear. They all wondered whether I was where I was—even though I wasn't very high up—because of that family tie. They were also afraid that anything they might drop in conversation would find its way back to Lasky's ear, so they were always on their guard when they spoke to me. Nothing deters a good social arrangement more than if one party must be careful about what he, or she, says to the other party. Jesse Lasky had told me, that first day in his New York office, not to say anything about our relationship. I hadn't, but Hollywood is no place to keep secrets. Everybody knew that I was Jesse's cousin, and it became a cross for me to bear.

Despite it, I kept on working. I went from *Prodigal Daughters* into a couple of auto-racing pictures with my friend, Wally Reid, called *Top Speed* and *Double Speed*. Each part I got was bigger and better paying. They still weren't leads—far from it—but good-sized supporting roles. Reid and I became very close. In fact, I felt the time had come to improve my standard of living and leave Mrs. Grover and her boardinghouse. Reid invited me to share his home and I did. There was some regret at parting from Mrs. Grover, who had always been so kind to me, but I could afford a bit more comfort now and felt I was entitled to it. So I moved in with Wally at his home on Van Ness, just off Hollywood Boulevard. It was a big change.

There were always girls around with Wally, even though he was married at the time. He was so good-looking and had such an engaging personality that he had to fight them off. I got some of his leftovers.

There was a different atmosphere in Hollywood then than there is today. Stars were STARS!!! You knew it from the way they walked, the way they dressed, the way they behaved. I knew them all—John Barrymore, Richard Barthelmess, Bryant Washburn, Francis X. Bushman, Richard Dix, Douglas Fairbanks, and, of course, Reid. The men always wore the finest clothes and the girls always had an air of glamour about them. They took time to get dressed and made up properly before they went out to the store. Nowadays, you see some big-name stars in bare feet, dirty slacks, and T-shirts at premieres. I can't get used to it, and don't want to.

It was an era of burgeoning promise, of enthusiasm, of joy. More and more, as my pictures came out, I was part of this exciting and electric world. There were parties almost every night and I got invited to bigger and bigger, better and better ones.

At one of them, I found myself seated, at the dinner table, next to a man I immediately recognized. He was Rudolph Valentino, then at the height of his career as the world's leading romantic idol. In such films as *The Sheik* and *Blood and Sand*, he had made the ladies faint in ecstasy. At the dinner table that night, however, he was anything but what I had expected. He was a little shy, but basically a very nice, unconceited, thoroughly charming man. Rudy and I became good friends. We would often visit together and talk, as everybody talked then, about films and the film business. Actually, despite his immense popularity, he impressed me always as being a rather lonely man. He had few friends and seemed to welcome our relationship. It was only about three years later that he died, a death that would cause thirty thousand women to riot outside the funeral home in New York where his body lay. I was in Hollywood at the time and I wept, too, for this sad friend who had passed away at the peak of his success.

Perhaps it was seeing Valentino close up that hastened my decision to leave acting. I knew I could never compete with that most dazzling of men. Or maybe it was the words of Reid, who kept telling me he didn't feel that it was in acting that I would find the key to my future. I was slow to convince, however.

I did those two films with Reid, and I got some nice notices in some reviews. For a while, I thought that maybe he was wrong about my acting future. I looked about for other parts to play and I found them. The one that came along first was not at Famous Players–Lasky. This, I felt, was a plus in its favor. That old label—"He's Jesse Lasky's cousin"—kept haunting me and hurting me. There was a film with a part in it for me at Warner Brothers, and I decided to take it.

COLLEEN MOORE:
I WANT YOU TO
DIRECT ONE OF
MY PICTURES

I had first met Jack Warner in San Francisco. At the time, I was working for Sid Grauman at the Pan-Pacific International Exposition, and he was in San Francisco running the Warner Brothers' office there. My vaudeville days were yet to come, and his were behind him. Jack and a man named Pike Rickard had had a comedy song-and-dance act that played the Gus Sun Circuit for a few years.

Jack and Pike used to steal their act. I'm not making any wild, sensational accusation—Jack admits it. In his day, there was a book of vaudeville routines called Madison's Budget, which sold for one dollar. It had all the routines of the leading vaudeville acts in it, and Jack and Pike took their material right out of that book. This wasn't unusual—everybody stole in those days. Obviously, however, an act based on borrowed material could never reach the top, and Jack and Pike soon recognized their limitations. Besides, Jack's older brother Sam caught their act one day in Youngstown, Ohio, and waited for him outside the stage door.

"You were okay, Jack," Sam said to him. "But let me give you some advice. Get out in front of the theater where you pay the actors instead of the other way around."

Jack took Sam's advice and joined Sam in what was destined to become one of the all-time greatest movie companies, Warner Brothers.

It was at Warner Brothers Studio that I was to get my next big break. It started one day at the studio's radio station, KFWB. The brothers had set the station up early in the studio's existence as a means of locally promoting their own pictures. Radio was still new and experimental then and nobody knew much about it. This was long before the networks, of course, and long before the big stars discovered it, or vice versa. When the Warner brothers started KFWB, they didn't know what to put on the air, so they tried everything. One of the things they tried was a singer named Leon Zuardo, who was really Jack Warner in disguise. He wasn't much of a singer and he knew it, so he'd often interrupt himself and tell jokes—and he still tells those same lousy jokes today. Whenever any of Jack's old vaudeville friends were in town, they would drop around and join Leon Zuardo on the air. They would tell their rotten jokes, swap stories, kill time.

It was all so loose and informal that people used to come in off the street and talk to Zuardo/Warner. Once in a while, I'd drop in at the studio, too. I was an old vaudevillian, like Warner, and I had a raft of stories and jokes. That's how I met Warner for the second time, at the old KFWB studio on Sunset Boulevard.

We became friends.

One day at the studio, Jack happened to mention that there was a part he thought I would be right for. They were shooting a film called *Little Johnny Jones*, a racetrack story, and they needed somebody to play a crooked jockey. He thought that I was short enough to play a jockey and I guess he felt I looked crooked or something. Anyhow, he offered me the part and I took it. It was the chance to get away from under my cousin's shadow and prove to the world that I could make it on my own. I mulled Jack's offer over for a while—maybe fifteen minutes—and then I said okay.

"Great," Jack said. "Oh, there's just one thing—can you ride a horse?"

"Sure," I said. "I was born on a horse."

It wasn't exactly a lie. As a small boy, that summer when my father had sent me to the country for a vacation, I had been on the back of a horse. The ride had lasted perhaps ten minutes, but that was sufficient so I could answer Jack positively without lying about it. That ten-minute ride was not, however, long enough to make me feel secure about my prowess as a jockey.

Jack told me they'd pay me $125 a week while we were shooting, and I quickly agreed to that. It was more money than I had ever earned before. He told me to report to work at the studio the following week and see Minne Wallis, Hal Wallis' sister.

The next morning I took myself out to Griffith Park, where I knew there was a riding stable. I introduced myself to the old man who ran the stable. His name, he told me, was Davis.

"Mr. Davis," I said, "I've got a small problem. I'm broke and I have a chance for this part in a movie. Only thing is that the part is a jockey. I have to ride a racehorse. And I don't know how to ride."

"That is a problem," Davis said.

"I've got a proposition for you. If you will loan me somebody to teach me to ride, when I do the part I'll pay you back. I'll be making a hundred twenty-five dollars a week, so I'll be able to afford it. How about it?"

He went along with me. He laughed about it and called one of his workers over and told him to teach me how to be a jockey. I practiced in the Griffith Park stable a few days, going around and around the riding ring with my teacher at my side. Then he said I was ready to try riding outside on the park's bridle paths. My instructor led the way. I had to know how to gallop the horse, of course, if I was to play a jockey. By this time, I could sit him pretty well, but we had only been walking or cantering. Now I was to get a chance to see how it felt to go at full speed.

"When I drop my handkerchief," the instructor said, "you let him go."

He rode ahead of me and then he turned around and dropped the handkerchief. I did as he had told me to do, and my horse took off like a streak. The simple truth was that he was running away with me.

We passed the spot where my instructor stood, watching my rapid progress. I didn't want him to know that I had lost control.

"How'm I doing?" I called. Then I couldn't resist a little grandstanding. I took one hand off the reins to wave to him. Big mistake.

"You're doing fine," the instructor called.

That was the last thing I heard. I fell off and landed in a heap in some bushes at the side of the bridle path. I wasn't hurt but I had learned that I wasn't yet exactly a polished rider. I got back on and practiced some more, and by the time the picture started I felt reasonably at home on the back of one of those beautiful but immense animals.

Davis and I became good friends, and later on I'd occasionally go back to Griffith Park to ride for the fun of it. Horseback riding never became a passion with me; I much preferred to hire other people to do it, while I sat on the sidelines and watched.

Little Johnny Jones starred Johnny Hines as the honest jockey. I was the bad one, the one who would do anything to win. The climax of the film was the big race, as Hines and I thundered down the homestretch. The script called for me to reach across and squirt acid, from a rigged whip, into his face. Justice was supposed to triumph, however. I was the one who had to fall off, a few yards before the finish line.

That sort of worried me, when I read the script. Falling off a horse didn't sound too much like fun. I had visions of me landing on the track and a cavalry charge of horses stepping on me as they went by. I mentioned my concern to Jack Warner.

"You know horses," Jack said. "Right?"

"Sure, I know horses."

"Okay then. You know that horses don't step on people."

"I know it," I said, "and you know it. But the big problem is—does the horse know it?"

By now that's an old gag, but it was new that day, and Jack fell down laughing. It helped me convince him to use a stand-in for me in that scene. He turned out to be right—the horse didn't step on the stand-in, and none of the other horses did, either. Still I felt more comfortable about the whole scene, as one of the spectators.

After *Little Johnny Jones*, I did a few more parts but they were small and I was certain that I had no shining future as an actor. Being in front of the camera turned out to be a tremendous help to me, when I moved behind the camera as a director. Otherwise, however, I found acting to be rather bland work. It didn't seem to me to be particularly creative. I wanted to do something that was less interpretive, more inventive.

About that time, I met a director named Alfred E. Green. We first met one Sunday at Gilmore Stadium, where the old Hollywood Stars used to play their Pacific Coast League games. I was always a big baseball fan, and I'd go out to watch the Stars play whenever I had a chance. This one day, I found myself sitting next to Green. I knew who he was and began talking to him. Before the game was over, Green and I had become friends.

He asked me to play a small part in his next picture, *The Ghost Breakers*, and I did. I played a ghost. It was a comedy and, during the shooting, I suggested a couple of gags and funny bits to him that he liked and incorporated into the movie.

"You know, Mervyn," he said to me, as the shooting drew to a close, "I think you've got a real flair for gags. How about becoming my gag man?"

I didn't have to think twice. That was what I wanted—a chance to be in on the creative aspect of movie-making. It wasn't directing, but it was getting closer. It was inventing, not interpreting, and I liked it. I abandoned my acting career with no regrets.

The first picture Green and I worked on together was at First National, a thing called *Potash and Perlmutter in Hollywood*. Potash and Perlmutter—Alexander Carr and Barney Bernard— were a kind of imitation Weber and Fields, two old-time vaudevillians who had been converted into motion picture actors. I made up a lot of gags for the film.

Green was pleased with the gags, and with how they had helped the film. The picture was a hit, and had helped him and his career. He was approached to make some very big pictures, starring one of the biggest stars in Hollywood. He invited me to come along with him, as his right-hand gag man. He offered me a pretty good incentive—a $500-per-week salary. And screen credit, too.

Naturally, I quickly said yes. But I did ask for one change in my billing.

"Al," I said, "that title—'Gag man.' It doesn't do anything for me, and I know my mother wouldn't like it. It sounds like I'm in charge of choking people."

He laughed.

"Okay," he said, "what do you want to call yourself?"

I had been thinking about it for a while, so I had the answer ready.

"Comedy constructor."

"Okay," he said. "From now on, you're my comedy constructor. Nobody ever had one of those before."

Things were looking up for me. I had an imposing-sounding title—comedy constructor—and I had an imposing salary to go along with it. I was gaining experience every day, with every picture. As Green's comedy constructor, I was suggesting bits of business that were, in effect, directing. My contributions were all in the comedy field, yet they were bits of directorial business after all.

I knew it was harder to make the audience laugh than to make them cry. I've always said that an onion can make anybody cry, but there's no vegetable that makes people laugh. If I could create comedy routines on film, then surely I would be able to create tragic moments just as easily, or even easier.

It was a step up. There would be more steps, but I would have help in scaling the next one, the biggest one.

In everybody's life, there is usually some one person who is a major aid in his career. You could call the person a champion, someone who goes to bat for you and makes the path a bit easier.

I found my champion when I went with Alfred E. Green to work on his next film. Green had been a tremendous help, and would continue to be so, but he wasn't my champion. That role in my life is reserved for the wonderful lady who was the star of that picture.

Her name is Colleen Moore.

Colleen Moore was a remarkable girl who grew into a remarkable woman. She was the daughter of a fine Chicago family. When she grew up with a burning urge to act, her family politely bribed Cecil B. DeMille into giving her a chance. She capitalized on that chance and became, next to Mary Pickford, the biggest silent female star of them all.

Later, she would retire from the screen at the height of her fame, marry well, and spend the rest of her life doing important civic works in Chicago, writing books, raising her stepchildren, and doting on her grandchildren. She was never anything but a lady, throughout her career and her postcareer life.

At the time we met, she was at the peak of her fame, making box-office hit after box-office hit and earning thirty thousand dollars a week. Her fame, however, never went to her head in any way. Perhaps because of her affluent background, she was never spoiled by her wealth, never seduced by her notoriety, never changed by her success. She was always sweet—in the best sense of the word—and kind and pleasant to everyone she met. I doubt that there was a man who worked on her pictures who was not platonically in love with her.

We began to work together when I came along with Al Green, who had been signed to direct Colleen in *Sally*. This would be followed by others—among them *Irene, Desert Flower*, and *Ella Cinders*—and Colleen and I quickly became very close friends.

She was married, then, to John McCormick, who had risen with her from publicity director to the head of the studio in Hollywood. He was a big, good-looking, and thoroughly charming man. His only problem was alcohol. Periodically, he would take off on benders that would last three or four days, sometimes a week or more. Colleen wouldn't know where he was, until she would get a call from a hospital somewhere and they'd tell her he was a patient there, drying out. It was very hard on her. She really had had no experience with that sort of thing, and she never did get used to it.

I was the shoulder she cried on. Mine were the ears into which she poured out her troubles. It was my heart that would break, thinking about this wonderful girl burdened with a hopeless drunkard for a husband. Every time, after one of his sieges, he would swear that it would never happen again. At first, Colleen would believe him, but when he broke his promise time after time after time, it became unbearable. Maybe, if McCormick had had some help from people like Alcoholics Anonymous, he would have straightened himself out, but this was long before AA came into existence. I'm sure he tried but he couldn't make it alone. It got worse, and Colleen grew more and more troubled, as she tried to make her marriage work. I heard it all, day by day, week by week, year by year.

We went to New York once to make a film there called *Naughty but Nice*. The first day, we shot on top of one of the double-decker buses then in use along Fifth Avenue. After the day's work was done, I took Colleen back to her hotel. The plan was to pick McCormick up, and then we were all going to the Stork Club for dinner.

We got to the Ambassador Hotel, and went up to their room, on the sixteenth or seventeenth floor. When she opened the door and we went in, McCormick was standing by the open window, looking out and brooding.

"Drunk again," Colleen said, bitterly.

McCormick didn't say anything, but he turned and there was madness in his eyes. He grabbed Colleen and began dragging her toward the window. There was no mistaking his intention—he meant to throw her out.

He was five or six inches taller than I am, thirty or forty pounds heavier, and possessed with the fury of his alcoholic rage. But I had one advantage—I had been trained in street fighting as a San Francisco newsboy. I just picked up the closest weapon—a chair—and socked him over the head with it.

I took Colleen's hand and we ran out the door, down the elevator, and out into the streets. We walked, hand in hand, all night long, she crying and me trying to get her to stop. It was dawn when we got back to her room. McCormick wasn't there. He was off again.

None of this private tragedy affected her public performing, however. No matter how rough things were at home, at the studio she was always cheerful and polite, her scenes down pat, her face sunny. I don't know how she did it, and I like to think my ever-present sympathy helped. She says that it did.

Almost every day when we were shooting we would have lunch together. The funny thing about that is that Colleen would let me pick up the check, even though she made nearly one hundred times the salary I was making. I still kid her about that, but I really didn't mind. It was a pleasure to be in her company and, anyhow, even though I wasn't in her financial league, I was still making pretty good money. I could afford to buy her lunch. She wasn't a big eater.

She liked me, I think, for myself as well as for my listening prowess. I was doing well with the gags I created for her films.

In *Desert Flower*, for example, there was a gag in which she seemed to be bowing, as though to an audience. When the camera pulled back, however, the scene was something entirely different. She was pumping a railroad handcar.

On one of our first films together—*Sally*—I think I got in her good graces—and Al Green's as well. There was a scene in a little restaurant. Colleen was the dishwasher and Leon Errol was the waiter, who was helping her by drying the dishes she washed.

"Mervyn," Al Green said, "I want you to come up with a gag for that dishwashing scene."

So I went back and sat down and thought about it, and came up with a gag that worked pretty well. I had Colleen wash a dish and then throw it off camera. It came back, like a boomerang, and Leon Errol caught it and dried it. Everybody loved the gag and it worked. Colleen hugged me and I think our rapport dates from that silly but funny gag.

We were together every day and, during the times when Mc-Cormick was off on one of his benders, every night. I would try to console her, but what could you say at a time like that? I did what I could. The situation lasted for years and, even after I had become a director, Colleen would call me and I'd come racing over to her magnificent home and help her through the long, frightening night.

She was the one who first encouraged me in my desire—my dream—to direct. As we talked, on those nights when McCormick would be absent, we would think of our futures. I say "our futures" because Colleen generously included me in her own plans and dreams. She often said that she thought I would make a fine director, that she could tell from the way I created gags that worked on screen that I had a flair for creating visual images. Furthermore, she told me she felt I had a knack for getting actors to do their best. Often, Green would let me tell the actors what I wanted them to do when we were going to shoot one of my gags. It was almost directing, and Colleen told me she thought I could handle a picture myself.

"You can do it, Mervyn," she would say. "And someday I want you to direct one of my pictures."

Naturally, I was pleased. Who wouldn't be? If I could start my directing career with a Colleen Moore film, I would be halfway home. Everything she did was box-office gold, and directors are always measured (in Hollywood, at any rate) by what their films do at the gate. If I could do a Colleen Moore picture, I would be made as a director.

There was another reason why doing a movie with her would be a tremendous head start. For anybody who sets out to direct his first movie, it's a time for nervousness. Suppose I was to draw a star who wouldn't be cooperative? There were plenty of them around. Or, perhaps, somebody who was a veteran and felt he or she knew more about movies than I did? The whole experience might turn out to be a disaster. I knew, however, that if I could work with Colleen on my first directorial assignment, it would all go smooth as silk, because of the great rapport we had.

So I dreamed right along with her. Al Green encouraged us in our mutual dream.

Meanwhile, there were pictures to be shot, gags to be created, and a salary to be earned. Things moved along swiftly in those days. We went from one film to another. In *Sally*, I taught Colleen to tap-dance. The character she played was supposed to dance, but she didn't know how. McCormick was going to hire a teacher, but I said I could do it—every vaudevillian knows how to tap-dance. I did.

I always loved to have fun on the set. In *Sally*, there was a dream sequence in which Leon Errol had his own harem. There were around thirty beautiful girls and he was supposed to grab one of them and give her a big kiss. He came to me and said he couldn't do it, that the girl had such terrible halitosis he just couldn't kiss her.

"Leon, you have to do it," I told him.

Then I went to the girl in the scene and I told her that she wasn't doing the bit right.

"Look, honey," I said, "you're supposed to be crazy about this man. What I want you to do is look him in the eyes—and breathe harder. Remember that—breathe harder."

So they went back into the scene and the girl huffed and puffed right into poor Leon's face. You could see him turning green.

"Cut!"

I called the girl over and again said that she wasn't exhibiting enough passion.

"Breathe even harder," I told her. "It's your big chance, but you've got to be passionate. Big breaths, now, remember that, big breaths."

The next time we shot, Leon had had enough. In midembrace, he stopped, said, "Pardon me," went outside, and came back with some mints for her. I don't remember what happened after that, but I imagine we switched girls.

Other films followed, in pleasant procession, and there were a lot of gags and a lot of experience to be gained. It was a period of maturing, both for me and for the film business. Comedy was changing. It had always been the purest of slapstick—pie-in-the-face, banana-peel-on-the-sidewalk humor—but gradually the public demanded more, demanded some sophistication. I like to think I played a part in helping change the public's taste somewhat. The gags I created may not have been up to today's standards, but they were a cut above what the screen had seen up to that point. The continuing success of Colleen's films, while others were tailing off, appears to me to be proof that I had my finger on the public pulse, in the matter of what type of comedy they wanted.

Then, one morning, the telephone rang.

"Mervy!" I knew right away who it was—Colleen. She was the only person who ever called me Mervy.

"Hi, darling."

"Well, guess what. It's happened. You're going to direct a movie. John just told me."

We laughed over the phone like school kids. It was true. I think that it was at Colleen's urging that her husband, John McCormick, had assigned me to direct her next film, which was going to be called either *Peg o' My Heart* or *Smiling Irish Eyes*. I walked on air all that day, as everybody at First National came over to congratulate me and wish me well. Al Green said if there was anything he could do to help me, all I had to do was ask. Everybody was so generous with their offers of assistance and their pledges of friendship and good wishes.

I poured myself into preparing the film. I read the script and figured out all my camera angles. I added gags. I watched as the carpenters built the sets. I went with Colleen as she tried on her wardrobe. Everything was set to go.

The day before the shooting was to begin, I took stock of myself. I was twenty-seven. I decided that I had done pretty well, at that, considering my slow start in life. Here I was, still young, still in my twenties, and I was about to direct a major motion picture with probably the biggest star in Hollywood heading up my cast. I had reason to be proud—but I resolved that was just going to be the beginning, that I would make that picture a winner and go on from there.

We were to begin shooting on a Tuesday. Bright and early Monday morning, I was at the studio, going over the last-minute arrangements. There was one detail I wanted to talk to McCormick about, so I went to his office. He was on the telephone. I could only hear his side of the conversation, of course, but what I heard wasn't good. He was yelling and cursing and his face was a bright crimson. Then, abruptly, he slammed down the receiver and turned his back to me. For a minute or so, he stood there, looking out the window, and then finally he turned to me.

"It's all over, Mervyn," he said. "That was Rowland I was talking to, and it's all over."

Rowland, I knew, was Richard Rowland, the president of First National Pictures, who had his office in New York.

"What do you mean, it's all over? What's all over?"

"We're through at First National, Colleen and me. Those bastards tried to pull a fast one on us, and I'm taking Colleen and going to New York tomorrow. We'll do our pictures at another studio from now on."

"But what about my picture?"

"Canceled."

Just like that, the bubble burst. Because of some fight between McCormick and Rowland, he was taking Colleen, and my directorial debut was over before it had begun. It was the end of the beginning.

I walked out of McCormick's office and went over to the stage where we were going to make *Peg o' My Heart*. There was nobody there. The word gets around Hollywood studios fast and everybody knew the picture was canceled. I wandered around the sets I had watched being built a few days before. I touched the fabrics I had helped pick out, picked up the props I had so carefully chosen, fingered the pictures I had selected to hang on the walls. And I must confess that I cried, real tears streaming down my cheeks.

I was still there, on that deserted stage, when one of the studio policemen found me.

"Hey, Mervyn," he said. "I've been looking all over for you. You got a long-distance phone call."

It was New York. Richard Rowland was calling.

"Mervyn," he said, "I want you to know what happened. We had to drop *Peg o' My Heart*. No reason to go into all the details with you, but that picture is out."

"I heard," I said.

"I figured you probably had. But Colleen has been so enthusiastic about your potential as a director, and I have so much respect for her judgment, that I want you to do a picture for us anyway."

"But I heard that Colleen and John had walked out."

"That's right," he said. "They did. That's why the picture is out. But we still want you. And I want you to do another picture for the studio. It won't be with Colleen, of course, but it will be something. I'm taking a chance on you because of what she said."

"Another picture?"

"That's right. As I said, no Colleen in this one, but a picture is a picture."

I asked him about the picture. He said that he didn't have any specific property in mind yet. He wanted me to find something. He told me to look around, read scripts and books and see plays. When I found something I felt would make a good picture, I was to let him know.

Years later, I found out that what I had suspected that morning was true. My champion had gone to bat for me. When Colleen Moore had heard about McCormick's actions, quitting the studio after that vitriolic phone call, she had immediately phoned Rowland in New York and begged him to give me another film to direct.

"Just because you're mad at John," Colleen had told Rowland, "don't take it out on Mervyn."

Out of respect for her, he had gone along with her, and then called me to tell me.

My disappointment over not having Colleen to direct was assuaged somewhat by the fact that all was not lost. I would get a chance to direct, after all. The only thing that remained was to find a property.

I spent the next few weeks doing what Rowland had suggested I

do. I went to the studio story department and read every script I
could find. I bought dozens of books and devoured them. I saw
what few plays I could see in Los Angeles. This was to become the
habit of a lifetime for me. From then on, I was always reading,
reading, reading. I kept stacks of books and scripts by my bed, and
would read for hours every night. I would read while I ate, read
during breaks while shooting, read everything I could lay my hands
on.

It has paid off, over the years, and it paid off that first time, too.
I found the script of a play called *No Place to Go*. I thought it
would make a funny movie and, more important, I felt I could
handle it. I called Rowland and told him about it, and he read it, or
had someone in his office read it, and then I got the word back that
they liked it and had purchased it for me. Now I had a picture
again.

Once more, I threw myself into preproduction. I supervised the
writing of the script. I checked sets, costumes, everything. I had
nothing to do with the casting, but I was delighted when the word
came through that the First National people in New York had
signed Lloyd Hughes and Mary Astor to play the leads in my
picture.

My picture!

What a wonderful sound those two words had. A positive ring in
the ears. I said it over and over as the weeks of getting ready drew
to a close. "My picture, my picture, my picture." It was a rhapsody
in syllables.

Inevitably, the glorious day approached. Then, finally, it arrived.

I was a director. I even had my name on the back of a chair to
prove it.

It was 1928, a good year for America—and for me. The bubble
had not yet burst, peace seemed as though it would last forever,
prices were low, and hopes were high. I imagine that 1928 was
possibly the best of years for the American dream. A year later, we
would all wake up to the harsh facts of economic reality; but in
1928, it seemed as though there was no place to go but up. It was
the last year for naïveté, for innocence, for dreams-come-true.

I was, I suppose, a perfect illustration of that cheerful philosophy of 1928. Before I reached my twenty-eighth birthday, I would
be a director of a major motion picture for one of the top studios of
the day. I would be receiving a salary of a thousand dollars a week,

in the days when a thousand dollars a week was a grand. If I had stopped to think about it—which I didn't—I would have classified myself as being the most fortunate man alive. After all, I was in the greatest country in the world, in the greatest state in that country, in the greatest industry in that state, in the greatest job in that industry. What more could a man possibly want?

I was nervous the night before shooting was to begin. But, when I walked on the set early on the Great Day, I found my nervousness had vanished. Work is the best cure for fear. That set a pattern for all my future films—the nervousness was the anticipatory type, and it disappeared once the battle was begun. I found, to my great relief, that I was calm and cool and collected, and ready and eager to set to work.

No Place to Go was a comedy, dealing with a married couple who had a fight. It wasn't particularly original but it had an honest situation, characters who were real and believable, and, most important, a quality that I always strove for in my films—the quality that goes by the corny but descriptive name of "heart." Heart is difficult to define, but the audience knows when it's there and misses it when it's not. *No Place to Go* had it.

I don't remember too much about the plot, but I do remember one of the key scenes had the couple painting a white line down the middle of their living room. They had had a fight and the white line was to separate his half of the room from hers. When the picture came out, that was the scene the public talked about and remembered.

That was not, however, the first scene I shot. When I began work that very first day, I walked into a studio surrounded by flowers. All my friends had sent baskets of flowers as a gesture of good luck, and the biggest one of all was from Colleen Moore.

I used those flowers to help decorate the set, because the first setup we had was for a café scene. This was to be the opening scene in the picture, and I always liked to open and close with exciting visual effects. In this case, I had planned for the audience to see what looked like a bunch of Zulu natives with spears ready to skewer a girl. When the camera pulled back, they were all part of a dance act in the café.

I knew exactly how I wanted to shoot it, and just what angles I felt would be best. I carefully consulted with my cameraman, George Folsey, however. That's become a way of life with me because cameramen—or, as they call them today, cinematographers—know how to turn ideas into reality. That's their job and any director who tries to bypass them is in for a lot of grief. Work with them and they will do anything for you. Ignore them and the picture is certain to look terrible.

We rehearsed the first scene and I was just about to call "Action!" for the first time when I heard a carpenter hammering nails as he built another set at the other end of the stage.

"Quiet!" I yelled.

The noise persisted.

"Quiet! You, with the hammer, cut it out."

"Aw, come on," the carpenter called back, "my hammering ain't coming through on your picture."

He was right. Traditionally, in silent film days, there was always a lot of noise on the set. There was hammering, coughing, sneezing, laughing, talking, everything. I had a theory about that. It seemed to me that the noise was very distracting to the actors. Never mind that the audiences in the theaters would never hear it. The point was that it bothered the actors and, to me, that made it bad. Right that first day I established a precedent—I insisted on absolute quiet on the set, even in the days of silent films. I think the actors appreciated that fact, too, because it helped them concentrate on what they were supposed to be doing.

Later on, when I directed *Quo Vadis* in Italy, the first Italian word I learned was *silenzio* ("silence"). I used it very often.

The picture went smoothly. One thing I had done, which not many silent movie directors did, was to have a solid script before I began, and to stick to it all the way. I've done that ever since.

In those silent days, there was very often a haphazard, crapshoot attitude toward the script. The producer and the director would have a vague idea of their story line and shoot it without anything remotely resembling a finished script. Their approach was, "We'll shoot it and then see what we've got." Often when they finished they found they didn't have anything like what they had expected. Sometimes they started out to make a drama and found out that they had filmed themselves a comedy. Or the other way around.

What they could do, then, was to rewrite the titles so they could actually change it from drama to comedy. There was a man in town named Ralph Spence who made a fortune at that. He was brilliant and could look at a picture and make up a whole new set of titles.

One of the great title writers was Howard Hughes's uncle, Rupert Hughes. He was the man who saved Jack Warner from a major disaster in 1920. Warner told me the story. It happened when the Warner studio had filmed *Moby Dick*, with John Barrymore and Dolores Costello. When they looked at what they had, they were shocked. The film was well acted and well directed, but, as Jack put it, the whole thing didn't go together at all.

So Warner ran to Hughes, who took it apart and put it together again with a whole new set of titles, and turned a potential disaster into a hit.

Warner says that he and Hughes had never talked money—"I was afraid to talk money," Jack told me, "because I was afraid that it was going to cost me too much." So, when the work was done, Jack gave Hughes "a check of no consequence—fifteen hundred dollars"—as a kind of down payment. Hughes sent the check back. He told Warner that he had rewritten the titles as a favor to Warner and Herman Melville.

I had no such troubles with *No Place to Go*. Everything had been planned so precisely before the shooting that there were no snags, no bottlenecks, no difficulties. The titles had all been written ahead of time, and we stuck to them all the way. They worked, too.

Directing that film was, of course, a learning process for me. No matter how many directors I had watched directing how many films, it's still very different when you do it yourself. The responsibility was mine, the decisions were mine to make. It was exhausting. Physically, it's tiring work—you're on your feet all day long, and it's a long day—but the worst is that it is so taxing emotionally. There is first the emotion inherent in the story and you become wrapped up in your story. Secondly, there is the emotion of urgency, the need to get the picture done and done well.

I found that I was so tired at the end of the day I could barely eat a few bites of dinner and then fall into bed. I hadn't anticipated that. I had heard other directors complain about being tired, but I figured they were old men and it wouldn't happen to me. But it happened.

That was one thing I learned—never plan any social engagements during the time I'm shooting.

I learned, too, to exercise my authority, and that the final authority had to be mine. Dozens of times a day people—actors, crew, executives—would come to me with a question or a problem. I had to have the answer immediately. I soon learned that it really didn't matter if the answer was right or wrong as long as some sort of decision was reached.

No Place to Go cost between seventy thousand and eighty thousand dollars to make, about average for that era. It took us somewhere around five weeks to shoot it. It opened only a month or so after we wrapped it up. There wasn't the lengthy postproduction period that there is today. For a tyro director anxious to see his first film in front of a live audience, that month was plenty long enough.

It was previewed in Glendale. The night before the big day, I couldn't sleep. All that day, the hours seemed to be ninety minutes long. I paced, I walked, I jogged (long before jogging became fashionable). I drove around. I just couldn't wait for the hour to arrive when I would see those thrilling words—"Directed by Mervyn LeRoy"—flash on the screen. I ate dinner and got dressed and was about to leave for Glendale.

Then I threw up.

I think that was the most nervous time in my whole life. The process would be repeated for the next three or four films I directed, until my stomach caught up to my mind. I finally made it to the theater in Glendale, a little weak, but willing. I got to my seat just as the opening titles appeared on the screen.

The picture was successful. Nobody hailed me then as the savior of the screen, but neither did they boo and hiss, so I was content. People congratulated me in the lobby afterward, and that was a warm feeling. I learned, quickly, to distinguish between the sincere congratulators and those who were only paying lip service to me and really didn't mean it.

That whole scene—the postpremiere lobby—is one of the falsest things about Hollywood. The people who have made the film—the producer and director and stars—stand there as their friends file by and solemnly tell them how great they thought the film was. Even if it's terrible, you hear the same ridiculous comments—"A wonderful film" or "I was never so moved in my life" or "You've got yourself a sure Oscar winner there."

I can't do that. When I go to a premiere and I like the picture, I'm always delighted to be able to tell them so. But if I don't like it, I simply cannot lie about it. I try to sneak out, if I can, or, if I can't, I'll say something innocuous like "That was a very interesting piece of film" or "Well, Irving, you've done it again." Let them interpret my remarks to suit their egos.

That night in Glendale, however, I found that the audience—both the invited guests and the ordinary moviegoers who just happened to be there—were sincere in their praise. I could tell that I had made a good, solid film and that they all recognized that I had done my job professionally.

Most exciting, however, were the words of Al Rockett, who had succeeded John McCormick as head of the First National studio in Hollywood.

"Good piece of film, Mervyn," said Rockett. "When you get to the studio tomorrow, drop in to the office. We'll talk about your next one."

That was the greatest praise I could receive, the fact that the studio boss felt my first one was good enough to warrant talking about a second one. After all, studios are pragmatic about films, and should be. They are business ventures and are concerned primarily with dollars and cents. I knew then that if Rockett was willing to discuss a second film, he must have been convinced that I could turn out motion pictures that would be profitable ventures.

To some, that may seem to be too commercial a view of the business, and an admission that all that matters in movies is that they make money. When you think about it, however, it becomes clear that, for a movie to be a money-maker, it must appeal to the public. The broader its appeal, the more money it will make. I don't feel that that is sinful or disgraceful, as some people do. To me, what we in the movie industry are hoping to do is to bring entertainment to the millions. The better our entertainment, the more people will buy tickets and the more money the picture will make. Thus it follows that when we go after profits, what we are actually doing is attempting to bring entertainment to the most people we can. I think that's as it should be.

So I was happy that night in Glendale. And *No Place to Go* established a pattern for me. All my pictures—and I made seventy-five of them—have been money-makers. Some made more than others, of course, but there hasn't been one that flopped in a big way.

Once, years later, just before I married Doris Warner, Jack Warner threw a stag dinner for me. He wanted, he told me, to decorate the room with posters of all my flops as a gag—but he couldn't find one.

No, I never had a real flop. I've had a few that I didn't particularly like and that didn't make too much money, and quite a few that the critics didn't like. There has never been one, however, that the public hated enough so that it lost money.

No Place to Go was successful enough that I was immediately given another picture to direct. That one was *Harold Teen*, based on the then-famous comic strip. It almost proved the old cliché about the sophomore jinx.

I went into it with the supreme confidence of anyone who has had a first success. It wasn't exactly an I-know-everything attitude, but more of an everything-I-touch-will-turn-out-beautiful approach. With one success, I felt the time was ripe to do some experimenting, to show Hollywood that somebody new and daring and innovative had arrived on the scene.

There was a scene in the script in which my cast—headed by Arthur Lake (who later became famous as Dagwood) and Alice White—was supposed to be making a movie themselves. These were comic-strip characters, remember, so I reasoned that they should behave comically. Obviously, they would get everything wrong, and wrong in a big and funny way. So I decided that the movie they shot would come out upside down. That is precisely how I shot it, so the whole scene was upside down.

When the studio bosses—Al Rockett, producer Robert Kane, and the rest—saw my upside-down rushes, they exploded.

"Mervyn," Kane said, "that's dreadful stuff. Upside down! I'm going to take you off the picture."

I tried to explain that I knew the difference between upside down and right side up, that it was all supposed to be a joke to show how inept my characters were. He didn't get it. He kept insisting that he'd have to replace me and get somebody on the picture who could at least tell the top from the bottom.

I probably would have been kicked off the picture—and it would have been tough to get another one, with that sort of blemish on my record—except for the kindly and timely intervention of Allan Dwan. Dwan was one of the great directors of that era; he directed most of Douglas Fairbanks' swashbucklers. For some reason, he had seen my upside-down rushes. He got the joke right away and went to bat for me. He told Kane and the others that he thought the upside-down scene was very funny and was exactly right for the film's characters.

They had a great deal of respect for Dwan's judgment, so they let me finish making *Harold Teen*. In Kane's defense, I must say that when the picture was previewed—in Glendale again—he came up to me afterward and apologized. I have a feeling, however, that he didn't apologize until after he heard how the audience roared at that scene.

"You were right, Merv," Kane said. "That was a very funny scene, that upside-down scene."

"Okay, Bob," I said, "but you know you could have ruined my whole career if you'd kicked me off the picture."

He could have, too. Hollywood is a sentimental town in lots of ways, but it can't forgive failure. Once the word gets around that somebody has goofed and has had to be replaced, that's generally the end of that particular somebody. Second chances are as rare in Hollywood as ski tows.

I've remembered that lesson, that brush with disaster I had. Over the years, there have been several actors I've worked with who have started out doing poorly in some of my films. There has been the temptation to wield a quick, sharp ax and fire them, but I've always thought back to how I almost lost everything just when I was beginning to find it. I've held my tongue and my pink slip, kept the actors on, tried to explain what I wanted—and, generally, it's worked. There's too much hasty firing around this business but, of course, there are times when it is essential to the integrity of your film. As a producer, later, I had to replace a director and it wasn't easy, but it had to be done.

Harold Teen turned out to be my first big box-office hit. It made a million dollars and, in those days, million-dollar profits on a single film were rare. People particularly liked that inverted scene, because it was fresh and new.

Being innovative in films is good, although if you get too innovative nobody knows what you're doing. Some of today's directors try so many new things that they are, in effect, practicing cinematic masturbation. Others boast of their fresh techniques, but they are in reality only doing what some of us veterans have been doing for years. They talk today of the "newness" of slow motion and hand-held cameras and quick cuts. It's all been done before, many years ago.

Take hand-held cameras, for example. I used them often in my early days. They were called Akeleys then. I used them sparingly, only in scenes where I felt they belonged, scenes such as people walking through a forest. Nowadays, some young directors use them to look at people's pores. To me, that sort of usage throws the audience off. Like any other tool in any other trade, it has its function—but you have to know when to use it and, just as important, when not to.

With two hits to my credit, things were definitely looking up for

Mervyn LeRoy. I acquired a nickname that, over the years, became both a blessing and a curse.

I don't know who first pinned it on me, but I began hearing it all over town.

"The Boy Wonder."

At first, I was pleased. It implied that I was doing wonderful things and anybody likes to have that kind of adjective associated with his work. I could understand "The Boy" part, too, because I still looked younger than my twenty-eight years. Every few days, somebody would come on the set and ask to see Mr. LeRoy. I would say, "I'm Mr. LeRoy," and they would say, "Cut the kidding, sonny, I want to see the director."

The nickname hung on for so long, however, that it got to be an annoyance. Like all things, however, it gradually died out—or maybe I began to look not so boyish, so it was no longer appropriate. I outlived it, fortunately. It's funny, but nobody has ever called me "The Man Wonder."

The infant Mervyn with his mother, Edna.

Mervyn LeRoy (center), a San Francisco boy.

Harry LeRoy, Mervyn's father. They helped each other.

Making movies in the backyard. Mervyn LeRoy at right.

MY FIRST MOVING PICTURE 1909.

Mervyn as a San Francisco
newsboy.

For fans, a postcard portrait
of a young vaudevillian.

Yours
Vaudevillingly,
Mervyn Le Roy.

BOB MILLS

THE BOY WITH THE SUNNY SMILE   IN VAUDEVILLE

JOE   BEA
BRADLEY & EARLE
"THE TIDD-LE-WINKS"
U. B. O. TIME   Direction, NAT SOBEL

MATT   BILLIE
KENNEDY AND FAY
BITS FROM MUSICAL COMEDY
IN VAUDEVILLE

M'LISS & CO.
IN THE IRISH MUSICAL COMEDY
TIMMY'S COLLEEN

ED   ED
ROWLEY & MULLEN
Comedy Talks, Singing and Dancing
IN VAUDEVILLE

STOVALL   SEDGWICK   SEYMOUR
3 RED HOTS
In "Darktown Kapers"
Singing, Dancing and Comedy Talk—In Vaudeville

Frank—Rose & Thorn—Olive
A Sparkling Spatter of Song and Chatter
DIRECTOR—ALF. T. WILTON

WIKI
HAWAIIAN ENTERTAINER
DIRECTION—PAT CASEY

JIMMIE   AIMEE
COLLINS & NOBLE
In Comedy Oddity "Green and Gray." By John P. Mulgrew. Special Drop.

"PEGGY"
Some Dog! Nuf Sed

MAX   HAZEL
McDONALD AND CLEVELAND
"CLASSY CONVERSATIONALISTS"
LOEW CIRCUIT   Direction—JOE MICHAELS

Harry Fraser & Edward Finley
IN "SKIRTS" A MELODRAMATIC NOVELTY BY RITA WELMAN

FRANK SHERMAN
SINGING, TALKING AND COMEDY   IN VAUDEVILLE

ESTELLE SULLY
The Black-Eyed Susan of Vaudeville
Formerly Five Sullys.   Direction—Bruce Duffus

FIELD BARNES
XYLOPHONIST   IN VAUDEVILLE

Singing Military Travesty
JOE   JACK
BARRETT & RYNO
BATTLE OF FORT LIMBURGER

CHAS. LOWE & BAKER SISTERS
In Musical Comedy Bits
IN VAUDEVILLE

RUTH GOODWIN
THE SINGLE GIRL WITH THE DOUBLE VOICE

JOHNNIE   RENE
FRANCIS & WILSON
DIRECTION—SAMUEL BAERWITZ

BOB & ELVA STANLEY
COMEDY WIRE ACT   Direction—LEVEY & JONES

BABE ANDERSON presents
MAJOR, MINOR and SCALE
3 girls, 3 violins and a special drop

KENDALL'S AUTO DOLL
THE MAIDEN OF MYSTERY
The World's Best Mechanical Doll Act   Direction—Jack Flynn

BELLE   JAMES
BRANDON & TAYLOR
The Girl and the Yodeler—Playing U. B. O. Direction—Smith & Hughes

MORGAN   SADA
BROWN & SIMMONS
Coming in a New Act by Joseph Byron Tottens

AUSTIN   MAE
GOETZ AND DUFFY
Manufacturers of Melody and Mirth   Direction—Jack Lewis   U. B. O.

MR. PIPP & MR. PEPP
"A COUPLE OF HIGHBROWS"

VIOLET & LEWIS
COMEDY NOVELTY AERIAL.   NEW ACT TO THE EAST

MERVYN   CLYDE
LE ROY & COOPER
"TWO KIDS AND A PIANO."   Dir.—MAX HART
IRVING SHANNON HANDLES THE LAYING OUT FINS

E. PAUL   ESTELLE
SOUTHE & TOBIN
VAUDEVILLE SPARKS IN HARMONY
Direction—JAMES PLUNKETT

Vaudeville bill, 1918. (See lower left.)

Mervyn LeRoy (left) and his vaudeville partner, Clyde Cooper.

Two kids and a piano.

Mervyn LeRoy, actor, in *Little Johnny Jones* as the crooked jockey. (*Photo by Guy Coburn, Inc.*)

Mervyn LeRoy and his champion, Colleen Moore.

The early days in Hollywood. LeRoy (right) with Efe Asher, Charlie Chaplin, and Thelma Todd.

The first scene Mervyn LeRoy directed—the nightclub scene in
No Place To Go.

LeRoy (center) demonstrates action for Alice White and Arthur Lake in
Harold Teen.

The first blockbuster—LeRoy directs Edward G. Robinson in *Five Star Final*.

Mervyn LeRoy directs John Gilbert (both on stairs at left) in *Gentleman's Fate*, Gilbert's only successful talkie.

LeRoy and Gloria Swanson, shooting *Tonight Or Never*.

On the set of *Tonight Or Never*. Florenz Ziegfeld (left) visits Gloria Swanson and LeRoy.

Another blockbuster—Paul Muni (left) in *I Am a Fugitive from a Chain Gang*.

Paul Muni and Mervyn LeRoy clowning during filming of *The World Changes*. (*Photo by Van Pelt, Warner Brothers*)

Edward G. Robinson in *Little Caesar*. (© *First National Pictures, Inc. 1930, copyright renewed 1958*)

Marie Dressler in *Tugboat Annie*.

On the set of *Tugboat Annie*. From left to right: Wallace Beery, visiting prize-fighter Jimmy McLaren, Marie Dressler, and Mervyn LeRoy.

Cast and crew of *Tugboat Annie*. Front row from left to right: Wallace Beery, Marie Dressler, Mervyn LeRoy, and Norman Reilly Raine. The cameraman peering over Miss Dressler's shoulder is Gregg Toland.

Marion Davies and Mervyn LeRoy during filming of *Page Miss Glory*, probably her best film.

Mervyn LeRoy (under camera) directs a scene in *Anthony Adverse* with Claude Rains and Anita Louise. (*Photo by M. Marigold*)

Mervyn LeRoy (left) and Fernand Gravet jokingly crown Carole Lombard on set of *Fools for Scandal*. (*Photo by Madison Lacy, Warner Brothers*)

Visitors to the set of *The Wizard of Oz* are Mervyn LeRoy's mother and son, Warner, with Judy Garland.

Vivien Leigh and Robert Taylor in *Waterloo Bridge*. (*MGM Photo by Willinger*)

Mervyn LeRoy directs Greer Garson in *Random Harvest*.

Ronald Colman and Greer
Garson in *Random Harvest*.

Elizabeth Taylor during
costume test for *Little
Women*.

5

SAM GOLDWYN:
YOU WANT TO
FINISH IT
WITH DOGS?

I made four pictures during my first year as a director, 1928. Nobody keeps statistics about that sort of thing, but I think that must be a record. It's something like a rookie quarterback starting every game in his first season. Not only did I make four films, but they were four successful films—the rookie threw a touchdown pass in each game.

My third was *Flying Romeos*, starring two great comedians of that era, George Sidney and Charlie Murray. It was pretty much of a slapstick comedy, typical of that era.

The fourth of my first year's crop gave me my long-awaited chance to work with Colleen Moore. She owed the studio a picture and came back to do *Oh Kay!*, taken from the musical comedy of that name. Since it was still a silent movie, however, it was not a musical. We just used the plot line of the Broadway hit.

It was during the filming of *Oh Kay!* that I started doing something that was to become a tradition with me. I like a company that is relatively loose and relaxed. To me, tension on a set is detrimental to the work we do. If people are nervous and uptight, the finished product will reflect that. So I began thinking up practical jokes to lighten the atmosphere.

One day, late in the afternoon, we were shooting a scene outside on the back lot. Colleen drove into the set in a horse and buggy. We shot one take and it was good, but I made up some excuse so that we would have to do it again, something about the lighting being poor. I told her to go back and get ready for her entrance again. When she was out of earshot, I had the whole crew leave the set.

"Ready, Colleen?"

"Ready."

Then I called "Action!"—and ran off the set myself. When she drove in in her buggy, the whole street was completely deserted.

We were all hiding, but watching from behind buildings and trees, and the expression on her face was a joy to behold. You could tell what was going through her mind—"Where is everybody?"—but she got the joke. She laughed and then we all came back out and joined her in appreciating the gag.

It wasn't only for the actors that I did this. It also helped make the crew feel important. They were on the inside of something, at the expense of an actor. I've always gotten along well with my crews because I tried to make them feel important. They didn't just follow orders on my pictures, but they contributed with their ideas and suggestions. Maybe because of that, I have always had the crews on my side, working with me, not against me. You'd be surprised what a crew can do to spoil a film if they don't like the director and begin working against him. It's happened many times.

During the shooting of *Oh Kay!* Colleen's relationship with her husband, John McCormick, grew steadily worse. He still did his periodic drunk disappearing act. One day when he was missing again, we had Al Hall, our cutter, trying to find him. Colleen showed up for work, as usual, but she was not herself. She was in her dressing room, crying her eyes out. I took her in my arms and tried to calm her.

"I'll be all right," she said. "Just give me a few minutes."

"Don't hurry," I said. "I'll shoot around you the whole day, if you want. I've got a lot of stuff I can shoot without you. You just stay here and cry it out."

Except for that, and that wasn't her fault, working with Colleen was exactly as pleasant as I had expected. The picture was great fun to make and apparently the public enjoyed seeing it, too, because it turned out to be a hit.

Of my first year's product, I had made two that were very big— *Harold Teen* and *Oh Kay!*—and two that were modestly successful —*No Place to Go* and *Flying Romeos*. My salary was getting bigger and I was in demand. Still, I wasn't quite where I wanted to be. I wanted to do a film that was daring, fresh, new, exciting, important. My first films had been good, but they had been in tried-and-true traditional molds. I knew that before I could be considered one of the top directors in town—and that's what I wanted to be—I would have to be at the helm of a landmark film, something that would make them all sit up and take notice. I began searching for a property that would have that quality. It would take me three years before I would find it.

Those three years would not be barren or wasted, however. Far from it. They would turn out to be three of the most fascinating years for Hollywood, and troubled years for the country. During those three years, America would be plunged into a pitiless depression and, in Hollywood, film would find its voice.

The depression, curiously, had little surface effect on Hollywood. Money would be lost, of course—Adolph Zukor and my cousin, Jesse Lasky, lost millions in the stock market—but the business itself survived and, in fact, thrived. This may seem to be a contradiction, but it wasn't. It was a very logical development. The public demanded entertainment, escape from its tragic situation, and movies and radio were the only sources of that escape. The people went to the movie palaces by the tens of millions and the studios were as busy as they had ever been. The advent of sound helped keep the public interested in films.

It was in 1927 that Warner Brothers made *The Jazz Singer*, in which my old Oakland friend, Al Jolson, spoke and sang and made talkies a household word. That was the real start of sound movies, although there had been some prior experimental work. Through 1928—my debut year—there were further attempts at combining sight and sound. It wasn't until 1929 and 1930, however, that sound became generally accepted, perfected to the point where it grew to be the standard and the audience came to expect to hear actors talk.

The depression was something that rolled off my back. For me, there was none at all. I was making a lot of money, and, for the first time in my life, I was able to save some of it. My standard of living kept improving. I moved out of Wally Reid's house and into the penthouse apartment in a building on Hayvenhurst. I bought a car. I could afford the clothes I used to envy on the backs of my rich friends. I ate at the finest restaurants, and didn't even look at the prices before I ordered—the hallmark of the affluent.

I think I started one fashion trend in Hollywood. Until I came along, all the directors affected a distinctive style of dress I considered outlandish—puttees. They all carried megaphones, too, which at least served a practical purpose. On most sets, workmen continued with their hammering during the shooting, so the directors shouted their instructions through their megaphones, to slice through that noise and the loud whir of the camera itself. Since, as I have said, I demanded quiet on my sets, I never had to use a megaphone. I never wore puttees or riding breeches, either. I wore an ordinary suit.

I dressed well on the set, and even better off. Everybody paid attention to clothes in the late twenties in Hollywood. It was a small circle still—although widening every day—and we all knew each other. It got so we knew each other's wardrobes, too, and we tried hard to find ways to outdress our friends. We would show off our latest outfits generally on Tuesday nights, which is when the Hollywood crowd of that time gathered regularly at the Cocoanut Grove. Somehow, that tradition got started and it kept up for years.

We would all have the same table, week after week. We went to see, and to be seen. You could look around and find the same faces in the same places—people like Wally Reid, Theda Bara, Ben Lyon, Nita Naldi, Barbara La Marr, Mary Pickford, Charlie Chaplin, Doug Fairbanks, all of them. Gus Arnheim's orchestra played for dancing, and there was a group of singers called "The Rhythm Boys," which included Bing Crosby, who supplied the vocals. There was no show—the audience was all the show we needed.

It was like one large but loosely organized club, the Hollywood set of the late 1920s and early 1930s. For kicks, just like a bunch of kids, we would pile into cars once in a while and head down to Venice to ride the big roller-coaster. Or we'd go to somebody's house—somebody was always giving a buffet supper—and play games. I remember there was one game, charades, which was the rage for quite a few years. It was a great life; everybody knew everybody else, and we would resent it if any nonmovie person— we called them "private people"—tried to elbow into our circle.

Another night each week, we would all go to the Biltmore. One night, I proudly escorted a gorgeous young German starlet named Marlene Dietrich. That was the night she shocked the place by walking in in a full dress suit and tails. I asked her why she wore that outfit.

"Why not?" she said.

I dated many girls, including Betty Compson—the girl I used to chauffeur around—and I dated dozens of others. I didn't feel like settling down and getting married yet; being a bachelor at that time in that place was too much fun. I must admit that I did as much dallying as I could, and I guess every young man in America envied me my fortunate position. Sometimes, I even envied myself.

Naturally, there were girls who offered themselves to me in exchange for parts in films, but I didn't play that game. I never have. Ambition can burn so brightly in some people that it completely overcomes their morals, something I have never been able to understand. I will say this, however—I never promised anybody a job without keeping my word.

I doubt that any of those business romances ever produced a lasting relationship—how could they, with that beginning?—but it was part of the Hollywood scene at that time. I am sure it still exists among people who place success above principles.

Those sleazy opportunities were only one of the by-products of success, and not very significant. Of paramount importance to me, then as always, was that I was doing work I enjoyed doing, and doing it well enough to be noticed. I was also among friends now, for, in 1928, Warner Brothers had bought First National. Jack Warner told me he was "going to make you one of the greatest directors in the business," and it's always a good feeling when your boss is in your corner. I always felt Jack was.

My fifth picture, in 1929, was my first with sound. I had been watching the experiments with talkies with tremendous excitement. It's hard to understand today, but in those days there were many people in Hollywood who decried the coming of sound to film. I think most of that was due to fear of the unknown. They had grown up with soundless movies and they wanted the status to continue quo. They understood films as they were, but they had neither the vision nor the experience to cope with that added dimension of sound.

I was fortunate. As a veteran of stage and vaudeville, I knew the value of the spoken and the sung word. I understood dialogue, because I had been an actor. I welcomed the coming of sound and couldn't wait until I had a chance to direct a talking picture.

Jack Warner gave me that chance. He asked me to direct *Naughty Baby*, a sound film starring Alice White. She was one of the earliest stars of the talkies. Alice and I had worked together before, in *Harold Teen*. She was hard to direct, primarily because she was never much of an actress. Somehow, I was able to get pretty good work out of her, so I think that may be why Warner selected me for *Naughty Baby*. Poor Alice. You had to tell her everything you wanted her to do, and then go out and practically do it for her. There was a dance scene in the picture, and I wound up waving a handkerchief at her when I wanted her to move one arm or the other. She couldn't remember her movements without that off-camera semaphore system, but she tried hard.

Early sound was on records, not on the film itself. We used very primitive equipment, of course, because this was a primitive period. The microphones were heavy and stationary. The actors had to be precisely on their marks, or else the mikes couldn't pick up what was said. Often, this meant the mikes had to be physically in the set—there was no way to avoid it—and we would have to paint them or camouflage them to match the scenery or to blend in with the background.

The first talking scene I ever shot in *Naughty Baby* was set in a hallway. We had done it once when the sound man came up to me.

"I don't understand it, Mr. LeRoy," he said, "but I get a buzzing sound in the set."

"Buzzing?"

"Yeah, you listen."

He handed me the earphones and, sure enough, there was a distinct buzzing sound. The sound men tore their equipment apart, trying to find the source of that noise. We dug up the hallway, looking for some defect in the wiring or something to account for that buzz. Eventually, we traced the trouble to one of the microphones. A bee had gotten trapped inside.

I wanted to try something new in that film—a rain shot. I thought it would make a wonderful effect, if I could capture the sound of rain in my movie. There was a scene in which two of my principals were walking down the street under an umbrella. I placed a microphone in the umbrella so it would, theoretically, capture the noise of the rain. When we saw the rushes, though, the noise of the rain beating down on the umbrella was like thunder—so loud you couldn't hear any of the dialogue. It all had to be reshot.

That's how we learned, through the hard teacher called trial and error. It would be some years before sound would be perfected, but in the interim the public was captivated by the new experience of hearing while it was watching.

I made three pictures in 1929 and four in 1930. Among them were *Hot Stuff*, one of James Cagney's first movies; *Numbered*

Men, with Conrad Nagel, which was a prison film we shot on location in San Quentin; remakes of *Little Johnny Jones* and *Top Speed*; and a picture called *Too Young to Marry*.

This last one was important to me because, in it, I starred my first discovery. We needed a very lovely girl in the lead, to play opposite Grant Withers. I had always admired the beauty of an actress named Sally Blane and I called her. She wasn't there, but her mother answered the phone and told me Sally was away, making a picture in Denver.

"That's too bad," I said. "I'm about to start a picture and I had a part I thought she would be right for."

"Well," her mother said, "obviously Sally can't do it. Her picture just started shooting a few days ago. But I do have another daughter."

"Is she pretty? Can she act?"

(In Hollywood in those days, that was the order in which you asked about the talent of potential leading ladies. Today, whether for good or evil, the questions are reversed.)

"I think she's just as pretty as Sally, maybe even prettier," Sally's mother said. "And, yes, she can act, too."

I said that I'd be happy to talk to her. The next day, Gretchen Young—that was the family name—came into my office at the studio. I was immediately struck by her beauty and her charm and I was sure she had a chance to be as good an actress as her sister. I liked everything about her, except her name. To me, she was not a "Gretchen"—that name always struck me as very hard, Teutonic. This girl was light and airy, flowerlike and dainty. I wanted a name more in keeping with her appearance and her personality.

"How about Loretta?" I said.

"I like it," she said, without any hesitation.

Thus Loretta Young was born, that day in my office. She was my first discovery—there would be many more—and she more than lived up to my first hopes. *Too Young to Marry* brought her romance as well as a career. She and her co-star, Grant Withers, fell in love as we shot that picture and were married during it, or shortly after we finished it. It didn't last, but it was nice to watch while it happened.

Top Speed, which also dates from that era, starred Joe E. Brown, and the great comedian and I did several films together after that. He was wonderful to work with. Many people don't know, or don't remember, that he was a great athlete as well as a comedian. Before he turned to acting, he had been a circus performer and he had great command of his body which, of course, enhanced his comedy routines. I remember once, in a picture we did called *Local Boy Makes Good* some years afterward, he was required to dive into the back lot lake. He surveyed the lake quickly, then backed off and was ready to plunge in.

"Watch out, Joe," I said. "That lake is a lot shallower than it looks."

"Okay, Mervyn. I'll take it shallow."

He dove in, but with a trajectory such that he didn't go too deeply into the water. Still, when he came up, his face was covered with blood from where he had scraped the bottom. I passed out—I never could stand the sight of blood—but he just mopped it off and got ready for the next shot. He was a wonder.

We did *Elmer the Great* together, too. In that one, he played a baseball star. We used some UCLA athletes as extras and one of them was Mike Frankovitch. Joe E. Brown and his wife, Katherine, raised Mike, who grew up to become a wonderful Hollywood producer. When we shot *Elmer the Great*, however, he was just one of the extras. I did give him one line, though, to please Joe. It was a simple line: "Good morning, Elmer. Had your breakfast yet?"

A simple line, but poor Mike was so nervous it took us a dozen takes until he got it right. Whenever I see Mike these days, I kid him about that line and he kids me back.

Through 1929 and 1930, through those seven pictures, and well into 1931, I worked hard. I lost weight—I never have been too heavy, but at that point I guess I was down to 120 pounds or so—and I didn't sleep much. It wasn't insominia, it was just that I was too busy. When I wasn't doing a picture, I was preparing one. When I wasn't preparing one, I was reading an endless parade of books, scripts, galleys, plays, searching always for that one special story that would help me make my mark. When I wasn't shooting, preparing, or reading, I was out for a night on the town.

Always, though, it was fun. Everything was fun. In the early days of sound, going to see the rushes of the previous day's filming was a constant adventure—you never knew what you would see and hear. We would sit there, in the preview room, howling over the way the sound came out. Then we would have to go in and redub it, to get it right.

Gradually, the technicians worked the bugs out of the sound apparatus. Sound improved. So did the technique of shooting the visual scenes. Movies became more sophisticated. We didn't realize it, certainly not consciously, but the time had come for the cinema to tackle more important themes—the techniques had matured to the point where they could handle something other than comedies and frivolous romances.

So we were both maturing, the movies and I. Together, we would come of age.

I found that special story I had been searching for for so long. As it turned out, I found it at precisely the right time. Hollywood, and the audience, were both ready.

One hot summer evening in 1930, I was getting ready to leave the studio. Jack Warner called me into his office. He held out the galley proofs of a new book.

"Might be worth your time if you read this," he said, and tossed the bundle on the desk. "I've got too much to do to read it tonight. You read it and tell me what you think."

I took it home. In an hour or so, I was supposed to go out to dinner with some friends. There was time to do a little reading before I had to get dressed. That was always my style; any free time, I read. So I picked up the galleys Warner had given me. The book was a novel by a man named W. R. Burnett. I began reading.

It was called *Little Caesar*.

I never did get to the dinner party. I read straight through the night, my excitement heightening with every page. I didn't even go to sleep. I just had time to shower, shave, and change my clothes; then I rushed back to the studio and headed directly for Warner's office.

The boss, as we called him, wasn't alone. His two young right-hand men—Darryl Zanuck and Hal Wallis—were with him. I was so keyed up about my discovery that I didn't bother about protocol, and anyhow, Warner never stood on ceremony. Of all the Hollywood tycoons, he was the least formal. He seemed to like his people to barge in on him, so in I barged.

"This is what I've been looking for, Jack," I said. "This guy Burnett must have written this for me to do."

I threw the galleys on his desk.

Warner did not immediately respond to my enthusiasm. He told me that some other people on the lot had already read *Little Caesar* without a positive reaction. He was hesitant about buying it, and with good reason. Until then, nobody in Hollywood had ever done anything like it. The usual Hollywood product, before *Little Caesar*, was sweet and innocuous. Most of the studio heads,

Warner included, felt that that was what the public wanted in that era of gloom and desperation that was the world of 1930. The key word was "escapism"—"The public wants to escape from its problems, not see them on the screen" were the words you heard, with slight variations, all over the industry then. Hollywood responded to that supposed plea and turned out film after film of pure escapism, fables that were as unlike real life as they could possibly be.

Little Caesar was something else again. It was harsh, rough, brutal. It was a tale told against the background of the Chicago mobs, and it focused on one supremely egotistical mobster, Caesar Enrico Bandello. Perhaps, in its own way, it went too far in the other direction and was something of an exaggeration. Even so, it was a lot nearer the truth than most of Hollywood's films up to that point. There really were mobsters. There really was brutality and savagery. There really were people like Bandello.

I felt that the public was more mature than we had given them credit for. They would, I firmly believed, pay money to see a film like *Little Caesar*, a film that wasn't escape but more a mirror of truth, a look at life as it actually existed. It might shake them up, but perhaps they needed to be shaken. They were aware of the existence of gangsters—Al Capone was a household word and the Saint Valentine's Day massacre had happened only a year before.

I am not sure if I would have conceived of the idea of a gangster picture on my own. Once I read *Little Caesar*, however, I knew for a certainty that the public would go to see the movie by the hundreds of thousands. My intuition told me the time was right.

For an hour or so, I pleaded my cause with Jack Warner. I think it must have been my persistence, rather than my logic, that finally turned the tide. By the time I left the office that morning, Jack had agreed to buy it and had given me the assignment of directing it, with Hal Wallis producing.

Our first big problem, when we began turning my golden dream into reality, was casting. Somebody—I don't honestly remember if it was Warner or Zanuck or Wallis or me—suggested Edward G. Robinson for the lead. Once the suggestion was made, however, all four of us immediately realized that Eddie was exactly right. He had been brought out to Hollywood from Broadway less than a year before. Hal Wallis had seen him in a play on Broadway. I had seen him there, too. We all knew him, off screen, as a kind, gentle, brilliant young man. We also knew that he was an experienced professional actor who could play any type of part and that he had the physical properties we felt would be right for Rico Bandello, alias Little Caesar.

Once the leading role was cast, there were the important secondary parts to consider. Too often, I feel, pictures are cast with only the major roles carefully thought out, but I've always believed that even the smallest secondary parts must be cast with equal care. For the gun moll, we dipped into the pool of Warners' contract players and came out with Glenda Farrell. Although primarily a comedienne, she was, like Robinson, a pro who could do anything. I was satisfied she could handle the part.

The biggest stumbling block, however, was who would play the part of the racketeer, Joe Masara. Warner wanted to go with Douglas Fairbanks, Jr., but I felt he had too much polish and urbanity. I wanted a real tough guy, not somebody who looked as though he had just stepped out of some elegant drawing room.

I kept looking, seeing everybody the agents brought in, watching every movie I could, going to the few plays that came to Los Angeles. One night, I went to see *The Last Mile*, done by a touring company at the old Majestic Theater. I found my Joe Masara that night—only to lose him just as suddenly as I had found him.

The Last Mile was a story of convicts in jail and, in one scene, the stage had five cells across it. In the center cell was a character called Killer Mears, and the actor playing the part looked like a killer. He was stripped to the waist and he was powerful, brutal, animal-like. No drawing room for him. As I watched the play, I could visualize him in my movie. He was the perfect Joe Masara.

I was escorting some long-forgotten blond starlet that night, and as the curtain came down, I turned to her and said, "What did you think of Killer Mears?"

"He's the most exciting man I ever saw," she said, and her eyes were dreamy.

Her reaction confirmed my hunch, so I checked my program for the actor's name. It was Clark Gable. I had never heard of him. I sent my date home in a cab—she didn't like that a bit—and went backstage.

The stage doorman pointed me in the direction of Gable's dressing room. I knocked and he said, "Come in." He had his back toward me, as he sat at his dressing table taking off his makeup.

"Mr. Gable," I said, "I want to congratulate you on a great performance tonight."

"Thanks," he said. He didn't even turn around.

"My name is Mervyn LeRoy. I direct movies at Warner Brothers."

That reached him. He swiveled around and studied me.

"Would you be interested in a film test?" I asked him. "I'm putting together a movie now, and I think you'd be right for one of the important parts."

"Sure, I'll test," he said. For the first time, I saw his big, friendly grin.

We arranged to make the test three or four days later. Gable did some scenes from *The Last Mile*, and I also had him read a few of Joe Masara's lines from *Little Caesar*. It turned out excellently. Gable had the same quality on screen that he had on stage, only magnified, as only a screen close-up can magnify.

The rest of the studio's brain trust saw the test, too. I was confident that they would see in Gable the same thing I had seen. I was very wrong.

It was Darryl Zanuck who summed it up for the anti-Gable faction: "What the hell have you done, Mervyn?" he said. "I'll tell you what you've done—you've just thrown away five hundred bucks on a test. Didn't you see the size of that guy's ears?"

I can remember being so stunned that for a few seconds I couldn't speak at all. I just stood there with my mouth open. How could they be so blind? What difference if a man's ears stick out if the overall effect is so strong?

"Are you seriously telling me," I said, when I was able to talk, "that you can't see that this guy Gable has really got something extra special?"

"We don't agree with you," Zanuck said. (I've never known for sure who he meant by "we," but Jack Warner, in his own autobiography, shoulders the blame for the decision.)

"Okay," I said, and my voice was trembling. "We—or you—don't agree. But I think Gable is perfect. And I'm the director. It's my picture."

I knew it was futile to argue—the mighty had spoken—but I just couldn't help myself.

"There's no point in discussing it any further," Zanuck said. "Gable is out. The decision has been made. Fairbanks will play the part."

He was right. There was no future in any more discussion. It would just be a waste of breath.

"All right, all right. It's Fairbanks. But listen. You take my advice—sign Gable. If we lose him now, we'll be throwing away the biggest thing to come along in years. This guy is going to be a star!"

For a few days, I debated whether or not I should put my money where my mouth was. I had the opportunity to sign Gable to a contract during that period. I finally decided that personal management wasn't my trade and, besides, I really couldn't afford it at the time. So I didn't do it. It was a costly mistake.

Gable always gave me credit for discovering him, even though I wasn't able to use him. He gave me a book once, with this inscription: "To Mervyn—Thank you for giving me my first break. I appreciate it." He also autographed a picture to me with these words: "Thanks for thinking and believing I could always make it. Clark."

Once the cast was set, I had to oversee the writing of the script. Hal Wallis and I did it, and it was hard. There had been nothing like it before. There were several rewrites, by several writers. They didn't seem able to grasp what we had in mind. Eddie Robinson felt strongly that it should be the story of a man, as the book had been, and not concentrate solely on his crimes. That's a concept that is difficult to get across on film, but eventually we worked one up that we all liked.

I threw myself into the shooting, and so did everybody else. There was a feeling that infused the whole company, a knowledge that we were creating something special. Even the extras seemed to sense it, although there were some extras who looked like they came right from the Chicago mobs. I have always thought that they probably did, that the big Chicago mobsters wanted to know what we were going to say and had sent some of their boys west with instructions to infiltrate the movie. At one point during the shooting, one of these types came up to me and said, "Hey, Mr. LeRoy, I gotta go to Chicago for a few days." He left and, a week later, he was back. I have always firmly believed that his bosses had sent for him, to get a firsthand report on what the picture was all about.

Little Caesar was a film about violence, yet it was not a violent film. It was a film about tough guys, yet it had no tough language —at least no swear words, not even a single "damn." Today's gangster movies and tough movies show every scrap of blood and brutality they can, use every possible dirty word they can find an excuse for squeezing into the script. I don't believe it is necessary to show violence graphically; you can get your point across with as much strength even though you really show nothing.

I have always been proud of one scene, as an example of what I mean. Eddie Robinson is talking to another hood who is wearing a distinctive diamond stickpin in his tie.

"That's a nice pin," Eddie says. "I'm going to have one like that someday."

I dissolved from a close-up of the pin in the hood's tie to the pin in Eddie's tie. The implication was clear—Rico knocked the guy off for his diamond stickpin—but I didn't show any killing.

That was Rico—Little Caesar—at work. He was a man with a driving ambition to be on top. As Robinson explained him, "He was a little punk trying to be big." He always tried to copy the man higher up, in hopes that he would thus assume the characteristics and eventually the job of that man. We worked that gimmick well, and we even used cigars as a device in that context. Both Eddie and I smoked cigars, and I had an idea that we could use cigars in the film. Rico doesn't smoke cigars, until the top man in the mob offers him one. He tries to smoke it, very amateurishly, but from then on he uses them in his pathetic effort to copy the style of that top man.

I used Eddie's cigar-smoking, too, in my continuing off-camera attempts to keep the set cheerful. I've mentioned practical jokes as a device to relax my company, and that technique was never more necessary than in *Little Caesar*. We were dealing with death and greed, and there was the ever-present danger that the company would become upset by it all. It's surprising how a movie company can absorb the characteristics and the mood of the film they are shooting. It was a continual battle to insure that the *Little Caesar* company maintained its sanity.

One thing I seized on was Eddie and his cigars. Time after time, I'd call the prop man over and have him nail Eddie's cigar down to something wooden on the set. The rest of the company would know what was going on, and wait for Eddie's reaction. It's a simple little gag, perhaps silly, too, but it served the purpose—to keep the set light and the mood cheerful.

The only problem I had with Eddie was his involuntary blinking when he fired his gun. There was a very important scene in an alley, just a close-up of Eddie's eyes as he fired his revolver. The only problem was that every time he fired, he'd blink. He couldn't help it, but it looked odd and I wanted his eyes cold and unblinking. We tried everything we could think of—we even taped Eddie's eyelids—but nothing really worked. I never did get that scene exactly the way I wanted it.

The film typed Eddie, a gentle man, as a gangster for years afterward. There is nothing inherently wrong in typing—when you think about it objectively, typing is a tribute to an actor's skill in creating a part the public believes. Eddie lived that part of Rico. He put in all those grunts himself—they weren't in the script and I didn't suggest them to him. He said the lines with so much authenticity that they became real; lines like "You can dish it out but you can't take it," "Take him for a ride," and "big shot," which all became a part of our vernacular.

Then, of course, there was the picture's final line, as Rico is gunned down at the end of the film—"Mother of Mercy, is this the end of Rico?"—which has become one of the classic lines in film lore.

Little Caesar cost seven hundred thousand dollars to make in 1931. At today's prices, I think it would cost two million now. It would still be a bargain, because it was one of Warner Brothers' biggest hits ever. When it opened, at the Strand Theater in New York, it shook the country. There had never been anything like it, and the critics and the public loved it.

After the opening, Jack Warner and I gave a dinner at Texas Guinan's club. George Raft was the star of the floor show, technically, but although I remember being very impressed by him, to me the floor show was the rest of the audience. I'm sure that some boys from the mob were there, and Warner, Robinson, and I were all a trifle concerned over how they would react. There was one moment when our concern seemed justified. One of the hoodlums, big and surly-looking and oozing threat, sidled over to me and said, "I seen your pitcher." Then he reached under his jacket and produced a gun and showed it to me. I was scared stiff. But all he wanted to do, apparently, was exhibit it, because he put it back in its holster and walked away.

Little Caesar was a tremendous hit, both with the critics and the ticket-buyers. It brought a new facet to the screen. A year later, Howard Hawks would make *Scarface* with Paul Muni, William Wellman would film *The Public Enemy* with James Cagney, and hundreds of other gangster films would follow. *Little Caesar* started it all. I'd like to be able to say I realized I was blazing a trail, setting a precedent, revolutionizing an industry. In all honesty, I can't say I made *Little Caesar* for any such noble goal. All I wanted to do was make a movie with some meat to it, some substance where before all had been froth.

The film did for me what I wanted it to, which was a purely personal goal. It established me as a topflight director. From then on, I was noticed. Where I had been classed as a good, dependable, workmanlike director, now I was known as an innovator, and innovators are always a step above workmen.

We got a few complaining letters—"Why did you glorify gangsters?"—but they were far and away in the minority. Most people loved it and, anyhow, the film did not glorify gangsters, it merely showed them as they were and proved that crime doesn't pay. I still feel that movies should make that point. Films in which criminals get away with their assorted evils annoy me. I always think of an old saying when I see that kind of film today: If you lie down with dogs, you get up with fleas.

Little Caesar raised my salary by a thousand dollars a week, and now I was hot in town. Everybody wanted me. My next two films were at other studios, as first MGM and then United Artists borrowed my services from Warner. For MGM and Irving Thalberg I made *Gentleman's Fate* with John Gilbert and Louis Wolheim—it was the only successful talking picture Gilbert made—and for United Artists I made *Tonight or Never*, which was Melvyn Douglas' movie debut.

Poor John Gilbert. He had a fight scene in *Gentleman's Fate*, and John was no fighter. He didn't even know the right way to hold his hands. To make the brawl look realistic, I had to resort to trickery. I had my cameraman overspeed the camera and took a close-up of Gilbert's fist coming right at the lens. Then I cut, quickly, to a shot of his opponent, Wolheim, getting hit and falling down.

In *Tonight or Never*, I worked with Gloria Swanson, who was—maybe still is—a jigsaw-puzzle nut. This gave me a chance to exercise my penchant for practical jokes again. When we finished shooting, she was heading for New York on the train and I gave her a going-away present—a great big jigsaw puzzle. Before I gave it to her, I had had the boys in the studio carpentry shop play around with it a little—they cut the ends off some of the pieces. Then I rewrapped it and presented it to her. She thanked me and took the puzzle with her on the train. Of course she couldn't do it because of the doctoring. Finally she caught on and wired me a two-word telegram. You can imagine what it said.

After those two were done, there was no longer any doubt in my mind, or in anybody else's mind, about my feeling needed and noticed in Hollywood. *Little Caesar* had been the turning point— for both Hollywood and me.

Success is a teacher. I was successful after *Little Caesar,* by any yardstick—money, fame, respect of my peers. In my innocence, I believed that everything else would remain the same. I learned that with success comes jealousy. I suppose it is predicated on envy, but it hurt me when I found that there were those in Hollywood who begrudged me my triumph. Behind my back, I heard, things were said, cruel things aimed at cutting me down. They ranged from remarks about my "luck" to complete fabrications that were so ludicrous they were laughable. I have since discovered that this is a phenomenon common to any who achieve success, no matter what field it is in. Rather than feel anger, I feel pity for those who are so eaten up with jealousy that they cannot stand to see anyone else make it.

There is another by-product of success. I learned, after *Little Caesar,* that I could no longer do only what I wanted to do. There are demands made on successful men that must be met, demands to serve on committees, appear at functions, work for charitable causes. Until *Caesar,* I was able to go along my own path at my own speed. If I felt like going out at night, I went out. If I preferred staying home and reading, I stayed home and read. Now, however, it became impossible to please only myself. I was no longer my own master. I had the obligations that go with success.

For the first time, I had to have a secretary, to keep up with my engagements and to help with my booming correspondence. I bought my first tailor-made tuxedo. I was on the go constantly. While at first I rebelled against this infringement on my personal freedom, I grew to enjoy it. I found that I liked the work of helping out with various affairs, and realized that, in a small way, I was doing some good. I was one of the fortunate ones and here was a way of helping others who had not had my blessings.

None of this stood in the way of my career, however. I went eagerly forward. It was just after *Gentleman's Fate* was finished that I had my first close brush with Sam Goldwyn.

Sam had taken the name Goldwyn some years before. It happened when he was in partnership with Edgar Selwyn. He just took the first syllable of Goldfish and the last syllable of Selwyn and concocted his new name. I've always felt it was a good thing that it wasn't Selwyn who had had the urge to change his name. He could

have taken the first syllable of his name and the last syllable of
Goldfish's name and he would have been Selfish.

Goldwyn wanted me to do *Tonight or Never*, but before that
one started, one Sunday he called me up. They had been shooting
an Eddie Cantor movie, *Palmy Days*. Things hadn't gone too
well, and he asked me if I'd take over and direct some retakes for a
couple of days. The couple of days turned into three weeks.

One of the scenes was a song-and-dance routine set in a cafeteria. A group of waitresses—don't ask me what waitresses were
doing in a cafeteria, but they were there—did the number first, and
then Cantor came out and did it as a solo. Goldwyn came down to
the set and watched for a while, then he took me aside.

"Look, Moiphy," he said. (He always called me Moiphy.)
"What's this? Cantor alone? You'd better put a lot of girls behind
him."

"I think you should talk to Cantor about that," I said. "That's
how he wants it."

Goldwyn went over and talked to Cantor, but the comedian
balked.

"Sam, I was in the *Ziegfeld Follies* and I did solos and they
never had to put girls behind me," he said. "I can do a number by
myself and that's the way I want it."

Goldwyn left the set but he called me when he got back to his
office.

"Don't tell Cantor," he said, "but in that number when he's
singing the song have a few girls whiz by."

I didn't. The number was all rehearsed and we shot it that way
and, when it came out, it was the hit of the film. Goldwyn never
mentioned it to me again.

Even at that time, Goldwyn was already beginning to achieve his
reputation as America's answer to Mrs. Malaprop.

Once, I'm told, he said, "You gotta take the bull by the teeth."

Another time he said, "You think I'm gonna put my head in a
moose?"

There was the time he met an old friend and said, "Hello, Harry.
Plenty of water's passed between us."

There was the time he bawled out his publicity man, Harry
Brand, and ended the lecture by saying, "And I don't like the way
the publicity is going from the Coast. Send it all east and have it
degenerate from there."

There was the time his auditor told him he was keeping too

many of his old records and advised him to throw everything away. Sam nodded and said, "Okay, go ahead, get rid of it all—but make a copy of everything."

There was the time when I was a producer, too, and we both wanted the services of a particular writer, and Sam said to me, "Moiphy, we're both in trouble—you got a writer and I need him."

Once, I heard, he described his wife in these terms: "Frances' hands are so beautiful I'm gonna have a bust made of them."

One day, we were discussing movies in general. I said to him that, for me, the important thing about a film wasn't how much money it made, but that it was a picture I was proud to put my name on.

"You're like me," Sam said. "I don't care if my pictures make a dime, just so long as everybody in the world goes to see them."

One evening, I heard, he was host at a dinner party at which England's Field Marshal Montgomery was the guest of honor, and Sam got up and said, "I'm glad I have with us tonight Marshall Field Montgomery."

My collection of Goldwyniana began during the shooting of *Tonight or Never*. It was a romance, with Gloria Swanson and Melvyn Douglas as the stars. I always liked my endings to be unusual, and I had an idea for one in this film. The last sequence was at a railroad station. Both of the characters had pet dogs, so I felt I could get the idea across of their going away together by simply showing his trunk and her trunk on the station platform, with their dogs attached to their trunks.

I went to Goldwyn and explained my idea.

"It'll be nice, Sam," I said, "to have just those two trunks and the two dogs, and the sound of a train whistle. What do you think?"

"Look, Moiphy," Sam said. "I spend millions of dollars on a picture, you want to finish it with dogs?"

But he went along with me. I always found Sam Goldwyn to be a man of great taste, and truly one of the finest producers Hollywood has ever seen.

Little Caesar had been the turning point. It took Edward G. Robinson a while to realize that it had also been a turning point for him. He still considered himself primarily a stage actor. He went back to Broadway and did a few plays, but they were all flops. He told me it was that series of failures that ultimately weaned him away from the stage. Nobody likes to be associated with productions that flop. If another medium offers him a chance to succeed, he'll take it, even if he might prefer working in the first arena. That's how it was with Eddie. Even though he preferred stage work, he came to realize that films offered him better odds for success.

Eddie was in my mind often that year. I considered him a lucky talisman and I thought it would be good to do another movie with him. When Jack Warner sent me to New York to see a play he was thinking about buying, I realized I had found the perfect property for that venture.

That New York trip was exciting for me in many ways. At one theater, I found my next picture. At another, *Girl Crazy*, I found the girl I was to date for several years. She was a lovely, vibrant young dancer-singer-actress named Ginger Rogers. We hit it off at once, and dated often during that trip. It was inevitable that she would come to Hollywood, and when she did, we resumed our relationship. For a few years, we went together constantly and, although it never led to anything permanent, it was great fun while it lasted. She became one of the most popular girls in Hollywood— I think the title "Bachelor Girl" was coined for her—and she dated all the most eligible men in town, men like Howard Hughes and Lew Ayres and dozens more. For a few years, we were a steady twosome everywhere and, later, she played the lead for me in *Golddiggers of 1933*.

The play I saw that I decided would be my next film was *Five Star Final*. It was based on a true story by a man—Louis Weitzenkorn—who ran the scandalous New York *Graphic*. It was a play about yellow journalism, and how the dirt this paper printed destroyed a family. I recognized it at once as a yarn with substance to it—like *Little Caesar*—which would add luster to the screen. Hollywood had made an about-face since *Little Caesar*, and the studios—led by the courage of Warner Brothers—were anxious to do stories of significance. I think this was Hollywood's bravest era, and it was exciting to be part of it. Exposé films were the rule, but we were able, at the same time, to combine our exposés with entertainment, unlike the more recent history of message films that are so heavy and ponderous that they do not entertain at all, and therefore defeat their own purpose.

However, I almost didn't get to see *Five Star Final*. Warner had arranged for five tickets to be left for me at the theater box office. I forget now who was in my party, but it doesn't matter. All that I remember is going up to the window, secure in my self-confidence, and asking for the tickets for Mervyn LeRoy.

"Where is he?" asked the man.

"I'm LeRoy."

"Come on, kid, cut the clowning. Mervyn LeRoy is a big director. You're too young. Move along."

It still happened. Even then, when I had just turned thirty, I still looked about twenty or twenty-one. It was a constant source of embarrassment, but never as much as that night. Here I was hosting some people I wanted to impress, and I got put down like that. Ultimately, of course, I was able to identify myself and got the tickets, but it almost spoiled the evening for me.

Then I saw the play. I knew that another studio—I think it was Fox—had previously optioned it, but had been afraid to make it. I loved *Five Star Final* and immediately wired Jack to buy it. He took my word and got it.

There was nobody to play the lead but Eddie Robinson, and he jumped at it. In the relatively small part of a minister, I used a newcomer to films, an English actor who was an Oxford graduate. He had one of the most beautiful speaking voices I had ever heard. His name was Boris Karloff.

There was a young man in the Warner Brothers publicity office who, I heard, had been an office boy on the real New York *Graphic*. I thought it might be a good stroke of public relations if he acted in the picture, so I contacted him and he was willing. I tested him. The only problem was that he had a high-pitched voice. When he saw the test screened, he listened to his own voice incredulously.

"Is that me?" he gasped, and ran out of the projection room.

He was no actor but he matured into an excellent playwright and screenwriter—Norman Krasna. His first play, *Louder, Please*, would be written a few years later. Its setting was the house I then had at Malibu.

Five Star Final became a tremendous hit. Again, it blazed a new trail for movies, demonstrating conclusively that film could be used to shine a brilliant and devastating light on current evils. The picture showed that movies had a tremendous potential for public good—or public bad, depending on the subject matter. The film also gave me a chance to show my directorial individuality—I tried something brand new, introducing the cast before the picture began.

If *Little Caesar* put me on top, *Five Star Final* solidified that position. The first could have been a fluke. The second demonstrated that it wasn't. Hollywood is like that; when a new director makes a good film, the town is reserved in its praise, waiting to make sure that that first one wasn't just an accident.

I knew I had arrived at the pinnacle of film society one day soon after *Five Star Final* opened, when I received a telephone call.

"Mr. LeRoy?"

"Yes."

"This is Mr. Hearst's secretary. He would like you to come up to the castle this weekend."

It was like a command performance. You were invited and you went, unless you were dying or off in Zanzibar. Otherwise, you had better be on that train for San Simeon. I was delighted to make the trip.

William Randolph Hearst was then the leading figure in the Hollywood superhierarchy. And San Simeon, his incredible castle, was worth the visit. It still is, even though he's long gone. I went there many times during his lifetime, but the first one was the big treat. It was a sure sign—like the first falling leaf heralds the coming of autumn—that I was now among the Hollywood elite.

Rooms were assigned for the weekend. Everything was organized. You could play tennis or ride or swim or look at Hearst's private zoo. He would lead groups out into the surrounding countryside for picnics. Every night, he would run the latest movie in his private little gem of a theater.

He brooked no misbehaving. If he felt any of his guests were impolite or had gotten drunk or had taken liberties with him or his things, that guest would find his suitcase packed and left in the living room. That was an order: Go home.

I met his beautiful Marion Davies that first weekend at San Simeon. A few years later, we would make a film together, and I was charmed by her from the beginning. People are inclined to look down their noses at mistresses and automatically pigeonhole them as ladies of small worth. Marion Davies, however, always seemed to me like a delightful person, kind and gentle and witty, and a much-underrated actress.

I came home from that first weekend at San Simeon in a state of glow. It was a time to reflect. Now there was no longer any doubt about being a success—I had the monetary rewards, I had the great reviews, and I had the recognition from the dean of honors, Mr. Hearst himself. I went home to my penthouse apartment and I sank into my favorite chair and thought about the state of my life.

What more did I want? First, of course, was to continue making films, the best I could do, or even better than that. Second, I wanted to lead a good life, have fun, enjoy myself.

There was something more now, now that I was thirty. It struck me suddenly. I didn't want to stay a bouncing bachelor all my life. There was, for the first time, an urge to settle down, find a wife, have children. I think it was that weekend at San Simeon that did it. It was an incredible experience, but I discovered that part of the joy of incredible experiences is the sharing of them. I longed to turn to someone, someone close and dear to me, and say, "Honey, let me tell you what happened up there at that crazy castle."

But there was nobody to turn to.

I started looking for a girl to marry.

6

PAUL MUNI:
IS HE THE DIRECTOR,
THAT KID?

Right after *Five Star Final*, I made another film I was very proud of. In some ways, *I Am a Fugitive from a Chain Gang* was the most important film I ever made, because it had an immediate and profound effect on our culture. I can think of very few films that actually altered laws and corrected heinous conditions, and *Fugitive* is among that honorable handful.

Once again, my insatiable appetite for reading led to the picture. I had picked up an autobiography by a man named Robert E. Burns. It fascinated me, with its details of such sheer brutality as to be unbelievable—and yet all of it true. Burns was the real fugitive from the Georgia chain gang and in his book he told of the incredible tortures and the degrading practices used then in that state. I recognized it immediately as the stuff from which a great motion picture could be made.

Jack Warner agreed with me, and bought it. Hal Wallis and I located Burns in New Jersey. He was still a fugitive, but safe there, as there were no extradition agreements between Georgia and New Jersey. We asked him to come to California to work with us, but he was hesitant. Georgia and California did have an extradition agreement and he would be risking his freedom if he came to Hollywood. We promised to keep his visit secret, and he agreed.

Wallis, Burns, and I worked together on the screenplay, with writers Howard J. Green and Brown Holmes. At Burns' request, we kept him hidden to insure his freedom. We arranged a room for him on the lot, had his meals brought in, and only a very few people were privy to the fact of his presence. He was with us for a few key weeks and whenever any question arose about the authenticity of what we were writing, we consulted him. His help was invaluable.

We got Paul Muni to play the part of Jim Allen, the name we gave to the Burns character. Muni had done *Scarface*, which established him as one of the top dramatic actors in the business. He was a pro among pros. Of all the actors I've ever worked with, I think Muni threw himself into his parts more deeply than any other. He didn't merely act his roles, he lived them. Perhaps he erred too much in that direction. After *Fugitive*, he did *The Good Earth* for Irving Thalberg, which Sydney Franklin directed. One day, Thalberg called me in a panic.

"Mervyn, you've got to help me," Thalberg said. "It's your friend, Muni."

"What's the problem?"

"Well, you know Paul. He's playing a Chinese in this picture. So he's down in Chinatown every night. He even sleeps there. I want him to act Chinese—but he doesn't have to become a real Chinese. Talk to him, will you?"

I called Paul, but there wasn't much I could say, or wanted to say, for that matter. I admired the man so much that I wasn't about to tell him how to prepare for his role. I just mentioned Thalberg's concern, and we laughed together about it. I imagine he continued visiting Chinatown until he felt he had his character down pat.

On *Fugitive*, we had no major problems. There are always minor problems, of course. The picture was all shot in or near the studio. There was one day when we were filming a shot of the chain gang breaking rocks. I wanted a strange, eerie light, so we had gone out before sunrise to film as dawn broke. Obviously, that particular light doesn't linger long, so the shot had to be made quickly. The camera focused on Muni, supposedly hammering away at the rocks.

"Paul, you're not hitting them right," I said. "You're hitting them like a woman would. Put your back into it."

The next time he slammed down at those rocks with his sledgehammer, he did it so vigorously that he hit his foot and almost broke it. That ended the shooting for that morning. We had to go back at dawn the next day and do the scene over again.

I respected Paul, and I think he respected me. Our first meeting, however, had not been auspicious. I had seen him on Broadway in *Counsellor-at-Law* and on the screen in *Scarface*, but we had never met. When he was signed to do *Fugitive*, I was summoned to Warner's office to be introduced to my new star.

I walked in. Warner made the introductions, but Muni didn't say a word to me. Instead, he turned to Jack and said, "Is he the director, that kid?"

At first, he wanted no part of me, I suppose feeling that I was too young to direct such a tough, brutal film. Warner convinced him that he should go along with the project and with me. Eventually, we became friends, a compliment in itself, because Muni had few friends. He was a loner, as opposed to lonely. When he died, the only two people from the film industry who were present at the funeral were his agent and me.

One of the greatest moments in *Fugitive* was its dramatic ending. I've been taking bows since 1931 for that scene, but I'd like to confess now that it was achieved by sheer accident.

That last shot had Muni, as the unfortunate Jim Allen, saying a last good-bye to his girlfriend. He knew that he would never be free, that he would have to spend the rest of his days running from the law. The two were in the mouth of an alley and, during their last two lines of dialogue, Muni backed away from her.

"But, Jim, how do you live?" she asked him.

As he edged deeper into the alley, the screen grew darker and finally was totally black. Then he whispered his last line—"I steal"—out of the darkness.

That wasn't the way I had originally planned it. As we were doing the last rehearsal, however, before we went into the take, the fuse on the big klieg lights blew out, just as Muni said, "I steal."

It was an accident, but I immediately recognized it as an accident that worked. The boss electrician rushed over to me and apologized, and said the fuse was okay now. There would be no more trouble with the lights.

"Do it just that way when we roll," I told him.

Eventually, after some experimentation, I decided that a sudden blackout wasn't as effective as a gradual dimming of the lights, and that's the way it was done. As we led up to Muni's final two words, we had the lights gradually dim, until there was total blackness on the screen as Jim Allen edged away from his fiancée and whispered his final, tragic line.

Fugitive was a powerful picture, but here again I tried to show brutality without being brutal. There was a scene of Muni being flogged by sadistic guards. Instead of dwelling on the actual beating, I focused my cameras on the shocked and horrified faces of the other prisoners who were witnessing the beating, and on the shadows of the beating playing on the wall. I am convinced that this made a more terrifying sequence than actually showing a whip landing on flesh.

Everything was in the picture, however, all the grim and ghastly details that were in Burns's book. We showed the slop the men were fed. We showed their dreadful living conditions. Above all, we showed the awful chains they had to carry around with them constantly, the chains that were attached to their ankles even when they slept.

When the picture came out, it knocked everybody for a loop. The book had had a respectable sale, but you cannot compare the cold print of a book with the graphic drama of a movie in terms of impact. Where the book may have shocked people intellectually, the movie had an emotional punch that was a knockout blow.

The nation was collectively offended at the harsh Georgia penal code. Editorials were written in dozens of leading newspapers demanding immediate improvement. Reform committees were formed, petitions were circulated, congressmen were flooded with letters and telegrams. It didn't take long. As soon as it could be done, Georgia responded, and the Georgia chain gang system was renovated.

I don't take credit for that personally. The credit belongs, I believe, to the motion picture industry. I was just the instrument through which the industry acted. It was my picture, but the real honors should be given to movies in general for showing the truth about a deplorable situation.

As far as I was concerned, the great reviews and the tremendous box-office receipts were honors enough. For a time, however, Jack Warner, Hal Wallis, and I were made aware that we would not be welcome in the great state of Georgia. There were a few letters—anonymous, of course—telling us that if we ever set foot on Georgia soil, we would be arrested at the very least. I did not have the occasion to visit Georgia for more than thirty years, so I had no chance to put my courage to the test. When I finally made the trip, to help John Wayne direct *The Green Berets* in 1968, the *Fugitive* furor had, of course, long since faded away. The Georgians were full of that good old southern hospitality and there wasn't a lynch rope in sight.

Georgia, and a few other southern states, may not have liked *Fugitive*, but the rest of the world did. It was the biggest American hit, up to that time, in Russia. I imagine the Communists showed it with glee and propagandized that it was a true picture of American life in general. The Russians stole prints and the film was a resounding hit there.

It was also a smash in Japan, and I was invited to attend the premiere at a Tokyo theater that, with some justice, called itself "the world's most beautiful theater." They always had a stage presentation as well as a movie, and at the time of the *Fugitive* opening, there was a cheap, imported-from-America musical. It was pretty terrible, except for one young actor who played the part of an old man. This was the first time I had seen or heard of Danny Kaye, and I went backstage to congratulate him after the performance.

"You're going to go places," I told him. "You have a great personality."

"I sure hope you're right," Kaye said. "Right now, I'm only making twenty-five dollars a week."

I wanted to sign him up personally, but I was heading around the world and it was impractical at the moment. I did keep an eye on his career, however, and we became good friends. He made it first on Broadway and then in movies and, one day, after his first film, he came to dinner at our home.

"I'm going to have a nose bob," he blurted out, between the soup and the salad.

"Why?"

"Sam Goldwyn wants it done."

I could tell he was unhappy about it and just wanted someone to talk him out of it. Since I didn't think he should mess around with his face, I told him what he wanted to hear.

"Danny, if you fool with your nose," I said, "you'll be fooling with your personality, too. Your nose fits you. With another kind of nose, you wouldn't be you."

He smiled, and then he laughed in pure relief. And he never did have his nose remodeled.

Russia, Japan, everywhere—*Fugitive* was big all over, but I was most pleased with its reception here. There were raves from the critics. For me, with three sensational hits in a row, I was the man of the Hollywood hour.

I went to the premiere in New York, and the trip turned out to be a fateful one for me. The Warners' brass had asked me to come up to their office to sign a new deal—I would now be making three thousand dollars a week—and while I was there, I spotted a tall, attractive girl.

"Hello, Mervyn," she said.

I looked at her a second time. From her greeting, it sounded as if she knew me. For a few seconds, I didn't recognize her, but then it came to me. I had known her before, in Hollywood, when she was just a gangling, awkward teen-ager. Now she was a woman, and a lovely one.

"Doris? Are you really Doris Warner?"

She laughed.

"It's me. Didn't you recognize me?"

"The last time I saw you, you were a kid. All of a sudden you're grown up."

I asked her to go to the theater with me that evening, and she did. Doris was Harry Warner's daughter, which made her Jack's niece. We went out several evenings in a row and then I had to go back home. I couldn't get her out of my mind and kept writing to her, and she apparently had the same reaction. We kept up a hot and heavy correspondence, punctuated by visits, either when I had a chance to go to New York or when she came west.

I recognized the symptoms in myself, since I had directed so many actors and actresses in such moments. This had to be love. I discovered that it was a pleasant feeling.

I sounded Jack out on what he thought about my becoming his nephew-in-law. He tried to talk me out of it, not that he had any objection to my entering the Warner family tree. He just didn't think we were right for each other.

Love listens to no advice, however. Since I was in love, I didn't listen. I proposed. She accepted.

We were married at the Waldorf-Astoria Hotel in New York, and the wedding was the big event of the social year. In fact, it was one of the biggest weddings ever held at the Waldorf. Jack Warner was my best man and, typically, he got there late and held the whole thing up a good ten minutes. I was waiting anxiously in an anteroom.

"Hey, Mervyn, we're on," he said, as he raced in.

"You're not on, I'm on."

He did a little "Shuffle off to Buffalo," and then said, "Okay, let's go," and dragged me into the ballroom.

Our honeymoon was a round-the-world trip on the *SS Empress of Britain*, which will always be one of the high spots of my life. It was four months of heaven, seeing the world and basking in the bright, fresh glow of matrimony at the same time.

Even though it was purely a pleasure trip, I kept up with my reading. During that voyage, I saw many people reading the current best-seller, Hervey Allen's *Anthony Adverse*, so I borrowed a copy. As soon as I became immersed in it, I decided I wanted to make the film version.

I cabled Jack Warner: "YOU MUST READ ANTHONY ADVERSE."

Back came his reply: "READ IT? I CAN'T EVEN LIFT IT."

He did read it though, and he bought it and eventually I made it. My batting average at picking winners when I read new books has always been pretty good. Jack Benny, at a testimonial dinner the Friars Club gave me in 1962, said, "I don't admire Mervyn for the pictures he made as much as for the ones he didn't make." I did make one of the biggest boners of all times, however, in the category of films I didn't make. One year Doris and I took the train from New York to California and, as we were about to get on the train, Annie Laurie Williams, the literary agent, ran down the platform and handed me a fat package.

"Galley proofs," she said, gasping for breath. "Great novel. You have to read it."

I had many other books and scripts with me so I gave Miss Williams' galleys to Doris to read. For three days, as the train chugged west, she had her nose in that book. Finally, she was finished.

"How did you like it?" I asked her.

"It's one of the finest things I've ever read."

"What's it about?"

"The Civil War," Doris said. "The North and the South."

"The Civil War? There have been too many movies about the Civil War. The public is tired of it."

So I passed up *Gone with the Wind*, which must rank high on the list of classic mistakes in Hollywood history.

The months aboard the *SS Empress of Britain* passed swiftly and idyllically. At every port, the local representatives of Warner Brothers would meet us. Often, they arranged interviews for me with their local newspaper contacts. Jack Warner kept in touch via cable and phone. I remember once he called me and asked where we were.

"We're just coming into Bali," I said.

"Be very careful in Bali," he said. "I know about that place. The good girls are nude from the waist up, but watch out for the ones who wear sweaters."

He was right, too.

While we were away, the carpenters and painters were renovating a house I had bought on Saint Cloud Road in Bel Air, one of the nicer sections of Los Angeles. Each of the Warner brothers—Jack, Harry, and Abe—gave us a room and paid for the remodeling. It was a comfortable home and would eventually hear the sounds of children—Warner and Linda, our two wonderful kids.

The four months on the ship sped by, and then we were home. Scripts and books and offers had been piling up and I quickly found myself back in the cinema swim.

In the next few years, while the world was struggling out of the depression, I would turn out film after film after film. It was a period of tremendous activity for me—and for Hollywood in general. It was prosperity, not just "around the corner," but already there.

I threw myself into my work. In 1932, I directed several movies. I was busy, but we were all busy. We had to keep working, to stay up with the demand. The public was voracious in its appetite for movies. Neighborhood theaters had double features, and the bill usually changed twice a week. That meant they were showing four new pictures a week, 208 a year, and that's only one theater. Hollywood had to supply them.

I shot them so often and so fast that they tend to blend together in my memory.

There was *Heart of New York*, with Smith and Dale. I felt like I was back in my days as a comedy constructor. I dreamed up an old-time gag for the opening scene, right out of the past. There was an old lady running down the street, hollering "I gotta leak, I gotta leak," and then she runs into a plumber's store.

There was *Elmer the Great*, another Joe E. Brown picture. We used Eleanor Holm in it, since she was then hot from the publicity that came with being kicked off the Olympic swimming team for drinking champagne on the Berlin-bound boat. She was no actress, but we had another girl making her film debut who was an actress—Jane Wyman. I found her on the lot. Although Jack Warner had signed her, he hadn't used her in anything. I saw her walking around the lot one day—I'll always remember she was wearing a yellow polo coat—and I decided she'd be right for *Elmer* and put her in it. She did a beautiful job, and her career was launched.

There was *Three on a Match*. They gave me three unknown girls in that one—Joan Blondell, Bette Davis, and Ann Dvorak. I made a mistake when the picture was finished. I told an interviewer that I thought Joan Blondell was going to be a big star, that Ann Dvorak had definite possibilities, but that I didn't think Bette Davis would make it. She's been cool to me ever since.

Around that time, the new racetrack, Hollywood Park, was being planned by a group headed by Alfred E. Green, my old director friend. I was sure it would prove a sound investment. I told Joan, my pet of the three, about it and suggested that she put some money—twenty-five hundred dollars—in the park. She laughed and said she didn't have that kind of money; she had just signed a contract and wasn't making much. So I loaned her the money to buy some shares and she made a bundle on it, and has always said that I started her on the road to financial security.

There was *The World Changes* (another Paul Muni film) and *High Pressure* (with William Powell and George Sidney) and *Big City Blues* (with Humphrey Bogart and a girl named Ava Gardner in a bit part). There was *Two Seconds* (once more with Edward G. Robinson) and *Hard to Handle* (my second with James Cagney).

They came and they went. They all made money, but that had nothing to do with my directorial skill. It's just that everything made money in those days. You could have done a movie about a bunch of zucchini and it would have shown a profit on the ledger.

But I felt I was standing still. I was doing work I loved—making movies—but none of the films I made were major triumphs. With *Little Caesar, Five Star Final*, and *Fugitive* under my belt, I wanted every picture to be a blockbuster. Of course, I knew that was impossible. A picture is only as good as its script—the words are the important thing—and the scripts I had been getting were good, but not great.

It was time to turn my attention to another kind of movie, a kind I knew well because of my years in vaudeville—the musical.

I was part of the Warner family now. They were a mixed-up family, the Warners, but they were always and endlessly fascinating. Of them all, Jack was the one I was always closest to. He was the family showman, and I gravitated toward him; the others were strictly businessmen. But it was my new father-in-law, Harry, who helped me get started with what has become my greatest off-screen passion—horse racing. Harry got me started, and I soon became as enthusiastic as he was—and he was almost a fanatic. He had been the man who had put up the last money needed to make Hollywood Park a reality.

He and I raced together. He took me into his stables; we called it the W-L Ranch, and for quite a few years we raced on the major tracks. Our best horse—in fact the best horse he ever owned—was Paper Boy, who once won the Saratoga Cup.

After that partnership dissolved, I raced under my own name for many years—Mervyn LeRoy Stables—and now I own a few horses with Buddy Fogelson, Greer Garson's husband. In recent years, we've used the services of one of the top trainers, Charley Whittingham, and the great Willie Shoemaker as our jockey. My horses may not have been great ones, but there's no thrill quite like seeing my colors come around that last turn and head down the home-stretch.

I became president of Hollywood Park, a post I have held for twenty-two years. It is an honorary job, but I find it great fun. Whenever the track is open, and I am not shooting a film, I'm there. I only go on weekends unless I have a horse running during the week.

People expect me to give them tips, but I never do. I always remember what my father used to say—"You can beat a race, but you can't beat the races." The quickest way to lose a friend is to give him a tip on a losing horse.

I was out at the track one day with Jack Warner and the three Hakims, a set of Egyptian-born brothers who made movies, and Charley Feldman. The man who was training for me at the time had a horse entered in the last race, and he told me the horse had a good chance of winning. I whispered to Jack that I had a horse that day who might be worth a bet.

"What's his name?" Jack asked. "What race?"

"Look, I know you, Jack. If I tell you, you'll tell everybody here. I don't want this spread around. I'll tell you his name just before the race comes up."

Jack grumbled, but I was adamant. Before every race, Jack said, "Can you tell me now?" And I'd say, "No, not yet. I can't tell you now. I don't want you telling the whole world."

Finally, just before the last race, I told him the name of the horse. We both put some money on him—and, of course, the nag finished way back.

When I got home, there was a telegram from Jack: "NOW CAN I TELL?" it read.

Often, when I was directing a picture, and I knew I couldn't get out to the track in the afternoon, I would get up very early in the morning and drive out to the W-L Ranch or go to the track before

I went to the studio. I'd get there about six in the morning to watch my horses being exercised and rubbed down, and to talk to the trainers and exercise boys. Since I prefer being with somebody, I'd often invite people to come along on those early morning visits. Naturally, it would be better if that person was with me on the picture, because then we could go directly from the ranch or the track to the studio. It got to be a thing with me that I'd have my first assistant director accompany me to the track or the ranch at that early hour.

It served a dual purpose. Besides having company on the drive, we would also talk over that day's shooting. Howard Koch was my assistant on several films, and he often went with me on those jaunts. Koch later became one of the better producers in town and, for a time, was production chief at Paramount. I always remember him sleepily rubbing his eyes as we drove out to the park while dawn was breaking.

We talked about many things besides horses and movies. I was doing well enough, so I began doing some serious investing and I had acquired many friends with expertise in financial matters. Through them, I got frequent tips on the stock market. I liked Koch, and wanted to put him on to some of those potential good things. One day, I told him about a stock I'd heard was destined for the heights.

"Howard," I said, "if you can get your hands on ten thousand dollars, put the whole bundle into a stock called Polaroid."

He laughed.

"Never heard of it," he said, "and, besides, I'm just an AD. Where can I get that kind of money?"

To this day, he says he'll never forgive himself for not acting on that tip.

In 1933, Hollywood was changing again. I could feel it, although I couldn't actually define it in specific terms. All I knew was that the public wanted something different again. I think most of the top directors operate the way I do, in that we are not particularly introspective or intellectual about our work. We just function on the basis of intuition. I think one reason why I've been able to please the public so regularly is that I don't try to outguess them. I consider myself a member of the public, and I make pictures that I believe in, stories that I enjoy reading, and I feel if it's a story I like, the rest of the public will like it, too.

I know that many of my colleagues use that same kind of reasoning. We do not go deeply into an analysis of our films, we merely make them. As some critics have written, we direct by the seat of our pants, by instinct.

The key word is instinct. In 1933, my instinct was working overtime. I could feel the public was surfeited, temporarily at least, with the films of realism that had flooded the market since I opened the gates with *Little Caesar*. Now, with the depression coming to an end, I felt they wanted something gayer, splashier, more lavish. I know I had the urge to make that kind of movie.

I had my chance with *Golddiggers of 1933*. There had been one earlier *Golddigger* film, the original directed by Roy Del Ruth, but I wanted this one to be grander.

It also gave me the opportunity to work with my old girlfriend, Ginger Rogers. When I first met her, during her Broadway run in *Girl Crazy*, I tried to persuade her to come to Hollywood to try movies. She did make a film, but her first one was made in New York. Finally, she could no longer resist the contract offers and made the trip west. She did a couple of pictures, in minor roles, then had a smash in *42nd Street*, and then I grabbed her for my *Golddiggers*.

I had Busby Berkeley choreograph the big production numbers, and they were some of the most memorable moments in his illustrious career. One of those sequences was shown in the recent film, *Bonnie and Clyde*. Perhaps the one I'll always remember had a hundred girls playing neon-outlined violins on a long, curving ramp.

The first day we rehearsed that number, the Los Angeles area was shaken by a moderate earthquake. The ramp swayed and several of the girls fell. Fortunately, none of them was seriously hurt. The ramp had to be repaired, however, before we could shoot the scene.

After *Golddiggers*, which was as much fun as I had anticipated and a huge hit as well, I was borrowed from Warner Brothers by Louis B. Mayer. He wanted me at MGM to direct a film called *Tugboat Annie*. It was my first experience with Mayer, but it wouldn't be my last. I was glad for the chance, because I was familiar with the *Tugboat Annie* stories and felt they had tremendous possibilities for the screen.

The stars were Marie Dressler and Wallace Beery. Poor Marie. *Tugboat Annie* was her greatest film, but it was also her last film. When we made it, in 1933, she was dying of cancer, and she knew it. *Annie* was a part she desperately wanted to play. She could only work three hours a day, because of her physical condition.

Marie was always a lady, always kind and considerate, and she worked like a Trojan, to the limit of her health. That limit was very limited. Her co-star, Wallace Beery, was just the opposite—a bull of a man, crude, impatient, unable to understand weakness of any kind. Marie's three-hour-a-day schedule seriously hampered the picture, but I knew that if it was to be finished at all, it would have to be done to accommodate her pace. When she went home at night, I couldn't help wondering whether she would be able to make it to the studio again in the morning. She was in constant pain, and the pain mirrored itself on her face, on her bearing, but never on her professionalism when the camera was rolling. She never lost her skill.

I had patience with her. Beery didn't.

One morning he came on the set and Marie hadn't yet arrived. I was content to wait, knowing that she would be there—lines memorized, ready for action—as soon as she physically could. Beery's patience was exhausted.

"Where's Dressler?" he boomed, in his hoarse, penetrating voice. "Get the old bag in here. I'll be in my dressing room. Let me know when she gets here."

The rest of the cast and crew were shocked. You could hear a big gasp from fifty or more throats, simultaneously. His remark shocked and offended me, too.

"Wally," I said, "that's not worthy of you—and you know it."

To his credit, he immediately recognized his own coarseness, apologized to everybody, and actually blushed. He had, apparently, gotten his impatience out of his system. From that moment until the end of shooting, he couldn't have been nicer to Marie and was, in fact, the soul of courtesy.

We shot one of the movie's biggest scenes at the waterfront in Seattle. The tug was coming in and there was a huge crowd—ten thousand extras—with bands to meet them. Because of the size of the scene, we worked out a system of giving badges to everyone involved, so they could get through the police lines to where we were working. In the morning, I sent Wally and Marie to board the boat, which was coming in from Alaska, and the captain had instructions to arrive at the mooring about three in the afternoon, when the light would be right.

I went back to the hotel to work on the script, and let my assistant directors maneuver the crowds into position. About 2:30, the studio driver took me to the dock and I started walking over to where the cameras were. A policeman stopped me.

"Where's your badge?"

I looked at my naked lapel. I had forgotten my badge.

"I'm the director, officer," I said. "I forgot my badge."

"Sorry, Mac. Can't get in there without a badge."

I tried the next corner, but the cop there was just as strict about following his orders. I had to go back to the hotel, and my first assistant had to rescue me, because I never could find my badge.

For me, one of the great advantages of that assignment was the chance to work with Irving Thalberg. He was one of the few authentic geniuses in the movie business—I think he and Walt Disney are the only two who really deserve that word—and it was an education working with him on *Tugboat Annie*. There's one incident in connection with *Tugboat Annie* that perfectly illustrates how he operated.

He called me in one day, after he'd seen the preview of the picture.

"Mervyn," he said, "remember that scene in the school auditorium? Marie is making a speech and Wally tries to sneak down the aisle, because his shoes are soaking wet and he doesn't want Annie to know he's drunk?"

"Sure I remember it. What about it?"

"Don't you think it would be better if his shoes squeaked when he walked? Wouldn't that help the picture?"

"We've struck that set already, Irving," I said. "We've paid off all the extras and the bit players. To get what you want, we'd have to have the people turn around. We'd have to reshoot it all. It'll cost around forty thousand dollars."

Thalberg fixed me with his eyes. He could look stern when he felt like it.

"Mervyn, I didn't ask you how much it would cost. I asked you whether it would help the picture."

"Sure it would help."

"All right, shoot it."

We had to rebuild part of the set, rehire the extras and the bit players, and reshoot the scene—just because Irving Thalberg wanted everything just right.

His judgment was vindicated when the picture opened. I took Marie Dressler to the premiere at Grauman's Chinese Theater in Hollywood, even though her health was getting progressively worse. I have always been pleased that she lived long enough to see the film and hear and read some of the praise that was heaped on her for her performance.

It was another triumph for me, too. I knew that the Metro brass
—Mayer and Thalberg particularly—were pleased with the work
I'd done on the film. There were hints dropped that they might like
me to come over to the studio on a permanent basis. That would
happen four years later, but meanwhile it was back to Warner
Brothers and a very productive period of my life.

7

LOUIS B. MAYER:
WATCH OUT
FOR YOURSELF

When the definitive history of Hollywood is written, I imagine the mid-1930s will be called "The Glory Days." There were several factors that contributed to that glory. First was the fact that the studios were flourishing, and studios created stars. You can't have stars without a big studio to find them, teach them, nurture them, bring them along slowly and carefully. Second, the public was demanding more and more product, so the studios had to meet that demand. Much of what we made, of course, was just so many reels of demand-filling movies, but for every two or three average films there was generally an exceptional one. Third, Hollywood had attracted the top writers of the era. It was the center for talent of all sorts; but writing is the key to motion picture success, so it was the steady influx of great writers that pleased me most. I've always said that Shakespeare agrees with me—the play's the thing.

Of all the studios of that period, Warner Brothers was the most exciting. There was the famous Warner Brothers stock company, probably the largest and most varied group of talented actors ever assembled anywhere. Under contract to the studio then were stars and, even more important, a coterie of character actors, great supporting players who could do anything.

I enjoyed every picture I made (some more than others, of course), but I can honestly say that I never made a picture I didn't like. After *Tugboat Annie*, I made a dozen films at Warner Brothers over the next four years.

A few of them stand out in my memory, for varying reasons. There was *Hi, Nellie*, because it gave me a chance to work with Paul Muni again. It was an unlikely part for him—he played a man who wrote a woman's column, under the name of "Hi, Nellie" —but he handled it magnificently.

There was *Heat Lightning*, which was memorable because it was probably the most uncomfortable film I ever made—and the least successful. Fortunately, I have never had what is commonly called a "bomb," but *Heat Lightning* was the closest to being one. That was because it was shot just before I left on my honeymoon trip around the world, so I had to get it done in a hurry. The whole thing was shot in three weeks. It starred Preston Foster and Aline MacMahon, and we filmed mostly in Needles, California, where the weather was so hot we could barely breathe. Relatively few people saw it—I never have—but it made money. Not much, but something. In those days, almost everything made something.

Oil for the Lamps of China, a year later, was back in the groove again. This film was based on the best-selling novel by Alice Teasdale Hobart, and the stars were Pat O'Brien and Josephine Hutchinson. Later, when I went to work at MGM, Irving Thalberg told me that it was one of his favorite films of all time, and that he had a print and screened it frequently for himself.

To me, the most memorable thing about *Oil for the Lamps of China* was something that happened one day when I was shooting. In fact, I remember the exact date—March 5, 1935. I had some three-hundred extras that day, a crowd of Chinese for a big scene. We were working, and I was called to the phone to hear that Doris had been taken to the hospital. Our first child was about to be born.

Naturally, I dropped everything and raced to the hospital. The only problem was that in my excitement I had forgotten to tell anybody I was going. One moment I was there, telling my three-hundred Chinese extras what to do, and the next moment I was gone. Nobody knew where I was. The assistant directors, after a reasonable wait, called the front office and Jack Warner was frantic with worry. For a few nervous hours, there was even some fear that I had been kidnapped. Kidnapping was on everybody's mind those days. Eventually, they found out what had happened and where I was.

My son, Warner LeRoy, was born that day, and it was one of the great days of my life. I longed to stay and watch him. I had never met a baby before, and it was endlessly thrilling just to stare at that tiny being and to realize that I had created him—with Doris' help, of course. But I couldn't stay; those three hundred extras were waiting for me, together with the rest of the cast and crew. So I rushed back to the studio and my picture.

Oil for the Lamps of China brought me some advice I'll always remember. When the picture came out, it received praise from most of the nation's critics. One exception, however, was William Randolph Hearst's San Francisco *Examiner*. Since I still had many members of my family living in San Francisco, I felt that slap keenly. At the time, I was spending the weekend with Hearst at San Simeon. I unburdened myself to Marion Davies.

"Why, that's awful," she said. "Let me go upstairs and get Poppy."

Poppy—as she always called Hearst—summoned me to his library. He was wearing a nightgown. I told him that I was distressed about the *Examiner's* review. He looked at me with his steel-gray eyes.

"I want to tell you something, Mervyn," he said. "Just remember this—the newspaper of today is the toilet paper of tomorrow."

Another film from that period was *Sweet Adeline*, which gave me a chance to work with Irene Dunne. She was then one of the great girls on the Hollywood scene, and she matured into one of the great ladies.

I had a small romantic problem on my hands when I did *Page Miss Glory*, which co-starred Marion Davies and Dick Powell. Many leading ladies fall in love—at least for the duration of the filming—with their leading men. And, in *Page Miss Glory*, Marion developed a roaring crush on Dick. It's a very understandable development. Leading men and leading women are generally extremely attractive people. They are thrown together, closely and intimately, for many weeks at a time. It would be abnormal if something like love didn't occur. I believe it is this kind of situation that accounts for the failure of so many Hollywood marriages; they cannot stand up to the temptation their work flings in their faces.

In the case of Marion Davies and Dick Powell, nothing really came of it. Mostly that was because of Dick's fear. He knew, as everyone knew, that Marion was Hearst's property. Hearst, at the time, was a heavyweight. He wielded a lot of muscle in Hollywood. I didn't want Marion's infatuation with Powell to lead to anything either, because Hearst might blame me for it. So I took pains to keep then apart as much as I could. But I didn't have to worry. Powell was so scared himself that he wound up virtually not even talking to Marion. He knew that Hearst could—and would—ruin his career if the word got back to him that his girl had fallen for the actor.

Marion Davies was one of the good people on this earth. At Christmastime, she'd bring hundreds of her dresses—she dressed well, but seldom wore a dress more than once—to the studio. She would get racks and hang the dresses up on one of the empty sound stages. Then she would invite the extras in and tell them each to take a dress. These weren't cheap copies, either, but all one-of-a-kind designers' creations.

By the time 1936 arrived, I was slowing my pace somewhat. Gone were the assembly-line tactics, the grinding-them-out methods of a few years before. Now the emphasis was on each director making fewer, but better, pictures. I only made two films that year, but they were both bigger, more expensive, and took longer to make. Many directors were working so slowly, perhaps shooting no more than a page or a page and a half a day, that it was foolish. They would spend hours, literally, lighting a set, then do retake after retake. I never allowed myself to go overboard in that direction but, like everybody, I was working slower, trying to achieve more beauty on film, looking for cinematic perfection.

Three Men on a Horse was another film from a hit Broadway play. I tried, as much as possible, to use the original Broadway cast, augmented by Joan Blondell and Eddie "Rochester" Anderson. One of those I brought out from New York for the picture was the great comic actor, Sam Levene. Curiously, despite his wonderful on-stage comedy timing, he had little sense of humor off stage. In fact, he was naïve and extremely gullible, and a perfect foil for some of my keep-the-set-cheerful practical jokes.

I couldn't resist. He was such a natural butt for humor. It started right away, the first or second day he arrived on the set. He said that he would like to get some nice still pictures of himself, to send back east to his old friends. I said fine and then I called Elmer Fryer, the head portrait photographer at the studio, and we framed a gag. I set up an appointment for Sam with Fryer, and the actor happily headed up to the portrait gallery.

"All right, Mr. Levene," Fryer said, when Sam arrived. "Now, the first thing, would you please take off all your clothes, except your shorts."

"Take off all my clothes?"

"Oh, yes. That's the way we work here. Mr. LeRoy likes to see our subjects in shorts first, so we can see the body of a coming star first, then in pants, and so on."

So Levene took off every stitch of clothing and his first Hollywood portraits were naked, except for his shorts.

Later, Sam said he'd like to have a picture of himself kissing Joan Blondell, to impress his actor friends back east. We were delighted to oblige him. The picture was taken. Meanwhile, I had a shot made of Teddy Hart, the round-faced comic, whistling. Then, in the photography lab, we played around with the negative and took out Joan's head and inserted the shot of Teddy Hart, all puckered up. The pictures came back, showing Sam kissing Teddy.

"I can't figure this out, Mr. LeRoy," Sam said to me, showing one of those pictures. "To the best of my recollection, I never kissed Teddy."

There was a scene in the picture in a barroom, which came equipped with an old brass spittoon. Sam had to enter the bar and stand next to the spittoon, and he kept kicking it accidentally. I asked him to be careful, because when he kicked the spittoon it made a noise and ruined the take. He said he'd be careful, but he kept kicking it, take after take, as he ran to his position at the bar.

I pretended to be very angry.

"Look, Levene," I said. "Any actor who can't act his way around a spittoon isn't much of an actor."

Poor Sam was very nervous. I told him to go to his dressing room and relax for a few minutes, and then we'd try it again. While he was gone, I had the prop men take the spittoon away.

He came back into the scene and I called for action and he ran up to his spot by the bar. You could see that all he was thinking about was missing that spittoon. When he didn't kick it, he kept feeling around for it with his foot. Finally, he couldn't help himself —he had to look down to see where that spittoon was. It wasn't there—and then he knew he'd been the butt of another gag. Like all the other times, he took it well and we became the best of friends.

After *Three Men on a Horse* came *Anthony Adverse* and a different set of problems. For the first time, I had a brush with censorship. The Breen Office at that time controlled the morals of movies. We had routinely submitted our script to them, and it came back with forty pages crossed out.

Their notations said that we couldn't film those forty pages, because the hero—Anthony Adverse—was naked in one scene, when
he was a little boy. They said that made the picture offensive to the
Catholic Church. I was furious. I had never done a picture that
contained anything offensive in it—I never would—and I resented
their lack of trust.

I got together with the head of the office, Joseph Breen, and we
had three days of conferences. We were getting nowhere. Finally, I
said to him, "Look, Joe, there's only one thing I'm going to ask you
to do. Let me make this picture my way. I can make it so it won't
offend the Catholics, or anybody else. When I finish, if you don't
agree, you can cut anything out you want to."

"I'm afraid to do that," Breen said. "We've never given anybody
carte blanche."

"Please, Joe," I said. "Leave it to me. I promise you will love
this boy from the start. You'll feel very sorry for him. The Catholic
Church and every other church will be very happy with it."

"Okay, Mervyn. But if I don't like what I see, I'm going to cut
hell out of it."

I made the picture under the terms of that informal agreement. I
must say I was pretty nervous when it was screened for Breen and
his people. I would have been in serious trouble if he had found it
offensive. He didn't object to a single frame. Later, representatives
of the Roman Catholic Church saw it, and they were among the
first to give *Anthony Adverse* their official blessing. The little boy
was still nude, but he was a block away.

I tested the Earl of Warwick for one of the parts, but that was
pretty much a publicity stunt. It was better that he stayed the Earl
of Warwick. Although he was a very good-looking man, he was a
better earl than he was an actor.

Anthony Adverse was a romantic adventure film. It was successful and it starred that brilliant actor, Fredric March. He was always
good, but he needed a firm hand. I realized that right away, the first
day, the first scene. We began in an African hut, March emoting
with an African girl, played by Steffi Duna. He was overacting
terribly. With a man of his reputation, it was ticklish to get him to
stop. I've always felt that a director has to be a working psychologist. There must be an instinctive ability to tell your actors what
you want in ways that are best suited to the particular situation and
the individuals concerned. In March's case, I knew I couldn't come
out flatly and say, "'You're overacting." I just had a feeling that he

would respond more readily if the suggestion was couched in humorous terms.

So I turned to my first assistant director, Bill Cannon, and I said, loud enough for everybody to hear, "Bill, get the Shredded Wheat set ready."

March gave me a funny look.

"What's a Shredded Wheat set?" he said.

"Well, Freddy, if you're going to eat the scenery, we'll have to make it out of Shredded Wheat."

He got the message, laughed, and from then on his performance was controlled and disciplined and a joy to watch.

Through the mid-1930s, I continued making pictures I wanted to make. There are a lot of film critics who have criticized me for the type of film I made during those years. They point to my early films—*Little Caesar, I Am a Fugitive from a Chain Gang, Five Star Final*—and say that I began by making movies of social significance and that I sold out to the establishment. They say that my later films were merely done for the money involved.

I have two answers to those charges. First, some of my later films, such as *They Won't Forget* and *Blossoms in the Dust*, had deep social significance. More important, I made movies based on properties that appealed to me, properties I felt would convert into motion pictures of quality. If a property had come along of any sort, socially significant or otherwise, I would have made it—if I felt it would be a movie that would appeal to the vast majority of the public and to my own tastes. Any director who tries to pander to public taste while he ignores his own is riding for a fall. Similarly, a director who sets out to make a movie to please only himself is also asking for trouble. A director must believe in the property he is doing, but must also consider what the public wants and needs. The two go hand in hand.

So the films I did in that period were based on the best stories I could lay my hands on. Some came from best-selling novels—like *Oil for the Lamps of China* and *Anthony Adverse*—and some came from Broadway hits.

It certainly wasn't any conscious effort to avoid any type of movie. I was big enough in Hollywood by this time so that I could do virtually anything I wanted to do. It was simply a continuing search for the finest properties I could find. If those happened to be romances or adventure stories or comedies, rather than films of social significance, it was pure coincidence. It was simply that those were the stories that appealed to me at the time and had entertainment value.

In late 1936, Jack Warner handed me a copy of a novel he had just bought. It was called *Death in the Deep South*, and it had been written by a man named Ward Greene. Jack wanted me to do the screen version. The first thing I did was change the title to *They Won't Forget*. The novel was pretty powerful stuff for 1936, and the picture would be, too. It was the first time, I think, that a black man was ever shown in a favorable light on the screen.

It was the story of two men falsely accused of the rape and murder of a teen-age girl. Greene had written his novel, using a real-life case, the famous Leo Frank case, and embellishing it with the story of a prosecutor who used the case as a political stepping-stone. I got a wonderful screenplay from Robert Rossen, and I hired a fine cast—Claude Rains as the prosecutor, and Gloria Dickson and Edward Norris. The one big problem I had in casting was to find the right girl to play the victim. She had to be young and desirable, yet have a childlike innocence, an untouched quality. There aren't many teen-age girls who have that.

"Find me a girl," I told the casting office, "who is sexy and innocent at the same time."

They looked at me as if I had lost my senses, but they did their best. They sent up a parade of young things to my office. I must have seen fifty girls without finding the right one. Then, a few days before Christmas, Solly Baiano, the studio's casting director, came in to see me with yet another young girl in tow.

She was fifteen. She was wearing a cheap blue cotton dress. Her hair was dark, messy, uncombed. She was obviously very scared. She was so shy she kept looking down at her hands all the time we were talking. Despite those surface drawbacks, I sensed immediately that this was the girl I had been looking for. I felt it even before she opened her mouth. I asked her to read a few lines, and she did, but her hands were trembling so badly she could barely hold the script. I asked her to walk back and forth across the office. I asked her to smile. But I was just going through the motions. I knew she was the girl for me even before I asked her to do anything.

She had the sexy-innocent-clean quality I wanted, and it wasn't anything she had made up. That was the way she was—a youthful face but there was something smoldering underneath, and, besides, she had a fantastic figure.

"What's your name, young lady?" I asked.

"Turner," she said. "Judy Turner."

"Well, I like you and I think I can use you. But I'm not too happy with your name."

It's funny about names. I liked the name Judy, and certainly there was nothing wrong with Turner. Yet the two names, to me, didn't seem to go together. She reminded me of somebody I had once known, back in Oakland or San Francisco. I tried to remember that other girl's name, and then it came to me—Donna Gray, the chorus girl I had a crush on when I was a teen-ager. Donna. That was a nice name.

Donna Turner. No, that didn't sound right, either. I went through the alphabet in my mind, as the girl sat there staring at her hands. Bonna, Fonna, Gonna. Nothing. Then I got to *L*—Lonna Turner. That sounded just right. Only maybe it should be spelled Lana.

"How do you like the name Lana Turner?" I asked.

She just smiled and nodded. She didn't say anything, but she seemed to be happy. At least she wasn't unhappy. That is how Lana Turner was discovered and renamed, all in one brief interview. When I asked her if she wanted to sign a contract, she said she'd have to ask her mother. She did, and her mother said yes.

As soon as she began work, I realized that Lana was not merely right for this picture, but she was going to be a big name in the business. There was something about her, some magic that was obvious when you saw her on screen. Besides, there was that superb figure. When she walked down the street, in the film, her bosom seemed to move in rhythm, a rhythm all its own. When I added the musical score to the picture, I made sure that the composer emphasized that rhythm with his music. She wore a sweater in that scene, and that's how she got her reputation as a sweater girl.

We paid her, as I remember it, the magnificent sum of seventy-five dollars a week for her first film. I didn't make the same mistake with Lana that I had made with Clark Gable. I signed her to a personal contract and supervised her career during its first, critical years. It needed a lot of supervision, too, because Lana was incredibly naïve about life and really didn't know how to take advantage of her natural assets.

I bought her first evening gown, when she went to her first big affair. I should have sent the wardrobe lady over to help her get dressed, too, because when she showed up she was so overmade up and overjeweled it was ludicrous. On one finger, she was wearing the biggest—and the most obviously fake—diamond ring I had ever seen. The next day I called her in to my office.

"Lana," I said, "I think you're going to be a very important star. But you'll never get there unless you learn to look real. You have to avoid anything that is fake or phony. You're too beautiful to rely on false things. Wait a while, and you'll have real diamonds."

She took my advice and actually was grateful for it. Nobody had ever taken her in hand to explain matters of taste to her before. She never wore that hunk of glass again, but she once told me that she kept it in her jewel box—along with the real diamonds she began accumulating—as a reminder of the way she used to be.

The legend that she was discovered sitting on a stool in Schwab's Drugstore is, like so many Hollywood legends, a nice fable, but completely untrue. The first person to spot her was Billy Wilkerson, then the publisher of the *Hollywood Reporter*. He had seen her in a little café that sold only soft drinks, and he was the one who had brought her to Baiano. And Baiano brought her to me.

After *They Won't Forget*, I loaned her to Sam Goldwyn for a part in *Marco Polo*, and she was off and running. By the time I released her from her contract several years later, she was making five thousand dollars a week.

They Won't Forget won many awards, and I have always considered it one of my best films. I was proud of the film's content and also of the work of Rains, Lana, and the fine Negro actor Clinton Roseman, the first to play a realistic black role on the screen. Nowadays, film historians are writing about the emergence of the blacks, and they like to poke fun at the early Negro film actors—Stepin Fetchit, Hattie McDaniel, Clarence Muse, Butterfly McQueen—but they generally overlook Roseman and the work he did in *They Won't Forget*. He paved the way for Sidney Poitier, Richard Roundtree, Paul Winfield, Billy Dee Williams, and the other fine black actors of today.

One thing that film did for me was to give me the reputation of a film liberal. That wasn't precisely true. If *They Won't Forget* did appeal to the so-called liberal philosophy, it was accidental. I made that picture, as I made all my pictures, because it was a good story. Any sociopolitical message it may have had was purely a by-product of its story. I know that it's a cliché, but often clichés are true—if you want to send a message, you should go to Western Union. I have never felt that motion pictures were the place to try to champion any cause—political, religious, economic, anything. Motion pictures are to entertain, not to change somebody's mind.

If you have a fine story that deals with a social issue, that's fine. But the story should come first, not the philosophy.

I have never been particularly political—I have supported Democrats and I have supported Republicans—and I didn't want to be stuck with any particular label. I made a point that my next picture would be very different, so nobody could accuse me of using the screen to promote my views.

That was one reason why I was delighted when my next was *The King and the Chorus Girl*. This came about through my friendship with Norman Krasna, the ex-New York *Graphic* office boy who had tested for a part in *Five Star Final*. I met him on the lot one day, and he told me that he and Groucho Marx were writing a screen-play. I asked to see it, and he showed me what they had already done—barely twenty pages—but that was enough. It was so clever and witty that I bought it even before I knew how it was going to end.

To show you that not all discoveries work out, I give you my find, Fernand Gravet. He played the lead in *The King and the Chorus Girl*, and I thought I had another huge star. I had seen Gravet in a European picture and got very excited, and I had him fly over here and test. The test was exceptional and Gravet was a handsome and charming man. In the film, he played opposite Joan Blondell, and I was convinced he'd make it big. The public liked him, too, but he never did make it. The reason was that his wife ruined him. Gravet—his name was originally Gravey, but obviously that spelling would look silly on English-language marquees —was a nice human being. At the time, he was somewhere around thirty-five, and his wife must have been at least thirty years his senior. She controlled him completely, and she wanted to keep him all to herself.

That film and the next few, such as *The Great Garrick*, with Brian Aherne and Olivia De Havilland, and *Fools for Scandal*, with Gravet and Carole Lombard, were not great but good enough to keep my nonflop record intact. *The Great Garrick* was something new. I didn't direct it, but merely produced it, with James Whale directing.

One day, I received a call from Louis B. Mayer. He asked me to come over to see him. Irving Thalberg had died in 1936, and Mayer wanted somebody to take over the studio and run it. I had been very close to Thalberg and respected him immensely. A week before he died, we were in Monterey together, playing golf in the daytime and bridge at night, with Doris and Irving's wife,

Norma Shearer, and Harpo Marx, Sam Wood, and some others. During those few pleasant days, Irving and I had worked out the details of a deal, which was still in his desk when he died, for me to work with and for him. The idea of going over to MGM appealed to me. As Hollywood has often said, MGM was the Cadillac of studios. And, too, Thalberg had had respect for me, so I didn't feel that I would be stepping into the job of a man who wouldn't have wanted me.

Mayer offered me a fantastic salary—six thousand dollars a week, twice what I had been getting at Warner Brothers. There was one proviso; I wasn't supposed to tell anybody what I was making. That salary was more than anybody else in town had ever gotten, and Mayer didn't want the details to get out. Unfortunately, the details did get out. There was a lawsuit brought against Loew's, MGM's parent company, asking for an accounting, and Mayer had to reveal the salaries of all the studio executives, so my three hundred thousand dollars a year became public knowledge.

The salary embarrassed me. Nobody is worth that much. When I got my first paycheck, I couldn't help but think back to my poor father. I made more in that one week than he ever made in a year.

The money was put to good use. It brought me security, which is something I have always craved, far more than temporary material possessions. I was able to care for my mother and stepfather, and I bought them a comfortable house in Hollywood. For the first time, I was able to indulge my taste for art. I consider good paintings a great investment as well as an aesthetic experience, and I've been mad at myself for not buying more. There was a time when I could have bought Renoirs and Matisses—I recognized their talent—but at the time I had no money. Now, when I had the money, there were few of their works available. I did buy what good art I could.

At first, the money was secondary to the opportunity and challenge the new job offered. Here I was, at the top studio in town, charged with developing new film projects. The fact that I was also the highest-salaried film executive paled into insignificance (almost) beside that. The kid who used to sing songs in vaudeville for a few bucks a night was now on top. It felt good.

It also felt good to be working with Louis B. Mayer. We were always close, and our friendship grew with the years. In fact, later, when I had divorced Doris and was once again a bachelor, L.B. asked me to move in with him. He was lonely, I guess, and wanted companionship. I didn't, and I've always wondered whether I made a mistake. Maybe he needed me. Maybe it was wrong of me to say no, to prefer my own solitude and freedom.

Mayer is a much misunderstood man. He was a legend; and over the years, legends have grown up around the original legend. The result is that the truth has been pretty much obscured by the undergrowth. The truth was good enough.

L.B. was a big man, not in stature, perhaps, but certainly in deeds. He had the greatest taste and the ability to translate that taste into film. He knew what he wanted. But, in my year at the studio, he never once said "no" to anything I asked to do. Maybe that's because his taste and mine meshed, or maybe it's just because he had confidence in me. Or maybe I was just lucky and never suggested anything he disagreed with. Whatever the reason, it made our association fruitful and pleasant.

He was a sentimental man, not the hard-driving tycoon his name conjures up. He was the kind of man whose door was always open at the studio, and the little people on the lot often just walked right in and began chatting away about his current projects.

Over his bed, there was a portrait of his mother. Mayer was a man who dearly loved his mother and wasn't afraid to admit it. Even though she died when he was in his early twenties, he continued to speak about her as if she were still living.

One evening, when we were sitting in his living room, he began talking about his mother. He told me how she had been a tremendous influence on his life and the way he thought. He told me how his mother had been dying, and what she had told him as she lay in her bed with the realization that she had little time left.

"Do not grieve, Louis," his mother had said. "We must all die sooner or later. Now it's my turn. I wish I could have stayed a little longer, so I could see you do the big things I know you are capable of doing. But I will watch over you. I will know all about you and your work. And I will wait for you."

Mayer firmly believed that his mother was watching over him, as she had promised she would do. I felt a chill creep through me as he talked, but maybe he was right. Somebody was surely watching over him.

We used to have long talks. I think he came to think of me almost as a son.

"Look out for yourself," Mayer once said to me, "or they'll pee on your grave."

He was right. This town is cruel. Hollywood forgets past triumphs quickly, but remembers the unpleasantness about people.

Mayer is much maligned these days, and even the great Thalberg and his wonderful work is being forgotten.

When they took Irving Thalberg's name off the Thalberg Building at MGM, I thought it was disgraceful. I felt the same way about the failure of the Academy of Motion Picture Arts and Sciences to honor Walt Disney at the Oscar awards ceremony the year after he died. They simply ignored the passing of a true genius without even a bow in his direction.

"Look out for yourself or they'll pee on your grave." I've looked out for myself since Mayer's warning. I'm damned glad I did, because if I hadn't, nobody else would have.

It was easy to save money, when I was getting six thousand dollars a week. I could indulge myself, take care of my family, even give plenty to charity, and still have enough left over to provide for my own dubious future.

Futures in Hollywood are always dubious. I went to MGM with high hopes for a lengthy tenure there. I was full of plans and dreams. At least one would materialize into a major triumph, but I quickly became disenchanted with my new job.

I found myself chafing at an executive's desk. It didn't take long to realize that the fun of the movie business was in the actual directing. Producing was paperwork. There were many great and creative producers, and they obviously enjoyed it. Not me. I found it just a case of putting packages together, getting a property and a director and a screenplay and a cast, and then watching somebody else transform all that into a finished film. I missed that act of transformation.

About a year after I got there, I went to Mayer and said I wanted out. I volunteered to take a cut in salary if he would let me direct again. He never stood in my way, although I think he was disappointed.

However, that year at MGM was a successful one. One of the pictures I produced during that span was destined to be seen by more people than have ever seen any other motion picture—*The Wizard of Oz.*

As a boy, I had read and loved Frank Baum's *Oz* books. That wasn't unusual; children of my era and children of all the eras yet to come read and loved *The Wizard of Oz* and all the others. I was told at the time that the publishers estimated that more than ninety million people had read one or more of the *Oz* books. Each new generation of children helped to swell that figure.

It had long been an idle dream of mine someday to take those fantastic, enchanting characters and turn them into a movie. The dream remained merely a dream until I found myself at MGM and L.B. Mayer asked me what I wanted to make.

"The Wizard of Oz," I said.

He didn't look pained or upset or anything.

"Okay," he said. "Do it."

I learned that Sam Goldwyn owned the rights to Baum's book. MGM bought it from Sam for fifty thousand dollars, which must go down alongside the Louisiana Purchase as one of the biggest bargains of all times. I reread the book and marked the scenes and characters I felt should be in the picture. I worked with screenwriters Florence Ryerson and Edgar Allan Woolf, who did the adaptation with the help of Noel Langley and Arthur Freed.

The picture turned out to be one gigantic headache, but I guess any great work evolves through pain. If it's too easy, it can't be very good.

The only thing L.B. worried about was the cost, and he knew whereof he worried. By the time we were finished, *The Wizard of Oz* would cost $3.2 million, which was a lot of money in 1938. It has made so much more than that, through its theatrical and repeated television showings, however, that it would have been cheap at five times the cost.

At first, I wanted to direct it, but L.B. talked me out of it. He thought it would be too much for one man to produce and direct a picture of that magnitude, and he was right. We hired George Cukor to direct it.

The preparations for that film were enormous. Nothing like it had been done before. It was basically a fairy story, a fantasy. Everything that we were doing—sets, costumes, makeup—had to be created out of our imaginations, guided by Baum's descriptions in his books.

Cedric Gibbons was my art director, aided by William Horning. It was their province to conceive and build the two main areas where we would film, Munchkinland and Oz itself. For the former, Gibbons and his team built a model that was one-fourth life size. They fabricated an entire model town, 122 buildings. It took months to finish that alone, and some of the statistics boggle the mind. For example, there were 150 painters and they ultimately used 62 shades of colors on the models. When the full set was built, it covered 25 acres of the studio back lot, or would have if all the sets were up at once. We had 65 different sets in the picture, and each one of them was concocted out of whole cloth and hard work.

I found myself working eighteen hours a day as I had to sift through questions from makeup men, set designers, writers, directors, everybody. They all wanted answers and that's what the producer must supply, when you get down to the nitty-gritty; he's the one who has to make the decisions, with the help of the director.

How do you make a yellow brick road look really yellow? We tried all kinds of exotic dyes and fancy bricks and imported paints and photographed them and none of them looked right. Then one morning I suggested to Gibbons that he try some ordinary, cheap yellow fence paint. He did, and the yellow brick road finally looked like what a yellow brick road should look like.

How do you get a believable shot of a cyclone? Arnold (Buddy) Gillespie, our special effects man, was one of the geniuses of that highly specialized field. He tried everything in his bag of tricks, but nothing photographed like a genuine cyclone. Then he had a brainstorm. He took a lady's silk stocking, strung it up, and twirled it around with a fan to give it a blowing look. That shot of the Kansas cyclone in *Oz* is just a silk stocking.

There were problems with makeup, too. Buddy Ebsen was cast as the Tin Man, and Jack Dawn, Metro's head makeup man, affixed a rubber jaw and a rubber funnel to his head, covered his face with white clown makeup, and sprayed him with aluminum dust. It looked perfect, halfway between human and metallic. The only difficulty was that Ebsen kept inhaling the aluminum dust and one morning, a week after we began shooting, he woke up and he couldn't breathe. His wife rushed him to the hospital where they had to put him in an iron lung. Naturally, in her panic, she hadn't thought to call the studio. All I knew was that my Tin Man wasn't there. I finally tracked him down at the hospital. We waited a few days, but Ebsen was too sick to come back to the picture. We had to replace him with Jack Haley. Jack Dawn had learned a lesson the hard way. With Haley, he didn't use aluminum dust, but made a paste of the aluminum and spread that on Haley's face. Ebsen had been the guinea pig and had lost a great part because of it.

With one major exception, casting had been easy. For the leading role, Dorothy, the MGM brass was unanimous—they wanted Shirley Temple. I was the only one who didn't. I had nothing against her, but I had seen my Dorothy, sometime before, when I caught a low-budget Fox musical called *Pigskin Parade*. In it, I had seen Judy Garland, and she had the quality I wanted for Dorothy.

It took me a while, but I finally convinced L.B. to go along with me. When he agreed, I contacted Judy and signed her for the part. At the time, she had a gap between her front teeth, and I sent her to a dentist who gave her that winning, gapless smile.

Everybody agreed on Bert Lahr, Ray Bolger, and Buddy Ebsen as the three major supporting roles—the Cowardly Lion, the Straw Man, and the Tin Man—and they were no problem, until Ebsen got sick. For the Wizard, I wanted Ed Wynn, but he turned me down. He said the part was too small for him. We got Frank Morgan, and he turned out to be ideal. I think that *Oz* was one of the best-cast films ever made; there wasn't a false note in it. Arthur Freed helped a great deal with the casting.

About the time Ebsen got sick, we changed directors. Cukor, one of our greatest directors, just did a few tests for me but didn't want to do the picture. We next tried Richard Thorp, but eventually and finally settled on Victor Fleming. Fleming, always a great director, had that fantasy touch we needed.

The idea of starting the film in black-and-white, then going into color when we reached Oz, and back to black-and-white again for the return to Kansas, was mine. For a while, though, I wished I had never thought of it. It created huge problems. The makeup had to be different for the black-and-white portions, but that was a relatively minor matter. What caused the biggest difficulty was the actual moment of transition. Each frame of film had to be hand-painted to make the change from black-and-white to color a smooth one.

Another headache was assembling the Munchkins, the little people. We brought midgets from all over the world, and quickly discovered that they were a handful. We kept them in a Culver City hotel. I guess it's like any group who go to a convention in a distant city; somehow, their inhibitions are left behind. Or maybe the little people, as they prefer to be called, have little inhibitions to go with their little stature. Whatever the reason, they were wild. Every night there were fights and orgies and all kinds of carryings-on. Almost every night, the Culver City police had to rush over to the hotel to keep them from killing each other. I was very happy when their part of the picture was over.

We had to have "a horse of a different color" in the Oz scenes. That didn't appear to be a serious matter; we would just take a horse and paint it. But the ASPCA, which has jurisdiction over animals in pictures, said no. They wouldn't let us use paint on the horse. So we had to come up with something else, and finally dis-

covered that liquid colored candy did the trick just as well, and we
passed the ASPCA test.

It took six months to prepare the picture, six more months to
shoot it, and then a lengthy postproduction schedule for the editing
and scoring. Altogether, *The Wizard of Oz* was many months in
the making.

Finally, when we were ready, we arranged for a sneak preview
in San Bernardino. I went with L.B.; as we sat there, I sensed that
the audience loved it. Afterward, in the lobby, we stood and
watched the happy people as they filed out of the theater. As usual,
we discussed the pros and cons of the picture. It may seem unbelievable now, but the only criticism any of the executives had was
about the song "Over the Rainbow." Yip Harburg and Harold
Arlen had written a fantastic score, but all the other songs were in
a faster, catchier tempo. They were the sort of melodies the public
could latch on to quickly, whistle as they left their seats. "Over the
Rainbow," on the other hand, was a ballad, and it always takes a
private ear several hearings before it appreciates a ballad.

"That 'rainbow' song," one Metro producer said, "is no good. It
slows the picture down."

There were other comments in a similar vein. That's all some
jumpy movie executives need to hear, some adverse criticism. Too
often, that breed is motivated strictly by fear. If there is any negative opinion expressed, they are inclined to act on it in a state of
panic. Many good films have been ruined because of this instan-
taneous, frightened reaction. Directors and writers may have spent
months or years on a project, but because one minor executive says
he doesn't like something, the boss will cut or reedit and inflict
incurable harm on a film.

"That song has to go," some of the MGM executives said, as I
stood there in the lobby. I knew in my heart that "Over the Rainbow" would be a hit, but I had had the benefit of hearing it often. I
tried to persuade them that the song was a good one, but I seemed
to be arguing in vain. L.B. didn't say anything, but he listened to
me, Harburg, Arlen, and Freed on the one side, and to the anti-
"Rainbow" faction on the other.

Finally, after he had heard about ten minutes of discussion,
Mayer spoke.

"Okay, Mervyn," he said. "You win. 'Over the Rainbow' stays
in the picture."

He had the last word, of course. "Over the Rainbow" did stay in,
and now when we think of *Oz*, that's the first song that pops into

our minds. I hate to think of what would have happened if those other men had won out that night in San Bernardino.

I'm very proud of *The Wizard of Oz*. I think it will live long after I'm gone. I get a personal satisfaction out of the fact that, every year, my children saw it and, after they had grown up and had children of their own, my grandchildren saw it. It has become a fixture on television, and this is one picture TV hasn't hurt by cutting. When it was first sold, the network asked me to cut five minutes out of it. I tried but I couldn't find that much that was expendable. I did cut one minute, and they were very happy.

My children and grandchildren could see any picture I ever made, but I often wonder about today's directors, who make X-rated films. Those who have children must really be torn. Kids like to see what their fathers have done.

Linda, my daughter, was born on May 17, 1938, while we were making *Oz*.

I don't want to bore you with too many proud-papa stories, but there are two I'll tell you. They both concern Linda. From her earliest years, Linda was interested in horses. She did a lot of show riding and won her share of ribbons. When she was seven or so, one Saturday I took her to Hollywood Park. I let her pick out a horse and I placed a bet and her horse won. I've never seen a child as excited as she was.

"Take me to him, Daddy," she said. "Oh, I can't wait! Where will we keep him? How will we get him home?"

She was under the impression that, since she had won, the horse was now hers. It took a lot of fatherly tact and daughterly tears before she understood.

Around that same time, she came into my room one evening when I was dressing to go out. Like most small children, she was proud of the rate at which she was growing. So she came over and stood in front of me as I looked in the mirror, and she said, "Gee, Daddy. I come right up to your heart, don't I?"

"You sure do, honey."

I've always wanted to use that line in a picture, but so far the right situation hasn't come up.

Warner started out wanting to get into the film business, but switched his allegiance to the stage. He produced the hit play *Tchin-Tchin* as well as many off-Broadway plays in his own New York theater, the York Playhouse. Then he switched again and became a restaurateur, and now owns the very successful New York restaurant, Maxwell's Plum. He has been married twice, once to a girl named Gen, and now to Katherine, a former TWA stewardess he met in his restaurant. Interestingly, Gen and Katherine are today very close friends. Warner has a daughter by each of his wives, Bridget and Katherine Plum (after his restaurant), both dolls.

Linda is married to a skillful New York attorney, Morton Janklow, and she has a son, Lucas, and a daughter, Angela, both dolls too.

Even though my children and I were not geographically close when they were growing up, I feel we have always been emotionally close. One thing I feel about being a parent is that you have to tell your children over and over that you love them. They need that sort of reassurance and if you deprive them of it you are depriving them of something rare and precious. I always told Warner and Linda that I loved them, and they grew up knowing it. Even today, I call them at least once a week. Even today, both Linda and Warner kiss me when we meet—and I'd feel hurt if they didn't.

My wife, Kitty, had two daughters by a previous marriage. Among my children and her children, we have nine grandchildren. It makes it exciting at Christmastime and there's always somebody visiting, or somebody for us to visit, and we enjoy being around children. Those nine kids are the greatest, although it's tough to remember their birthdays.

I've always loved children. I think they help keep a person young. That's why my divorce from Doris—she went to live in New York with Warner and Linda—was hard on me, even though Doris and I have always remained friendly. That's why I welcomed Kitty's daughters, Rita and Eugenia, with love and affection. The fact that somebody else was their real father never troubled me. I am proud of the realization that my stepdaughters, Rita and Eugenia, love me. I remember when I celebrated my sixty-fifth birthday, for some reason I was all alone. I think Kitty was away somewhere and my own children were in New York and I looked forward to a barren and lonely celebration. But Rita and Eugenia got together and threw me a big surprise party, and it turned what could have been a sorrowful day into a joyous one.

We've had a lot of weddings, Kitty and me. Between our own and those of our children, it seems as though every time we turn around somebody is getting married.

When Rita, Kitty's daughter, married Dr. Herbert Roedling, in 1964, the ceremony was performed by the same judge, Edward Brand, who had married Kitty and me eighteen years before. Rita has two daughters, Anita and Kathy, both U.S. tennis champs, from her first marriage to David May, and a son, Alexander, the child of Roedling. Then there's Eugenia, who has also been married twice, both times to Italians, and she and her two children, Caterina and Cristina, now live in Rome.

Linda's one and only marriage, to Morton Janklow, was the most confusing of all. Maybe it would have been anyway, at least to me as the father of the bride, but what made it worse was that Linda came down with a mild case of chicken pox the day before the wedding. It had been scheduled as a big affair at the Beverly Hills Hotel—I'm on the board of directors there, with my good friend, Ben Silberstein, who is the owner—and we had invited some 250 guests. When she got sick, that was immediately canceled, but she didn't want to cancel the wedding. So we had a small affair, at our home, with only the immediate families present. The wedding wasn't postponed, but the honeymoon trip to Hawaii was put off until she recovered.

Linda's birth in 1938 was a joy to me. If people were allowed to dedicate movies, as they dedicate books, I would have dedicated *The Wizard of Oz* to her. It was a tremendous thrill to make such a well-received film, to have my name associated with a movie that has become a classic.

Despite the thrill of *The Wizard of Oz*, I missed directing. I missed the moment-to-moment excitement of being there with the actors, of saying "Action!" and "Cut!" and "Print it!"

I wanted to be back in the cinema trenches. I know that some of my crew called me "Little Napoleon" behind my back, but I didn't mind that. After all, Napoleon won more often than he lost. I considered that a tribute to the way I ran the set. Mistakes happen anywhere, of course, and you can forgive them, but what I never could forgive was somebody who made a mistake and then lied about it or tried to pass the buck to somebody else. Men who did that didn't last long on my set. If there was an error, and it was honestly admitted, the culprit always got another chance. We would talk it over and do something about it. But the liar and the buck-passer got a quick heave-ho.

I missed all that, the immediacy of the action that a director has, and so I voluntarily cut my salary from six thousand to four thousand dollars and went back to being a director. At various times, after that, I would also produce my own pictures, but I never again functioned only as a producer.

8

WENDELL WILLKIE:
WE WON'T BE AT WAR
WITH JAPAN

Even though I was no longer the highest-paid executive in town, I wasn't exactly poverty-stricken. Four thousand dollars a week is enough to keep body and soul together. But I learned that simplest of lessons: Money can't buy happiness.

My marriage to Doris began to deteriorate. It happens, even when you have a four-figure income. There was no particular reason, no one major bone of contention, just a gradual falling out of love. It ended unofficially when Doris and I had a long, final talk, and she left. This was during World War II; and on the surface, her motives were patriotic. She wanted to do something for the war effort, she said, and she had a chance to join the staff of the coordinator of inter-American affairs in New York. I knew that she had just seized on the offer as a way of ending the marriage without actually ending it. This was in 1943, and we announced our separation a year later and were divorced a year after that.

Naturally, the one thought uppermost in both our minds was the effect of the split-up on Warner and Linda. It's always that way, but I think sometimes it's better on the children when the parents separate than when they live in an atmosphere of constant acrimony.

When I knew there was no turning back, that the marriage was gone beyond recapture, I took Warner and Linda with me for a weekend to a cottage we had at Lake Arrowhead. Warner was ten and Linda about seven. I wanted to try to explain to them what was happening to their innocent lives. It wasn't easy.

"Kids," I said, "you know, at school sometimes, you have good friends and then one day they have to move away and you don't see them anymore. That's what's happening to your mother and me."

"We won't see you anymore?" Linda asked.

"Sure, you'll see me. And you'll see your mother, too. But we'll be living in different places."

"Don't you and Mommy love each other?" Warner asked.

"We'll always love each other," I said, "but we just won't see each other as much, that's all."

Linda cried. Warner just stared at me. They understood. Maybe they didn't quite comprehend the concept of loving-but-not-seeing, but maybe they did. Since Doris and I did not part with bitterness, there was never any hate for them to contend with. Neither of us tried to poison their minds against the other. It was all very civilized.

I missed them, when they had gone east, more than I believed it was possible to miss anyone. On my first birthday after they were away, I received birthday letters from both of them, and I don't think I've ever gotten anything that moved me more. Linda wrote:

Dear Daddy:
   Many happy returns and a happy, healthy and successful life to you. I am very proud of you and wish to heap up my love on you. When I am grown up I want to buy you the whole world.
                              Love and XXXXXXX
                              Linda

Warner's letter, as befitted a young man of eleven, was couched in much more formal terms:

Dear Daddy:
   Let me congratulate you on your birthday and wish you all the happiness in the world, a healthy and successful life. Since I am a mere child, I hope you will be satisfied if I promise you to love you always and to be a good boy.
                              Love, your son,
                              Warner
                              XXXXXXXX

It was over. I was a bachelor again. I went back to being the man about town. This time, I was a much-sought-after extra man at parties. I dated many of the greatest beauties of the time— Paulette Goddard was one of my frequent dates, and there were many others—and I must admit I enjoyed the life. But I had come to love married life, too, and I kept my eyes open for a potential wife. Unfortunately, Hollywood isn't the best shopping center for that sort of goods.

Around town, the rumormongers were cheerfully predicting the end of my career. They figured that since I was now divorced from the Warner family, I would go downhill fast. They forgot one thing and didn't know something else.

What they had forgotten was that I had been a very successful director long before I married a Warner. What they didn't know was that all the Warners—even Doris' father, Harry—may have been upset, but they had no antipathy toward me at all. They felt Doris and I had been wrong in separating, but they didn't blame me any more than they blamed her. There was never any ill will over the divorce. Quite the contrary; we remained very close friends. Eventually, I would return to their studio.

That, however, would be some years in the future. Meanwhile, I was still under contract to MGM and I went to work with a vengeance. It helped me forget the absence of my children. The next few years would be possibly the most productive in my career.

The first picture I directed after I went back on the sound stage was *Waterloo Bridge*. There are many who call it my best. My good friend, Jack Benny, says he considers it his favorite among all my films. Vivien Leigh, who co-starred in it with Robert Taylor, always said it was the best thing she ever did. Considering the fact that she had just done *Gone with the Wind* when she came to me, I consider that very high praise.

Naturally, after *Gone with the Wind*, Vivien was the hottest actress around. Everybody wanted her. She could have done anything she wanted to do. But she liked the property we had, which was based on the play by Robert Sherwood. It was a love story, pure and simple, and had been made before, as a silent film, by Universal. I had a great screenplay by Samuel Bierman. Sydney Franklin, whom I consider our finest and most sensitive producer, was our producer.

We had problems on the set with the fog; everything, or nearly everything, was supposedly set in the fog, and the sound stage was always full of the acrid smell of what the studio manufactured for the effect. But the fog worked to our advantage, too. We could suggest a locale, and the fog would be so thick we didn't have to be too specific with our sets. There was one scene of Vivien walking on a bridge. All we did was build part of the sidewalk and string some lights across it, then fill the set with fog, and we had our bridge.

One of the key scenes was the one in a nightclub on New Year's Eve, in which Vivien and Bob were supposed to meet and fall in love. He was leaving the next day for the front. It was a scene that Bierman, Franklin, and I had spent a lot of time on, and the dialogue between the two was, we had all thought, beautiful and tender. But on the set it just didn't seem to work too well. I knew something was wrong, but I couldn't put my finger on just what it was.

At four in the afternoon, after some hours of fruitless fiddling with the scene, I told everybody to go home. I sat there, in that make-believe nightclub, with just one small work light to give me illumination. Over and over, I read the scene, read the words that Sam, Sydney, and I had labored to get right. I was still there at two in the morning, when suddenly the answer came to me.

"No dialogue!" I said, aloud. "No dialogue at all!"

I realized at that moment what silent directors had always known, and what I should have known, too. Often, in great emotional moments, there are no words. A look, a gesture, a touch can convey much more meaning than spoken sentences. Since sound came in, we had become dependent on it, perhaps overdependent on it. It was time to go back to basic human behavior, and often human beings say nothing. This scene was one of those times when silence was more expressive than dialogue.

That's the way we played the scene. It started with a long shot of Vivien and Bob dancing on the floor, as the orchestra played "Auld Lang Syne." Then I cut to the orchestra; each musician had a candle on his music stand; one by one, they snuffed them out. Cut to a close-up of them dancing, looking deep into each other's eyes. Back to the orchestra and more candles being put out. Before all the candles were extinguished, the message was clear—they had fallen deeply, completely, in love. Not a word had been uttered.

Waterloo Bridge, old as it is today, still plays often on television and still brings tears to the eyes. Bob Taylor, in his later years, when he knew he was dying, grew sentimental. Most actors keep and cherish prints of their pictures, but Taylor had never had any. He told friends then that he would like a print of one picture he had made—*Waterloo Bridge*. The people at the Walt Disney Studio, where he was working at the time, got one for him, and he showed it often in his last few months.

I worked with Taylor again on my next film, *Escape*, with Norma Shearer, Alla Nazimova, Conrad Veidt, Albert Basserman, and Bonita Granville. Veidt had always been my first choice for the role but, at first, he was unavailable. We hired Paul Lukas, but he didn't play it the way I wanted. He was the only person I ever had to take out of a picture and it wasn't because he was untalented, but he simply was misinterpreting the part. I was lucky; when I had to make the change, Veidt was available.

I was lucky with Basserman, too. There was a small but important role for a German lawyer, the man who kept telling the hero (Taylor) to go back before the Gestapo arrested him. We tried several of Hollywood's German actors, but I wasn't satisfied. Then MGM's casting director, Billy Grady, heard that Basserman had arrived in Hollywood. Everyone in the movie business knew of Basserman, one of the greatest German actors, who had fled the evil that was Nazism. I said to Grady that we should ask Basserman out to see us at the studio.

"He won't do the part," Grady said. "He was a star in Germany. Don't forget, he won the Ring (the greatest prize for German actors) three years in a row. Why would he take a part that's only a couple of days' work?"

"Get him out here anyway," I said. "I'd like to see him."

So Basserman came to the studio, with his wife and an interpreter. I showed him the script and asked him if he'd do the part. I told him I knew the role was a very short one, but said it was terribly important that it be done right.

"It isn't how long the part is," Basserman said, through his interpreter, "but how good it is."

He read it and said, on the spot, that he'd do it. He was so professional that he did the part in one day—we paid him ten thousand dollars for the day's work—and he was so brilliant in it that he was nominated for an Academy Award.

I've always remembered what he said—"It isn't how long the part is, but how good it is"—and have often quoted him to lesser actors who balked at playing small roles for me.

Next came *Blossoms in the Dust* which began my association with Greer Garson. This was another picture that made an immediate and profound contribution to the world we live in. Between it

Little Women. From left to right: Elizabeth Taylor, Janet Leigh, June Allyson, Margaret O'Brien.

A scene from *Quo Vadis* with thousands of extras on hand.

Esther Williams in *Million Dollar Mermaid*.

On the set of *Mister Roberts*
—Mervyn LeRoy, James
Cagney, and Leland Hayward.

The Bad Seed—Patty
McCormack. (*Photo by
Bert Six*)

For *The F.B.I. Story,* J. Edgar Hoover arranged for Mervyn LeRoy (top center, with tie) to shoot from behind the Lincoln statue in the Lincoln Memorial, Washington, D.C.

The F.B.I. Story— Murray Hamilton (left) and James Stewart.

The Devil at Four O'Clock—Frank Sinatra, Barbara Luna, and Mervyn LeRoy in Hawaii. (*Photo copyright © 1960 by Columbia Pictures Corp.*)

Spencer Tracy in *The Devil At Four O'Clock*.

A scene from *Gypsy* with Rosalind Russell, Karl Malden, and Natalie Wood.

Mervyn LeRoy with *Gypsy* star Rosalind Russell.

Moment to Moment—Mervyn LeRoy and Jean Seberg. (*Photo by Gene Daniels from Black Star*)

Mervyn LeRoy working with John Wayne on *The Green Berets*. (*Photo by David Sutton*)

A gathering of Hollywood immortals: Mervyn LeRoy (top left). Middle row from left to right: Cecil B. DeMille, William Perlberg, Jack Benny, Gloria Swanson, Adolph Zukor, Mary Pickford, Arthur Freed, Jesse Lasky. In front: Samuel Goldwyn and George Jessel.

Mervyn LeRoy (right) with Louis B. Mayer.

Mervyn LeRoy (right) with Jack Warner.

Mervyn LeRoy (left) with Jack Benny in room on set of *Quo Vadis*.

Nancy Davis Reagan, introduced to her husband, Governor Ronald Reagan, by Mervyn LeRoy.

Discoveries—Lana Turner models for Mervyn LeRoy (right, back to camera). (*Photo by Art Weissman*)

Discoveries—Clark Gable.

A Hollywood dinner party. Seated: Joe E. Brown and Kitty LeRoy. Standing, from left to right: Mike Frankovich, Maurice Chevalier, and Mervyn LeRoy. (*Photo by Van Pelt. Copyright © 1965 Columbia Pictures Corp.*)

Mervyn LeRoy, sportsman, with Walter O'Malley, chairman of the board of the Los Angeles Dodgers.

Mervyn LeRoy, sportsman and president of Hollywood Park, with one of his yearlings.

Little Warner LeRoy, a small jockey.

Warner cuts his birthday
cake while Linda waits.

Linda (center), ballerina.

Proud father Mervyn LeRoy with his children, Linda and Warner.

Linda LeRoy, a show rider.

and *Fugitive*, I think I have contributed toward making this a better country.

The theme of *Blossoms in the Dust* was that our laws—in particular, the laws in Texas—were an injustice to illegitimate children. On birth certificates in Texas at the time, illegitimate children were so labeled. The book the picture was based on, and the picture itself, took the position that "there is no such thing as illegitimate children, only illegitimate parents," as my heroine said in the film.

The whole story was true, and it revolved around Mrs. Gladney's home for unwed mothers. Greer and I went down for a few days to visit the place and see how it operated. It was a remarkable experience.

During most of the shooting, the set was full of kids of all shapes and sizes. Because of California's laws, working with babies is particularly difficult—they can only be in front of the camera for a minute or two at a time. I've always been able to establish a rapport with children and that helped me. I was able to explain what I wanted—I talked to them as though they were grown-ups, and they liked that—and usually they did what I wanted. There were so many squalling infants on the set, however, that the crew began calling *Blossoms in the Dust* by another name—"Bugs in the Mud."

Greer's co-star was Walter Pidgeon, and the teaming of these two proved to be made in heaven—or wherever it is that great movie teams are conceived. Astaire–Rogers, Gable–Harlow, Powell–Loy, Pidgeon–Garson, Colman–Garson—there aren't many of them. That indefinable something called (for lack of a better word) "chemistry" has to be there, and you never know it's there or not until you try it.

Pidgeon would come onto the set every morning and the first thing he'd say would be, "When do we eat?" I've never met anyone who was so constantly and consistently hungry, yet he never seemed to gain weight, despite his appetite. I envied him his metabolism.

One problem I had with Walter was that, despite his suave and sophisticated air, he had never learned how to dance. There was a scene in *Blossoms in the Dust* where he was required to dance.

"Do I have to dance?" he asked. "You'll have to rewrite it, because I don't know how to."

"Why didn't you tell me that before?" I asked him. "You've had the script for two months."

The scene was vital, however, so I had to dream up some way for him not to dance while it looked like he was dancing. I had the carpenters build a low platform and we put roller skates underneath it. I put the camera on the platform, with Greer and Walter. There were other couples in the scene, and they danced off the platform. Greer and Walter just bounced up and down on the platform, which was revolved on its skate wheels. The result was that it looked as though my principals were dancing skillfully.

Greer Garson has the most beautiful speaking voice of any actress the screen has ever seen, and she is an exquisite-looking woman. On *Blossoms*, I was fortunate in having Joseph Ruttenberg as my cameraman; he is one of the best. He knew that Greer looks better with her chin raised. During rehearsals they worked out private signals. Whenever Greer lowered her head, Joe would signal her and she'd raise it again. Theirs was such a close and successful relationship that she refused to make a picture unless he was the cameraman.

I was back with gangsters again in *Johnny Eager*, and this was another winner. It was the first film I had done with Lana Turner since her debut. She was one among a topflight cast—Bob Taylor, Van Heflin, Pat Dane, and Mousie Lewis (which was what we called Diana Lewis, who was William Powell's wife).

Heflin's part was the juiciest. The day he walked on the set, I said, "Van, play this part the way I tell you to and you'll win an Oscar." He did, too.

Pat Dane was a gorgeous but strange girl who was later married for a while to Tommy Dorsey. I began to realize that she was a little unusual one day when she drew me aside on the set.

"Mervyn," she said, "I'm going east for a few days. Do me a favor, will you, and keep this for me."

She thrust a white envelope in my hands and began walking away. I looked inside and it was stuffed with cash—she told me later it was twenty thousand dollars. I don't know where she got it or why she wanted me to keep it for her. I only knew that I wasn't going to be stuck with the responsibility of walking around with all that money on me. I called her back, gave her the envelope, and told her to put it in a vault. I don't know whether she did or whether she got some other sucker to hold it for her.

Random Harvest, another Greer Garson film, followed *Johnny Eager*. This time, Sydney Franklin and I teamed her with Ronald Colman; between the two of them, the English language was never spoken more beautifully on film.

This was based on James Hilton's huge best-seller. I've done many adaptations of novels and plays, and never once have any of the authors or playwrights complained about the way I transferred their works to film. Too often, as we all know, films take books and plays and produce something that is only a fraction of the worth of the original. When I do a movie based on a work that is popular in another medium, I feel almost a sacred responsibility to keep the spirit of the work as it was. It's hard work to make a good movie out of a great book. Some authors write in visual terms, but most do not. You must take what the author has only hinted at and bring it to life.

Hilton, for example, loved the movie version of *Random Harvest*. In fact, he was so pleased with the way it turned out that he offered to speak the narration that opened the film. I was delighted to have him do it, and even more delighted to know that he was happy with the job I had done on his book.

After *Random Harvest*, there were two more very successful films, giving me a string of seven solid hits since I had resumed directing. These were *Madame Curie* and *Thirty Seconds Over Tokyo*. The former is one of my own favorites among my films, because it was the true story of a remarkable woman. Eve Curie, the daughter of the amazing Polish-French scientist, Marie Curie, never visited the set, but she did write a letter later and told me how much she had enjoyed the movie.

Even though the subject—the discovery of radium—was somewhat highbrow for a popular film, we were able to simplify it and romanticize it so the public understood it. I was very careful; I didn't let a scene go by unless I understood it myself. If I didn't understand it, I knew that the audience wouldn't understand it either. We wound up with a film the public loved.

Madame Curie reunited Greer Garson and Walter Pidgeon. By now, they were a solid team, and they knew each other's pace and reactions so well sometimes they had to shake each other up a bit to preserve their freshness. One incident illustrates the way they operated together.

A key scene in *Madame Curie* was the one where the Curies, late at night, go out to the shed where they were conducting their experiments. In the blackness of the night they see the strange glow from the pitchblende, proof that there was radioactivity and an indication that they had discovered a new element, which turned out to be radium. Naturally, this was a scene that needed great drama. We rehearsed it and rehearsed it so the audience would have goose-bumps when it flashed on the screen.

I called for action, and the cameras were rolling—and then, from out of the darkness, I heard Greer laugh.

"Cut," I yelled. "Come on, Greer, what's so funny? Why the big laugh?"

"I couldn't help it," she said. "Walter just told me the funniest joke."

The tension that had built up during the long rehearsal period was gone. I waited about fifteen minutes, until Greer and Walter stopped their giggling, and then shot the scene. It worked perfectly.

Pidgeon had become a cigar-smoker by this time. One day, I bought him a box of fine Havanas, in those glorious days when it was politically acceptable to smoke Cuban cigars. Later that day, I ran out of cigars myself and asked him for one of his.

"I should say not," he said. "These are all for me."

Then came *Thirty Seconds Over Tokyo*, my first war film. This was another true story, based on the daring raid on Tokyo by Jimmy Doolittle and his men. We shot much of it at the Naval Air Station in Pensacola, Florida, where Doolittle's men had trained for their historic mission. Doolittle was there through much of the filming, and so was General Hap Arnold. Hap was a lot of help in technical matters.

One day, he came up to me and said, "Mervyn, if you won't say anything, I'll show you something exciting."

He had me put on a major's uniform and taught me how to salute, and to whom. Then he took me deep down, underground, beneath the base, and showed me the first B-29 bomber. He was right, it was exciting. It was the biggest plane I had ever seen—two stories high, and it dwarfed anything around in those pre-747 days. He led me in and let me sit in the pilot's seat in the cockpit.

"Just one word of caution," the general said, as I stared in fascination at all the dials and switches. "Don't tell anybody how this plane works."

I laughed. I am the world's all-thumbs champion.

"General Arnold," I said, "you have nothing to worry about. I don't even know how an electric light works."

There were many aerial shots in *Thirty Seconds Over Tokyo*. For the biggest one, we had fifty B-25s flying in. This kind of scene is always tricky. I was in contact with the lead plane by radio. I had to have the right light and the right cloud formation, or it wouldn't look the way I wanted it to look. That day was an odd weather day, with fast-scudding clouds darting in front of the sun. At last, there came a moment when I thought everything—the sun and the clouds—looked perfect. The planes were circling, about fifty miles away, and I radioed the message: "Bring them in." I repeated it: "Bring them in while the sun's out."

What I didn't know was that my words were being broadcast to all the airport towers in Florida. Dozens of ground-control men were suddenly confused when they heard a strange voice saying, "Bring them in while the sun's still out." They hadn't the foggiest idea what that voice—my voice—was talking about. The next day all the Florida newspapers wrote about it.

Besides Doolittle, we had hired one member of his original squadron, Ted Lawson, who was the subject of the book the film was based on. He was our official technical adviser. Lawson told me that when Doolittle had led his planes over Tokyo that day in April, 1942, they had been under strict orders not to bomb the Imperial Palace. Some of the men, apparently, had wanted to disregard those orders and aim a few big bombs down the Mikado's throat, but Doolittle had commanded them to follow instructions and just bomb their assigned targets.

My cast was headed by Spencer Tracy and Van Johnson, but I found a young and interesting actor among the bit players. His name was Robert Mitchum and I had him play a small scene with Johnson on the deck of the aircraft carrier. It was his first role in films, and I sensed that he had something special. I begged my bosses at MGM to sign him up, but they ignored my advice and let him go, much to their future regret.

You might think, as I go down my list of the films I have done, that every one of my plans materialized. On the contrary, throughout my career, there have been films that have been planned and have then fallen through. There was one around this time that was a particularly bitter disappointment. I had read Ayn Rand's monumental novel, *The Fountainhead*, and had persuaded the studio to let me do it. For weeks, we had gradually whittled away at the book's 754 pages and had forged what I think was an excellent screenplay. We had cast Humphrey Bogart and Barbara Stanwyck in the leading roles. Nothing came of it, however; that production would have to be classed as a war casualty. Many films were similarly scratched by the War Production Board, because the sets for them would use too many strategic materials.

Similarly, I worked for some weeks with Irving Wallace on a screenplay we were calling *The Helen Morgan Story*, but we could never lick the problems inherent in the story. Later, it would be made by others, but it was obvious that they couldn't lick the problems, either. I was impressed with Wallace, however, and have followed his career with great pleasure ever since, as he has become one of the most successful novelists America has produced.

It wasn't all work. There were many moments and days of pure fun. When I worked with Wallace, for example, it was in Palm Springs, and there were hours when we just sat around the pool and soaked up sun. There were times I played tennis and times I went off on trips with my friends. One of those jaunts developed into something of a classic outing, the kind of thing that has become legend in Hollywood circles.

On the surface, it was just a duck-hunting expedition. A big group of us were off to Mexicali. There were Jack Warner, Darryl Zanuck, Jack Haskell, Bill Koenig, Bryan Foy, myself, and several others. I don't know how many of the group had ever been duck-hunting before, but I hadn't. I went to Kerr's, the leading sporting-goods store in Beverly Hills, and told the clerk I was going duck-hunting and to give me everything I would need. I bought all the proper clothing and a rifle, an instrument I had never before held in my hands.

When we got to the hunting lodge, we went to bed late and they had the audacity to wake us up at four in the morning. The ridiculous idea was that we should be outside, in our positions in the duck blind, when the ducks flew over. They were scheduled to arrive at dawn, which is maybe why ducks aren't considered too bright.

When the first light of daybreak appeared, our scout or guide or whatever you call him began tootling on his little horn, a maneuver that proved successful. A flight of ducks began to fly overhead. I did as I had been told by the clerk at Kerr's. I put my rifle up to my shoulder and began squeezing the trigger. The clerk had left something out of the lesson—he had failed to show me exactly where to put my thumb. I had inadvertently put it somewhere it didn't belong and it got caught when I pulled the trigger. It was caught so badly that it was cut and began to bleed, and I hate blood, especially my own.

"Hey, somebody," I called into the gloom, "give me a hand. I hurt my thumb. It's caught in the trigger."

"Quiet!" came several outraged voices.

"Hey, come on, fellows," I said, in a loud whisper, "this is serious. I'm wounded."

"Keep it down, Mervyn," called Zanuck. "We're trying to shoot ducks and you're distracting us."

So, while everybody else popped away at the ducks, I sat there. I finally extricated my thumb from the rifle's evil grip, and spent a few cold and miserable hours sucking the blood off my poor damaged thumb. I never did take a shot at a duck. When I got back to Beverly Hills, I returned everything to Kerr's.

The point of the duck-hunting safari wasn't ducks, however; it was fun. We had plenty of that. We were a bunch of city boys and we behaved like a den of cub scouts on their first overnight excursion.

The first night, we ganged up to pull a trick on Haskell, a noted dance director. We began warning everybody, being careful that he heard us, about the multitude of dangerous snakes in the area. We kept that up all evening; meanwhile, we had secreted a rope in his bed, arranged so that one of us could pull it from the outside. When he went to bed, we twitched the rope so it moved sensuously under his mattress, and he leaped up with a scream that could be heard in Acapulco. He ran out—and took the tent with him.

I masterminded another nasty little trick. I got a red lantern and hung it about a quarter-mile down a lonely road, on a tree limb. As we were all getting ready for bed that first night, Jack Warner asked me where the bathroom was.

"See that red lantern?" I said, and pointed off to where the red pinprick glowed in the dark. "It's right down there."

Jack walked down the road until he got to where the red lantern —and nothing else—stood.

It was Warner, in turn, who planned a nice gag for Darryl Zanuck's benefit. Zanuck was proud of his marksmanship and eagerly leaped at the bait when Warner bet him he couldn't hit a wooden duck decoy out in the lake.

"That decoy?" Zanuck said. "I'll blast it out of the water."

He put the rifle up to his shoulder and fired off several rounds. Nothing. The decoy floated blissfully on the lake, as it had before. Zanuck paid off the bet, but he never did understand why he hadn't hit it. I don't know if he ever found out that Warner had loaded his rifle with blanks.

So Hollywood life wasn't all movies and movie business.

One morning in 1945, I had a telephone call from Frank Sinatra.

"Mervyn," he said, "I've got an idea for a short that I want to talk to you about."

We got together and he told me his idea. There was a song he did called "The House I Live In." He said that he and Frank Ross thought a movie version of that song would be a good thing to do, during those wartime years. He asked me if I'd help them with the project and, since I agreed with him about the worth of the idea, I quickly said I would. After I played the record a few times, I became very excited about it. Ross had a script written, and he and I coproduced it. Axel Stordahl directed, and Frank Sinatra was the star.

Sinatra is an old friend, and a much-maligned and much-misunderstood man. He does some foolish things sometimes, but I consider him one of the outstanding men in America. He's done so much for others, given so much of his time and money, and most of the things he does are done anonymously. His greatest joy is doing something for others. Many times I've come into my office and found a box of cigars on my desk—no card, no name—but I knew it came from Frank. It isn't a big thing, but it's typical of the way he operates.

It was a pleasant experience, working with Frank on *The House I Live In*. We shot it all in one day. Our little film was well received and then, the next spring, I found myself owning an Oscar. I had been nominated many times, but that was my first and, so far, only Oscar. Winning it was a tremendous thrill but even more thrilling was to listen to the heartwarming round of applause that came from the audience when my name was mentioned. I must admit that I basked in that sound.

I had never dreamed of winning an Oscar. There is a lot about the Oscars that the public doesn't know. There is, for example, the tradition of bloc voting. That's a device whereby the big studios get behind their own pictures and urge—in the strongest of terms—that all their employees vote for that picture. Naturally, the studio that has the most employees has the most voters and, therefore, a pretty fair head start toward winning. That doesn't exist as much today, because the studios have lost much of their power. Throughout the 1930s and 1940s, however, bloc voting was the rule.

I have always felt that if somebody in my pictures—whether it be an actor or a technician—wins an Oscar, that is enough of a tribute to keep my ego functioning.

I was always very active in the Academy. For some years, I staged and produced the Oscar shows. The year that Walt Disney won for *Snow White and the Seven Dwarfs*, I designed the special Oscar—the big one and the seven little ones—that Disney was given.

The House I Live In was the only short subject I ever made for commercial exhibition. I did make some others, when World War II came along. Like most of Hollywood, I did something extra for the war effort.

I worked for Nelson Rockefeller, who had been assigned by Washington to supervise the making of shorts for civilian defense and some for the Army. Rockefeller came out to Hollywood; and, even though he admitted that he knew nothing about the picture business, he did his best. He knew enough about being an administrator to hire experts to help him. Rockefeller had an office at the corner of Hollywood Boulevard and Vine Street, and many of the greatest talents in the film business would go there to consult with him. I was only one of many whose assistance he called on.

All the studios cheerfully pitched in and helped, giving him facilities, supplies, personnel. I found Rockefeller a fine man to work with, and it felt good to be doing something to help.

In the few years that I worked on the project—sandwiching that work in between my regular films—I did somewhere between ten and fifteen shorts. They were on such subjects as how to put out fires and how to contend with bombs. The whole point was to prepare the civilian population for the possibility of attack.

Hollywood survived the Second World War, as it had survived the First, and such other calamities as the Depression and the Red Scare. I survived, too. I've always been pleased that my parents chose the year 1900 to have me. That was a great year for missing wars—the class of 1900 was too young for the World War I draft and too old and settled for World War II. We were just right, however, for the hectic days of the Red Scare and the blacklist, and I was right in the middle of that.

Suddenly, it was upon us. I don't know where it came from or how it happened, but, seemingly overnight, there it was. It was a sorry period for human relationships. Out of fear and self-preservation, men and women informed on their friends, even on their husbands or wives.

I was never deeply involved. There was never any personal worry, because I am not a political person. I am, however, strongly pro-American and I had come to recognize that some Communist propaganda was creeping into movies. I felt it was a good thing to root that out, but I deplored the excesses that went with the rooting-out process.

There was a time when I wanted to use a certain actor. Marvin Schenck, who was Nicholas Schenck's nephew, said I couldn't use him, because he was on the blacklist. I was surprised, but felt that if he was on the list, I shouldn't use him. The incident nagged at me. I thought about that actor. He was, I had always believed, a decent person, and I knew that he had a fine family and was a good, churchgoing Catholic. I just couldn't imagine him being un-American in any way. So I went back to Schenck and asked him to check it out further. He did check, and found that the man on the suspected list was an entirely different person, who just happened to have the same name as the actor. That's the way things were in those uneasy days. If I hadn't pursued the matter, that actor would have been blacklisted, out of work, merely because of an accident.

On the other hand, there was the case of a particular writer, a friend of mine. Louis B. Mayer asked me about him one day.

"Ask your friend to tell you if he is a Communist," Mayer said. "If he is clean, we'll try and help him. Otherwise, he's going to be blacklisted."

I went to my friend, the writer, and I put it to him bluntly.

"Do you have a Communist party card?" I asked.

He laughed and said that was ridiculous, he wasn't a party member. He lied to me. As it turned out, the investigators already had his card. He ended up in Mexico.

There were writers who were supposedly on the list that I trusted anyhow. Sam Zimbalist and I had used Dalton Trumbo, one of the Hollywood Ten, as the writer on *Thirty Seconds Over Tokyo* in 1945. He turned out a great American story for me, and it had not the slightest hint of anything subversive in it.

Through it all, through the wars and the depressions and the periods of unrest, I went on about my primary business.

World War II never touched me directly. Like everyone, I had minor inconveniences to live through, but we were glad to do what we could. The beginning of the war, however, found me in sudden trouble, and for a few spooky days I was suspected of being a spy.

The day before the Japanese attacked Pearl Harbor, I was in New York. I was in the upstairs room at the 21 Club on the evening of December 6, 1941. Albert Lasker, the big Chicago advertising man, came in after the theater with his son Edward and a large party of friends. Before I had gone to the restaurant, I had been shaving in my room at the Waldorf-Astoria Hotel and I had turned on the radio. I wanted to listen to the news. There was a report that said something disturbing about the international situation. I worried about it, and was still worrying later when I met the Laskers.

I couldn't concentrate on my dinner. Somebody started talking about the world crisis.

"You know, Albert," I said to Lasker, "I feel we'll be at war with Japan within forty-eight hours."

The others scoffed. They reminded me that the Japanese had peace negotiators in Washington at that very moment. How could there be war?

The next day, Sunday, December 7, 1941, I went to the pro football game at the Polo Grounds with Doris, William Randolph Hearst, Jr., and Bryan Foy of Chrysler. The Laskers were there, too, with Wendell Willkie and General William ("Wild Bill") Donovan. At half time, Albert Lasker went to the men's room with Willkie and told him what I had said over the dinner table the night before.

"I met the damnedest kid last night," Lasker said. "He thinks there will be war within forty-eight hours."

"Albert," Willkie said, "we won't be at war with Japan within forty-eight hours, within forty-eight days, within forty-eight years."

At that precise moment, there was an announcement over the field's public address system.

"Telephone call for General William Donovan, telephone call for General William Donovan," the speaker blasted.

Donovan raced to the phone and came back, white as a sheet. His caller had been someone at the War Department who had told him what had happened at Pearl Harbor. He whispered the news to us, and we all left.

I went with Bill Hearst, Jr., down to the office of the New York *Journal-American*. Together, we watched the terrible news unfold over the wires. Hearst's first order was a simple one: "I want American flags all over the front page—in color!"

None of us knew what to do. Foy had invited us all to his home, and so we gathered there—Willkie, Hearst, the Laskers, myself, some others. We talked about the war we suddenly found ourselves in. After we had been there about an hour, a man appeared at the door, asking for me. Foy's butler showed him in.

"Are you Mr. Mervyn LeRoy?" the man asked. I said I was. He pulled out his wallet and flashed a silver badge.

"I'm from the FBI," he said. "We heard that you told somebody yesterday that we would have war within forty-eight hours. We're very interested in how you knew that."

"It's simple," I said, and I explained how I had heard a news broadcast, the previous night, which had reported that Japanese battleships were heading for Hawaii, and how I had put two and two together and how I had been worried about it all day.

"Did that really happen, that news broadcast?" the agent said, with suspicion dripping from every syllable.

"Of course it did," I said. "I heard it up in my hotel room last night while I was shaving. You don't think I could make up a thing like that, do you?"

"What time was that news broadcast, Mr. LeRoy?"

"It was about seven-thirty, I think."

"Well, we'll check it out, Mr. LeRoy." He left.

A few days later, I got the word. They had checked it out and the broadcast had occurred, just as I had told him. I hate to think what would have happened if they had not been able to find a record of that newscast. I might still be in some cell, doing my directing with the prison dramatic society.

Like every American, I found the war years long and tragic. Many of my friends, of course, were in one service or another, and there was always the sad news that someone I knew had been killed in action. I felt lucky that my son was too young to be active in the war.

For me, those years were busy ones. Most of my time went to the films I did, both the commercial ones and the service-connected ones I did for the government. Hollywood's social life was, of course, greatly curtailed during the war. It was no time for partying.

There were some affairs, naturally. You can't just curl up in a cocoon. There must be some moments of release. It was to achieve one of those moments that I accepted an invitation to a cocktail party given by Doris and Jules Stein one evening.

I was introduced to Kitty Spiegel who was, I was told, the widow of Sidney Spiegel, who had owned a chain of theaters in Chicago. Before that, she had been married to Ernest Byfield, a restaurateur and hotel executive. I remember being impressed by her attractive face, cheerful manner, pert airs. That was all. Or so I thought.

I went home, and curiously I found myself thinking about that beautiful little blond I had met at the Steins'. It was odd for me, because there were so many of Hollywood's glamour girls around, yet for a couple of days all I could think about was Kitty and the way she looked at me.

Two days later, I called Doris Stein and asked her where I could reach Kitty. Doris told me that she was staying at the Bel Air Hotel, so I called her there and invited her to have dinner with the Steins and me.

She told me then that we had met before. There was a party a few years earlier, she said, at Darryl Zanuck's and we had met there. I didn't remember that at all, but I sure did remember meeting her this time. It was a pleasant dinner, and we told each other all about our families, me and my two children, she and her two daughters.

We began to see each other as often as I could manage it. For a while, it wasn't easy. She was still living in Chicago, and my work kept me tied down in Los Angeles. I was able to manage to get there once in a while, and she arranged a few trips to the West Coast.

There was a point when we broke up. It didn't last too long. We got together again, when we both happened to be in Lake Arrowhead. There was one thing about her that made me sure I wanted to marry her. She had absolutely no desire to be an actress, a lack of ambition that made her particularly attractive. When a man is a director, he is never sure if girls like him for himself or for what good he might be able to do for their careers. With Kitty, I was sure. Since she didn't want to act, the only reason she could be interested in me was because she honestly liked me—for myself.

We were married on February 1, 1946. As Kitty says, "There hasn't been a dull moment since." It was a small wedding, in her Bel Air home. I was pleased because my children, Warner and Linda, were there. So were her children, Rita and Eugenia, and my mother and stepfather. We had a brief honeymoon in Palm Springs and quickly settled down to what has been a long and extremely happy marriage.

There is one thing about our wedding that Kitty has never gotten over. She always teases me about it. It had been planned to take place on a certain Saturday. About a week or ten days before the date, I called the man who was training my horses, and he told me that he had entered one of them in a race. That evening, when I saw Kitty, I told her about it.

"Wise Eagle is going to be running a week from Saturday," I said. "And we'll go see the race."

"A week from Saturday? But, Mervyn, don't you remember—that's the day we're getting married."

It hadn't exactly slipped my mind, it's just that I was very excited about Wise Eagle running and simply hadn't placed the two events in any kind of context.

Kitty was—and is—very understanding. We got married on Friday, went to the track to see Wise Eagle run (and lose) on Saturday, and left for our honeymoon after the race.

"I think," Kitty has often said, "that I was the only bride whose wedding was planned around a horse race."

We lived in Bel Air for almost twenty-five years, then sold the house (to Johnny Carson) and moved down to a smaller home in Beverly Hills.

It is a curious thing about Kitty and me and our respective charities. I am Jewish, she is gentile. Yet she does a great deal of work for the Cedars of Lebanon Hospital, among many others, and Cedars is a Jewish institution. On the other hand, I am a regent of two Roman Catholic institutions—St. John's Hospital and Loyola University. Perhaps we are both subconsciously trying to thank our spouse's faith for each other. I know I want to thank somebody for Kitty.

When the war ended, I found myself with new responsibilities. So it was back to work, to an intensely productive period. First, though, I had Howard Hughes to contend with.

9

ELIZABETH TAYLOR:
CAN YOU HIDE ME,
MERVYN?

When I made my Oscar-winning short, *The House I Live In*, I worked with Frank Ross of RKO. That wasn't exactly the first time we had done something together, but it was the first time what we had worked on was actually finished.

Ross and I had planned to do *The Robe* together. He had bought the property and had a screenplay written. Our plans were very far advanced, when Howard Hughes bought the studio. For reasons he never told me, and I never learned, Hughes cancelled *The Robe*. He paid me two hundred thousand dollars for my efforts. Ross kept the property and eventually filmed it.

For a while, Hughes was very friendly. At that point in his life, he was devoting most of his time to the movie business, as the head man at RKO, and he was part of the Hollywood scene. He would quite frequently drop by at our house, unannounced and unheralded, just to talk about the business. I imagine he wanted to learn what he could and felt that the best way to learn was by talking with people who had been around the business for a while. He was trying to pick up knowledge through conversation.

One morning, he came by in his little, unpretentious car and asked me if I would drive into Hollywood with him. We were riding along when he suddenly pulled over to the curb. He said he had to stop for a minute and asked me to come with him while he did an errand.

We went into a haberdashery and he bought a set of underwear. Then he went into the back of the store and put on his new, seventy-five-cent underwear and threw the old ones away.

"Sorry to hold you up, Mervyn," he said, "but my underwear was dirty."

Then there was the morning when he called me up and it was so early—about four o'clock—that he woke me out of a sound sleep.

"Hey, Mervyn," he said, "what are you doing?"

"It's four in the morning, Howard," I said. "What do you think I'm doing? I'm playing polo."

That just rolled off his back.

"Tell you why I called, Mervyn. I want to get in touch with Janet Leigh. I'm going to make a Russian picture and I think she'd be right for it."

I told him where he could reach her, although I've always suspected that he had something else in mind, other than a part in a picture. But there was a picture made at the studio with a Russian background, and Janet was in it.

The only picture I did for RKO, besides *The House I Live In*, was a frothy little comedy called *Without Reservations*. It starred John Wayne, Claudette Colbert, and Lana Turner. My cousin, Jesse Lasky, produced it. There was another actor of note in it, although he got no billing. We were doing a scene in a café and, on the day we were shooting, Cary Grant walked by the set. I asked him to sit at one of the tables, since he had nothing better to do, and he did.

Claudette Colbert was an interesting lady to work with. For one thing, she had a strange habit of never looking where she was going. She kept bumping into things. I remember one day seeing her heading straight for the side of her trailer–dressing room.

"Watch out, Claudette," I called, but she kept right on course and banged into the wall. It happened all the time.

Another problem with Claudette was that she insisted on having only one side of her face photographed. I think it was her left side. I thought she looked very good on both sides, but she was adamant about it. So every scene had to be arranged so that only the side she considered good was on camera.

Without Reservations began my friendship with Duke Wayne. I'd known him before, but this was the first time we worked together. We became very close, and our friendship culminated in our association on *The Green Berets*.

I was glad when my brief sojourn at RKO was over, and I could go back to MGM, where I felt much more at home. Working around Hughes was too nerve-wracking; you never knew when he would call up, at any hour, with some minor problem to discuss at major length. I haven't seen Howard for twenty years, and I probably will never see him again. He really wasn't cut out for the movie business anyhow. I don't think his heart was ever in it.

Back at MGM, I began another string of films that proved to be hits. The first was *Homecoming*, in which I finally got my chance to work with Clark Gable and my other discovery, Lana Turner. John Hodiak and Anne Baxter were in it, too. I think *Homecoming* showed Lana at her sexiest. There was one scene where she came out of a swimming pool, water dripping from her hair. It was accidental at first—the same as her sweaters were accidental at first—but it was a happy accident.

We tried something new on my next film, *Little Women*, an adaptation of Louisa May Alcott's classic novel. There was one scene in the snow. Until then, Hollywood had always used artificial snow, and I thought it always looked phony, too. Somebody suggested using ground-up ice, so I decided to give it a try. The ice was fed into a machine, which chopped it up and sprayed it out, and it did look more real. Besides, it had something else that was helpful: It was cold, and that made my actors cold, and therefore they looked cold, which was all to the good.

Little Women had been one of my daughter Linda's favorite books, and I had enjoyed it myself. David O. Selznick owned the rights, but I persuaded L.B. to buy it for me. Selznick had even built some sets for his production, which MGM bought along with the rights to the book.

Ever since Kitty and I had married, I had tried to adhere to a strict routine while I was shooting. We never went out. We would have dinner and then I'd plan the next day's setups. Then I'd go over the dialogue and often Kitty would read it to me. During *Little Women* we did that. One evening Kitty was reading and the emotion of the story got to her and she began to cry.

"I can't finish this," she said.

"My God," I said. "Is it that good?"

I had a fine cast in *Little Women*. One of my actresses was Elizabeth Taylor. A few years before, I had directed her screen test for *National Velvet*; and, like everybody else who saw her, I was struck by her potential beauty. I've made a lot of tests, as all directors have. Years earlier, I had directed the screen test for Errol Flynn, when Warner Brothers was considering him for *Captain*

Blood. His test turned out well, and so did Elizabeth's. At the time we made *Little Women*, she was seventeen and that potential had flowered; she was exquisite. She was easy to work with then, and easy to photograph. There was no bad side, no good side—all sides were fantastically beautiful. I have found, with rare exceptions, that photographing really isn't hard—if your subject has talent. Marie Dressler, for example, was very easy to photograph. Her face may not have been a thing of beauty, but it was alive. If they have talent, they're easy to shoot. If they don't, nothing helps.

We also had cute-as-a-button June Allyson, Janet Leigh, Margaret O'Brien, Peter Lawford, and Mary Astor, who had been in my very first picture. It was a big cast and many of them had reputations for temperament, but everybody got along swimmingly. I've really never had any major temperament problems on any of my sets. I've come to believe that temperament and other personality problems start at the top and filter down through the cast. If the director takes things calmly and instills a sense of fun on the set, problems of that sort will rarely develop.

Any Number Can Play, which followed *Little Women*, is one picture that didn't turn out as well as I had hoped. I don't know what went wrong. You start out with what you think is a good script and you get a good cast—in this case I had Clark Gable and Alexis Smith—and you end up with a film that is less than you expect. Something happened or, more likely, something didn't happen—the chemistry didn't work and the emotions didn't explode. Whatever the reason, *Any Number Can Play* was a disappointment to me.

While I was shooting, a young man with directorial ambitions asked me if he could stay with me on the set while I worked. I remembered how I had learned by observing, so I agreed. His name was Richard Brooks, and he was on the set every day. Brooks became a fine director and I hope that watching me at work was of some help to him.

After that, I did *East Side, West Side*, which worked better. My stars were Ava Gardner, Barbara Stanwyck, James Mason, Van Heflin, and Cyd Charisse. They were all pleasant and capable people; but, of them all, Miss Stanwyck was the easiest. I suppose, if you took a vote among old-timers on Hollywood crews for the most popular star, she would win the election by a landslide. If she had a nine o'clock call, she would be on the set by eight, her makeup already on, every line memorized, a smile on her face. Once in a while, I would look for her and couldn't find her. She would be up

on the lights, talking to the electricians. She was a very earthy
dame, and she could talk to the crew in their own language. They
all loved her and—not that that was her motive—they would do
anything to help her and make her look good.

The press was on the *East Side, West Side* set continually. I
never closed my sets to the press, but this one, because of the big
names we had, attracted reporters and columnists in droves. I had
always had excellent relations with the press—with one exception.
The exception's name was Hedda Hopper.

Hedda and Louella Parsons were the queens of the press corps. I
guess if one liked you, the other felt obligated to hate you. Louella
adopted me right from the start of my career and always wrote nice
things about me. So, I suppose, Hedda decided that she would take
the opposite tack. That was peculiar, because I had given her a job
in one of my first films, *Harold Teen*. Despite that, she began taking potshots at me in her column whenever she could. I'm not one
to ignore a fight, if a fight is forced on me, and one day I had one
of those once-in-a-lifetime chances to shoot back. It was a perfect
setup.

I was at Hollywood Park; and, as I made my way up to the pari-
mutuel window to place a bet, I noticed Hedda Hopper in the line
right behind me. I ignored her. She didn't ignore me.

"Who do you like?" she asked.

I didn't even turn around.

"Louella Parsons," I said.

Naturally, after that, the barbs were flung at me even sharper
and more often in her column. I just waited. I knew that there
would come a time when she would go too far, and then I could get
back at her.

It happened. I picked up the paper one morning and there was
Hedda Hopper's column. She had written something about Victor
Fleming, the man who had directed *The Wizard of Oz*.

"Victor made the great picture, *The Wizard of Oz*," she had
written, "the picture Mervyn LeRoy was taken off of as director."

My first reaction was anger. My second was joy. I picked up the
phone and called my lawyer, Arnold Grant.

"I think we've got her, Arnold," I said, and I read him that
sentence from her column. "Isn't that a statement that can be held
to be damaging to my career?"

"Damn right it is," Grant said. "I'll take care of it."

He wrote a formal letter, full of those nice legal terms, demanding a full and immediate retraction. He sent it to the paper in New

York—Grant was in New York—that printed her column. A few days later, the editor called Grant.

"What does LeRoy want out of this?" the editor asked.

"Mr. LeRoy doesn't want any money," Grant told him. "All he wants is a complete retraction of that statement, printed in a prominent position—just as prominent as the original untrue statement."

She was forced to do just that, run an item that admitted she had been wrong. It ran in all the papers that carried her column.

She had to do it, but she didn't like it. One MGM executive, who was friendly with her, told me she called him.

"How dare one of your directors threaten to sue me?" she asked him.

"There's nothing in Mervyn's contract," my friend told her, "that bars him from protecting himself legally when he is attacked."

That ended it as far as I was concerned. I had made her eat a little crow, and I must say she got the message. She stopped sniping at me. Ultimately, after some years, she even became nice to me. Just before she died, she wrote a very nice article about me. I called her to thank her, and I've always been happy that I did.

As the 1940s drew to a close in Hollywood, the whole business was changing. It's hard to be conscious of change, when it happens slowly. Television was the vehicle of that change. You could call it the devil or the angel, depending on which office you were sitting in. Movie people hated it, but naturally the TV producers were ecstatic about their steady growth.

My own feelings were distinctly positive. I was crazy about TV, as I was about most new things. I had seen sound come in and radio come in and all those things that had been predicted as spelling doom to the movie business. Instead, the movie business had prospered. So I felt motion pictures could survive television, as well. I was, therefore, not antipathetic toward television, in theory.

I had one of the first TV sets in town. I loved it. I recognized immediately what a tremendous thing it could be, bringing moving pictures, as opposed to motion pictures, into the home itself. I had many offers to do television, but I wanted to stay in pictures. I felt no hatred toward the new medium, as some Hollywood veterans did. Of course, our business would have to change to accommodate it, but change can be beneficial.

One of the major changes, I felt, would be that certain types of movies would soon become a thing of the past. Television would do the types of programs it could do best and cheapest, programs that required little outdoor action, no huge casts, no vast sweeps of sets. They would stick pretty much to intimate things.

During TV's early years, I thought more about that and realized that it left the field open for the movies to do the bigger, broader type of film.

One thing I had never done in my career was a gigantic spectacle. I had watched Cecil B. DeMille work—I had even been in one of his colossals—and I had always harbored a secret yen to make one of them myself. I felt this was the time to do it. It was now or never.

So I welcomed the opportunity to do my biggest film—*Quo Vadis*. *Quo Vadis* had actually been in the works for some time before I became associated with it. Arthur Hornblow was producing it for Louis B. Mayer and he had been working on it in Europe with John Huston. They had already spent two million dollars, gone through several writers, and built some sets, but it never jelled. I never knew what happened among Mayer, Hornblow, and Huston, but something did. There was a falling out and the whole project seemed doomed. Mayer wasn't the kind of man who takes lightly to losing two million dollars. With that kind of money already spent, he wasn't about to abandon the picture.

He assigned Sam Zimbalist as the new producer and Sam Bierman and John Lee Mahin to write a new script. Then he asked me to direct. It was Bierman who gave me a copy of the book, as I left for Rome with Mahin.

"Here's a book you won't be able to put down," Sam said.

I found the book heavy going, so I cabled Bierman: "I HAVE FINALLY FOUND A BOOK I COULD PUT DOWN."

Nevertheless, I finished it and realized there was a story buried in it that would make a wonderful movie. It was a spectacle, and I wanted to make a spectacle. Sam, John, and I went to work, did a lot of research, wrote and rewrote the script. It was a tough job, whipping that monumental story into a script that was possible to film and yet would have the vastness the tale demanded.

Before it was all done, I would have spent fourteen months in Rome, with nine and a half of them in shooting. The studio would spend twelve million dollars, making it one of the most expensive movies ever filmed up to that time. Despite that huge nut, it would prove to be a profit-maker. By now it has grossed about fifty million dollars.

I was more nervous before I started *Quo Vadis* than I had ever been. I knew the enormity of the project. I knew the logistics were such that it could easily go wrong. I knew a picture of that magnitude could, if I erred badly, wreck the studio. There was a lot riding on it, and I had the jitters in a big way.

Mayer gave Zimbalist and me carte blanche—almost. It's curious how the executive mind works. Here I was with millions of dollars to spend and yet there was penny-pinching. I wanted to use Howard Koch as my first assistant director. He was eager to do it, but he knew it would mean almost a year away from home. Naturally, he wanted his wife to be with him. Routinely, I passed along the request. It was denied. Because of the cost of a plane ticket and a hotel room, he couldn't bring his wife. So he refused to go, and I can't blame him. That kind of thing irked me, but it isn't unusual. All too often, studios toss hundreds of thousands of dollars around, like so much confetti, and balk at spending a few hundred dollars on something meaningful. My other assistant director, Bill Cannon, was available, however, so I used him.

This was one of those pictures that could literally boast of having a cast of thousands. There was one period that lasted about three weeks when there were sixty thousand extras in the amphitheater every day. I borrowed from my experience with DeMille in organizing that mob.

As I was about to leave for Rome, I called DeMille.

"Master," I said, using the form of address most of us reserved for him, "I'm off to Rome. Before I go, I'm curious about one thing. I've always wanted to ask you why you like doing biblical films."

"I'll tell you, Mervyn," the old man said. "The Bible has been a best-seller for centuries. Why should I let two thousand years of publicity go to waste?"

When I had my arena sequence in *Quo Vadis*, I remembered how DeMille had done things in *The Ten Commandments*. The place was decorated with banners, and one of them had the Roman numerals LXII, or 62. In all my films, I've used the number 62—from the house at 62 Geary Street where I was born—but it was hardest to squeeze that lucky number into *Quo Vadis*.

The stands were all arranged alphabetically. The crowd was broken up into groups of fifty, with a man—the Italians called him a *capo groppo*—in charge of each group. He had the responsibility of feeding them, seeing that they were in their proper costumes and had the right props, marshaling them at the right time to the right place. It was all done in a military manner and, after a few expectable mishaps, it all worked with amazing smoothness. The Italians, I found, were born actors. They loved being in front of a camera, even if they were with 59,999 others, and each one of them felt it was his picture.

My stars were Robert Taylor, Deborah Kerr, Peter Ustinov, Buddy Baer, Finlay Currie, and Leo Genn. The only casting difficulty we had was with the part of Lygia, the Christian girl who believes in Jesus and what he stands for. Originally, I felt an unknown actress would be best, and for three months we tested hundreds of girls. In London, I thought I had found her when we tested a young actress named Audrey Hepburn. I thought she was sensational, but the studio took one look at the test and turned her down. Eventually, we decided we couldn't use an unknown after all, so we got Deborah Kerr, who is always good.

Actually, the cast included several unbilled stars. One day, I got a call from Elizabeth Taylor. She was in Rome with her husband, Nicky Hilton. She said they had had a fight and she wanted to keep away from him for a while.

"Can you hide me, Mervyn?" she asked. "I don't want him to find me."

"Sure," I said. "What better place to hide than in a crowd? Come on over to the set."

When she arrived, I sent her down to wardrobe. They put her in a toga, just like all the other extras, and for a few days Elizabeth Taylor was one of my mob scene. I was careful to keep her in the back, however, so nobody could see her.

There was another girl, however, whom I just as carefully placed in the front where she could be seen. I had spotted this girl, a tall, dark-eyed Italian beauty, and felt she was such a glorious specimen that I wanted my cameras to be certain to pick her up. I promptly forgot all about her until, years later, she reminded me.

It was after I shot *Moment to Moment* in Monaco, and Princess Grace gave us a farewell party before we all left for home. Sophia Loren and her husband, Carlo Ponti, came in and Princess Grace and Prince Rainier introduced us.

I was startled—and pleased—when Sophia impulsively gave me a big kiss.

"You're responsible for my being a star, Mr. LeRoy," she said.

"I am? What do you mean?"

Then she told me that she was the girl I had placed in the front ranks of the crowd in *Quo Vadis*. From that, she went on to her phenomenal career.

"My mother and I needed money," she said, "and you hired us. None of the rest of this would have happened, except for you."

"I had good taste even then," I said.

It seemed to me that we hired almost everybody in Rome at one time or another. There were down-on-their-luck actors, newcomers like Sophia, even impoverished royalty. Very often, some of the extras bore titles such as Count This or Prince That.

There was one day when one of the extras came up to me and said, "Hey, Mr. LeRoy, how would you like to be a count?"

"A count?"

"Sure. It's easy. For ten thousand dollars, I can have you made a count."

I laughed.

"For five thousand dollars, can you make me a half-count?"

The actors weren't nearly as much a problem as the lions. One of the biggest scenes in the picture was in the Roman Circus, when the lions were supposed to eat the Christians. It's easy enough, back in Hollywood, to write something in the script: "Enter fifty lions who proceed to attack and eat the Christians."

Then you get to that little sentence in the shooting and obviously you are faced with some distinct problems. Before you can do anything else, you have to acquire some lions. My scouts rounded up all the lions (more than fifty of them) they could find in Europe, from circuses and traveling shows. We had to hire their tamers, too, and dress them as Christians.

We were in the Circus, and I was up on top of an eighty-foot boom, because this had to be a long shot, at least at the beginning. I wanted shadows on the arena, so I waited until late in the afternoon, when there would be long and photographically interesting shadows. I had set up a series of cues, using a revolver—one shot meant everybody get ready, the second shot was the signal for the cameras to roll, and, on the third shot, the lions were to be released.

The sun began to sink and the shadows grew. It was time. I lifted the revolver and fired—once, twice, a third time. I was scared to death. Would the lions take their roles too seriously and actually eat the poor pseudo-Christians?

The lions came out of their enclosures—the Italians called them *spinas*—and they looked meancing and growled and swished their tails. But that's all they did. They took one look at the hot sun and turned around and went back into their *spinas*.

"Cut!" I yelled. Then I called the lion tamers over and asked what went wrong.

They explained, via their interpreters, that the poor lions couldn't act ferocious because it was too hot. Besides, they weren't hungry. We had been feeding them too well. Their advice was to starve them for a couple of weeks and then try again.

"Two weeks?" I said. "My God, they'll be so hungry they'll eat up all the actors and the set, too."

The lion trainers assured me that they wouldn't, that by the end of two lean weeks they'd be just right, hungry enough to attack and not yet so underfed that they'd be weak.

So that day's shooting was canceled; and, for two weeks, I shot other things while my fifty lions were on their involuntary diet. Whenever I went near the Circus set, I could hear them roaring. It was eerie. I had visions of them, the next time we shot, coming racing out of the *spinas* and devouring everybody in sight. I even wondered if they could climb up an eighty-foot boom.

When the two weeks were up, we set the whole scene again— Circus, crowds, lion tamers, everything. Once again, I was on the boom. Once again, I waited for the shadows and the hot sun and then fired my revolver three times. Here came the lions, those starving, terrifying animals, roaring out of the *spinas* with a three-course meal on their minds.

The same thing happened. The lions came rushing out all right, but then they apparently decided the heat and the sun were too much for them, and turned right around and went back. I still don't know how the ancient Romans staged their bloody circuses. I am probably the only living soul who ever tried to coax a lion into eating somebody, and I tell you they just won't do it.

We had to fake the scene. I wound up having the prop men stuff empty clothing with meat, so it looked like a Christian lying on the ground, and we brought the lions out forcibly and they ate those "bodies." I augmented that with close-ups of fake lions, which the technicians built, jumping on real people. It worked, although I never did get the scene exactly as I had wanted.

In the more than a year I was in Rome, many things happened to me. To begin with, I lost twenty-two pounds. That was curious, because my diet consisted almost entirely of pasta, which is supposed to be fattening. I have discovered my own secret for losing weight, based on my *Quo Vadis* experience. If you eat the same thing every day, no matter how caloric it may be, you will lose weight. At least I did.

Then there was the question of our relations with the Roman Catholic Church. They were, of course, very interested in the production. They had assigned a Jesuit priest, an American named Father Mara, to us as technical adviser. He was a great deal of help.

I also had two audiences with Pope Pius XII while I was in Rome. The first was a group affair, with Kitty and her daughter (Eugenia, now the Countess Bucci-Casara, lived in Rome and worked in the film as an extra), Frances and Sam Goldwyn, and Robert Sherwood, the playwright, and his wife.

The only thing memorable about it was that Goldwyn, who, as we were all getting ready for the audience, called Kitty in our hotel room.

"Say, Kitty," Sam said. "Tell me something. When we get to the Vatican, where do I find him?"

The second audience, however, was private. Kitty had become friendly with the Prince and Princess Puccelli. He was the head of the Vatican guard and he arranged the private audience for me. It lasted twenty minutes and was a memorable experience.

Around my neck, I wear a medallion that has the Jewish Star of David on one side and a Saint Christopher medal on the other. It had been given to me by Frank Sinatra when we did *The House I Live In*. The pope noticed the Saint Christopher medal.

"Mr. LeRoy, are you a Catholic?" he asked.

"No, I'm Jewish."

"Well," he said, "that happens to be very close to the Catholic religion."

I found myself staring in fascination at the pope's hands—thin and expressive and forever making gentle gestures in the air. For some reason, my father's hands came to my mind. I asked him if he would bless my *Quo Vadis* script, which I had with me. He put his lovely hands on the script, murmured some Latin words, and then said, in English, "May your film be a successful one."

He showed me his bedroom, which, I subsequently learned, was a rare privilege. The walls were white and unadorned, except for the crucifix that hung above his simple bed. There was nothing else in the room, merely the bed, the crucifix, and a small window. The contrast between the richness of the Vatican and the spareness of the pope's own quarters was startling.

"I like the cinema," the pope said.

"I am glad," I said. "And, Your Holiness, let me tell you that I will never make a film I'm ashamed of."

"That is good," he said. "By the way, do you remember a movie called *Going My Way?*"

"Of course," I said. "One of my friends, Leo McCarey, made it."

"I have a print of it," he said. "Don't you love that scene where the priest takes a little drink?"

The twenty minutes sped by, and then I left. I have always felt enriched by that audience. I still wear my Star of David–Saint Christopher medallion. Something has been bringing me luck, and maybe that's it.

During the *Quo Vadis* shooting, however, there were some moments when I felt luck was deserting me. First, it was Kitty's illness. It was quite serious, and we had nine doctors to consult about her, and then I had another specialist brought down from Switzerland.

In my own experience Italian doctors carry no bags, use no instruments, seem to work entirely on intuition. They just lean down, put their ears to your heart, and listen. The doctor who visited Kitty did just that, then whispered, "*Ella è morente,*" which means "she is dying." Immediately I knew I had to have another, non-Italian opinion. That's when I had the Swiss doctor flown in, but he wasn't too comforting, either.

We were shooting at night at the time, but I didn't sleep during the day either. I was too worried about Kitty. It's a cliché, but the only thing that really matters in this life is the health of those you love. I could see that Kitty was suffering and that her condition was worsening.

She made up my mind. She decided she had to get back to New York at once. I arranged for a TWA flight, I hired a nurse, and I got her passport. Within two hours, Kitty, her dog, and her nurse were airborne. I called Jules Stein, who was in New York, and he met her and took her directly to a hospital. She was operated on immediately and, I was later told, the operation saved her life. I dread to think what might have happened had she stayed in Rome.

The airline was wonderful to me. They knew my concern and had someone call me every other hour while the plane was in the air, to keep me informed about her condition.

When she recovered, she went home to Los Angeles to recuperate. It had taken a lot out of her. I missed her in Rome, but her health was the important thing. As it turned out, it was a good thing that she was back in California then, because it was my mother's turn to have physical problems.

Over the years, my mother and stepfather had grown closer to me. I had come to appreciate her bouyancy and love of life. She and Percy went to the track every day and, religiously, she would place her two-dollar bet on every race. Her system was simplicity itself—she bet on jockeys she liked. Her favorite was Johnny Longden; and, if he had a mount, she would put her two dollars on his horse to win. Since he was a great jockey, she had her share of winners. All the employees of the tracks knew her and called her by name. When she had a winning ticket, she'd always give some of her profits to the clerks at the window. Even today, some of the older clerks talk about her.

I had come to appreciate Percy, too, and for many years he handled my business affairs. He had his quirks. His patriotism was so strong that he had written a book about the American flag. He also thought that he had invented the outside toilets used in service stations. Despite his idiosyncrasies, he was a dear man, and what mattered to me most was that he and my mother were happy and content together.

Four days after my fiftieth birthday, when I was in Rome, my mother suffered a stroke that was eventually to prove fatal. Kitty was called and got there as fast as she could. She was in time to hear the last words my mother ever spoke.

"How's my boy?" she said.

She lingered for a few months. Kitty was torn. She didn't know whether to send for me or not. She knew that my presence in Rome was vital and that my presence at the bedside of a comatose woman could not really do anybody any good, and yet she thought I might want to see my mother once more, no matter what her condition. She called Dore Schary, who was then in charge at Metro, and alerted him to be prepared that I might have to leave Rome. Then she called me and told me the situation, although she minimized the seriousness of it.

I decided to stay in Rome. Kitty said she would let me know if there was any change in my mother's condition. In Rome, there were thousands of people depending on my presence. So I stayed and, as it happened, my mother lived on until the film was over. I reached Los Angeles in time for Christmas and immediately went to my mother's bedside. I thought I saw a little smile on her tired face.

"Ma," I said to her, although I knew she couldn't understand, "you've got to get well. The boys at the mutuel windows are waiting for you."

That was when she smiled. It was her last.

On New Year's Eve, we were at a party at the Bel Air Hotel. A few moments before midnight, I was called to the phone. My mother had died. I shed a few quiet tears, and we went to her house immediately.

Soon after the funeral, my business manager asked me if I wanted to send the same amount of money to Percy each month, now that my mother was gone.

"Of course," I said. "After all, he was so good to my mother." Percy lived another four years, passing on in 1954 when he was seventy-four. He had been my stepfather for forty-five years.

Those were the sad moments, Kitty's illness and the news of my mother's imminent death. Over a fourteen-month period, some sad moments are inevitable. Just as, inevitably, there will be cheerful moments, and there were.

I remember particularly one day when I was shooting a scene with a huge crowd. Everything was ready. Over the public address system, I called *"Silenzio!"* The thousands of extras slowly quieted down. There was not a sound, as everyone waited for me to say *"Via!"* which meant to turn over the cameras.

Then I heard one voice, from way back in the crowd.

"Hey, Moyvan!"

There was no mistaking that voice. Nobody else called me Moyvan, at least not with that particular intonation. It had to be Jack Benny, one of my best friends for many years.

I broke up. I could see him, pushing his way down through the crowd. They didn't know what was going on; Jack is a peculiarly American comedian and he is not well known in continental Europe, so the Italian extras had no idea who he was. They figured he must be important, the way I stopped the shooting and ran through the crowd to meet him, and the way the Americans in the crew applauded.

Jack and his wife Mary were on a vacation trip to Europe and had decided to surprise me. Jack stayed with me that day, while I directed that big scene. It was a terribly hot day and I was wearing a new, lightweight shirt I had had made for me in Rome. I was very pleased with the shirt and I kept saying to Jack, "You must have some shirts made while you're here."

"No, I don't think so," he said. "I really don't need any shirts."

"Look at this shirt," I said. "Feel it. Italian shirts are great. And they're so cheap. You have to get some."

Jack thought for a long moment when I used that word "cheap" but he still said no, he didn't want any shirts. All day long I pushed the shirts, all day long he said he didn't want any. As we drove back to the hotel, after we had wrapped for the day, I said if he wanted to, we could stop at the shop where I'd had my shirts made.

"Will you stop with the shirts?" he said.

At the hotel, Jack went to his room. I ran to my room and got some of the shirts and took them down to show him.

"Jack," I said, "will you please look at these shirts? Just take a good look. And they have my initials on them."

"I've got shirts just like that at home," Jack said.

"What? You've got shirts like that—with my initials on them?"

He laughed until I thought he'd get sick. Ever since, whenever we meet, he wants to know if I'm wearing one of those Italian shirts with my initials on it.

One night while he was in Rome, we decided to attend the opera. Jack is a great music lover, so I thought the opera would be a treat. They were singing *Madama Butterfly*. I had my secretary get two of the best seats in the house, but the best seats turned out to be fifty rows back from the stage—the orchestra alone takes up thirty rows. I imagine the real, knowledgeable opera lovers like to be that far back for acoustical reasons, but all Jack and I knew was that we were so far back that the stage seemed three miles away.

"Which one is Koko-San?" Jack whispered to me.

"From here," I said, "they all look like Knute Rockne."

Jack laughed so hard that the benches we were sitting on shook. People around us gave us dirty looks. I thought maybe we'd be the center of an international incident—the Italians take their opera very seriously—so I tried to keep a straight face. Neither of us could; we had the giggles. Jack gave up and ran out of the Opera House, and I followed. That was all we saw of *Madama Butterfly* that night.

Through it all—the tragedies and the cheerful moments—I kept shooting. It was a terribly difficult production in every way. The first time we turned over the cameras, they went backward—somehow, they were in reverse. The crowds of job-hunting Romans were so vast and so vigorous that they once nearly overturned my car, and I eventually had to have them build a special gate for me at the back of the studio, so Sam Zimbalist and I could slip in and out unmolested. For a big, triumphant Roman parade, we had to rebuild a quarter-mile of the Appian Way. Along the route, we had to rebuild Roman ruins and other structures that had lined that historic thoroughfare. Every day was a problem to be solved, decisions to be made, orders to be given. That's true of all pictures, but here the problems, decisions, and orders were on a much grander scale.

Eventually, however, it was finished. I went back home to Los Angeles and collapsed for a few weeks. Then, with Zimbalist, I had to supervise the postproduction, which was on a large scale, too. Altogether, about eighteen months of my life went into *Quo Vadis*, but I think it was a worthwhile investment.

The premiere was held at the Warfield Theater, in San Francisco. That was, for me, a nostalgic evening. After I had seen the film, and thrilled to the pleased reaction of the audience, I walked the six blocks to the Alcazar Theater, where I had once stood and sold newspapers. I remembered back to when I had been overjoyed to make a few dollars. Now I had just seen a movie I had made at a cost of some twelve million dollars.

It was almost too much to grasp, the differences that a relatively few years can make. I stood there, in the darkness, and I cried. Then I walked back to my hotel and decided never again to look back, only forward.

How do you follow a picture like *Quo Vadis*, a picture with that scope and impact? The answer is you don't try to top it with another film in the same genre, you do something far removed from it.

In my career, I have successfully avoided being typed. Typing can happen to directors as well as to actors. There are some directors, like the late John Ford, who are typed as directors of outdoor adventure films; some, like Frank Capra, who are labeled comedy directors; and some, like George Cukor, who are considered primarily directors of women. They are all capable men and, presumably, could do many different types of films. However, since they have been so successful in their particular areas, the powers-that-be ordinarily refuse to give them a shot at other things.

I have been fortunate in that respect. Even at the start of my career, I was selective. As I grew in stature, I could pick and choose my own properties. For me always, the sole criterion for selecting a film was that it had a good, solid story and that it had the quality I call "heart." So I ran the gamut of movie types.

My most important films illustrate the extent to which I was able to escape being typed:

> *Little Caesar*—gangster
> *I Am a Fugitive from a Chain Gang*—melodrama
> *Five Star Final*—newspaper drama
> *Golddiggers of 1933*—musical
> *Tugboat Annie*—comedy
> *Oil for the Lamps of China*—adventure
> *Anthony Adverse*—romantic adventure
> *They Won't Forget*—drama
> *The Wizard of Oz*—fantasy
> *Waterloo Bridge*—romance
> *Blossoms in the Dust*—biographical
> *Johnny Eager*—gangster
> *Random Harvest*—romance
> *Thirty Seconds Over Tokyo*—war
> *Mister Roberts*—comedy
> *Quo Vadis*—spectacle

I have made seventy-five films, as this is being written, and I never repeated myself. I never made the same story, or anything like the same story, twice. There was never any such thing as "a Mervyn LeRoy-type" picture. You could always tell a Lubitsch picture, or a Hitchcock picture, or a DeMille picture. I'm not saying that's bad, I'm just making a factual statement: My films were all so different that there never was a LeRoy trademark.

So, when *Quo Vadis* was in the can, I decided it was time to shift gears again. It wasn't easy. Dore Schary had another epic he wanted me to film. He called me in and showed me the script of something called *The Plymouth Adventure*, and asked me to read it. I did, and I couldn't believe it, it was so bad. I just couldn't bring myself to report back to him because I found it so dreadful. Finally, he called me.

"What did you think?" he asked.

"I don't want to make it," I said, "and, what's more, you shouldn't make it, either."

"Why not?"

"It's a bore, that's why. It'll be a boring picture. Look, Dore, history has its place but right now I'm not so much interested in who discovered America as I am in who can save it."

He didn't take my advice, however, and the studio made *The Plymouth Adventure*, with Clarence Brown directing. I was right; it was a bore. It bombed.

With that little episode out of the way, I looked around for something else to do. I had been thinking that I hadn't done a musical in some time. I knew MGM was planning on a remake of *Roberta*, so I asked Mayer if I could do it. He agreed, and that film became *Lovely to Look At*.

We had a superlative cast—Kathryn Grayson, Howard Keel, Red Skelton, Marge and Gower Champion, Ann Miller, and Zsa Zsa Gabor. Miss Gabor had only one line in the picture but, on the first day of shooting, it seemed like she must have been the star, judging from the quantity of flowers that were delivered to the set for her. There were baskets of flowers, bouquets of flowers, vases of flowers. The stage smelled like a florist's shop, and so did she.

Lovely to Look At was a film that really was lovely to look at, which is what I wanted. Everything was beautiful. One of the high spots was a fashion show and that caused something of a logistics problem. When you make a movie, you know the public won't be seeing it for between a year and a year and a half later. You have to try to outguess the public's taste and make a movie with the hope that your subject matter will be popular twelve to eighteen months later. In the case of the fashion show, I wanted all the clothes to be the latest thing—at the time the public was actually seeing the picture. I went to one of MGM's top designers, Adrian, who had done the costumes for *The Wizard of Oz*, and dumped my problem in his lap. I told him he had to think ahead and gamble on what would be fashionable at the time the film was released. He whipped up a series of gowns that were breathtaking and, more important, they were right on the button. When the movie came out, Adrian's styles were up to the minute.

This was one film where the cast problem wasn't that they didn't get along, but that they got along too well. The girls—Kathryn, Ann, and Zsa Zsa—became an instant sorority. They were always off in some corner, giggling like schoolgirls. Red Skelton, one of those comedians who is always on, recognized their potential as an audience and he played to them constantly. He's a funny man and he had them laughing all day long.

I like a happy set, but I also like a quiet set when there is work to be done. I had a devil of a time trying to get those girls to simmer down.

After the film was finished, many of us were invited to Rio de Janeiro for a film festival. I can't remember all of the people who went along, but Errol Flynn was there, and so were Edward G. Robinson, Walter Pidgeon, Irene Dunne, Irene Powell, and Ann Miller and I represented *Lovely to Look At*. We were all staying at the Tropicana Hotel, and it was a delightful week or ten days.

For me, the most memorable part of that trip was the day I rescued Ann Miller from the crooks. It began when I got a call from her, while I was in my room getting ready to go to bed.

"Mervyn," she said, "come up to my room right away. I've got some rocks here worth millions."

So I went up to Ann's room and found her with a couple of oily-looking South American types, the kind I immediately recognized as con men or hoodlums or worse. On her couch was a big pile of ordinary-looking rocks.

"What are those rocks?" I asked.

"That's what I wanted to show you," Ann said, bubbling as only Ann can bubble. "I'm so excited."

"You see, *señor*," one of the oily ones said, "those are gems in the raw. Inside those rocks there are precious jewels—diamonds and emeralds and rubies and—what do you call them?—amethysts. My friends and I are so enamored of the *señhorita* that we wish to make her almost a gift of these valuable rocks."

"Oh, Mervyn," Ann gushed. "Think of all the jewels in those rocks! I'll have more jewels than Zsa Zsa."

"What do you mean when you say 'almost a gift'?" I asked.

"Well, *señhor*," the man said, with an inexpensive shrug, "we have incurred certain expenses in obtaining these rocks."

"How much?" I asked.

"Practically nothing."

"How much?"

Ann took me by the hand and drew me aside and told me that her "friends" would let her have all the rocks for five thousand dollars. She was so excited by the prospect of outjeweling Zsa Zsa that she was all set to go for the deal.

I excused myself on some pretext and went downstairs to my own room. Kitty was there, and we discussed what I should do. I picked up the phone and called Ann.

"Look, Ann," I said, "you're being taken. Those characters are nothing but hoodlums. Crooks. Chiselers. Get 'em out of your room before you throw five grand out the window."

She was disappointed, but she took my advice and told the men to take their rocks and go. In the years since, she's managed to amass enough jewelry so she's able to hold her own with Zsa Zsa, although I doubt if anybody—except perhaps Elizabeth Taylor and Tiffany's—is quite in Zsa Zsa's jewelry league.

Around this time (this was 1952) one of MGM's hottest properties was Esther Williams, but there was a problem of what to do with a swimmer. The studio had tried several different approaches that had worked, in varying degrees. Mostly they were farfetched, and the way they got Esther into the water (where she was unsurpassed) had all the subtlety of a kick in the head. It seemed to me that something more appropriate could be found for her.

I remembered the story of Annette Kellerman, one of the most famous woman swimmers who had ever lived. It was, I knew, an intensely dramatic tale, and I felt that perhaps this was the way to get Esther into the water logically.

That's how *Million Dollar Mermaid*, which Esther has always said was her best picture, came into being. It was essentially a true story. It told of Annette Kellerman's life, and it wasn't so much the story of a swimmer as the story of a woman.

Annette Kellerman had polio as a girl and began to swim simply as a means of strengthening her muscles. She became so proficient at it that she developed into the foremost woman distance swimmer in the world. She fell in love, she had money and prestige and fame; but, when everything seemed to be perfect for her, she had an accident in a swimming pool and once again faced paralysis.

Here, for once, was a chance for Esther Williams to swim within the confines of a legitimate plot. Besides Esther, I had Victor Mature and Walter Pidgeon, and there was one big production number I got Busby Berkeley to help with.

For the swimming numbers, Esther did much of the staging herself. She was a bright girl, and she had a good sense of the camera, to go along with her natural rhythm and obvious swimming ability. The picture worked well and played the Radio City Music Hall in New York for eight weeks.

I have directed more pictures to play the Music Hall than any other director. One of them, *Random Harvest*, still holds the record: It played there for twelve weeks and could have played longer except that Nicholas Schenck, MGM's New York boss, wanted it to play the Loew's circuit. Russell Downing of the Music Hall told me he thought *Random Harvest* could have stayed on at the Music Hall another ten weeks. All told, I have had twenty pictures open at the Music Hall.

After *Million Dollar Mermaid*, I did only two more films for MGM. Things were beginning to bother me at the studio, in particular Dore Schary. We never did really see eye to eye on most things. Gradually, our divergence of opinion widened until it became what we have come to call a communications gap. Since he was then running the studio, it didn't seem to make much sense for me to stick around.

I did those last two films. One was *Latin Lovers*, with Lana Turner and Ricardo Montalban. The other was a remake of the old Jeanette MacDonald–Nelson Eddy hit, *Rose Marie*, with Howard Keel, Ann Blyth, and Fernando Lamas.

Then I left. I gave out the story that I needed a rest, and I guess that was at least partially true. I had been working steadily for years, with practically no time off between films. I had been scheduled to make *The Student Prince*, but I just couldn't take the bickering anymore. I gave up my contract—five thousand dollars a week at the time—and walked out the door. Security conscious as I am, I knew that I could go back to Warner Brothers, but I didn't tell anybody at MGM that. I just told them that I was tired and that I wanted to take a long vacation.

One thing I hated to leave behind was my secretary, Rose De-Luca. She couldn't afford to leave with me, because of all the seniority she had built up at the studio and the pension plan she had been contributing to for so long. Things always work out for the best, however, for at Warner Brothers later I would begin an association with another secretary, Ruth Bridges, which still exists. She has been my right arm since 1954. Her job interview consisted of two sentences:

"Honey, do you want to work for me?"

"I sure do."

She's the kind of person I can trust to write much of my correspondence on her own. I'll just give her the broad outline of the idea I want to convey and tell her to write the letter and she'll do it, then I'll read it over. I am inclined, too, to be overgenerous in arranging tickets for people and it's poor Ruth who has to do the dirty work. She often says that she isn't sure whether she's a secretary or the proprietor of a ticket bureau.

There was one day when a group of Japanese dignitaries were visiting the studio. I asked her to take them on a tour, but she didn't want to. She said she couldn't speak Japanese and there was no way she could communicate with them. I blew up; I have a temper that explodes quickly and just as quickly goes away and then I feel contrite about it. Ruth reacted in a typical feminine fashion—she cried. So we arranged for the studio's foreign department to take them around, something they should have done in the first place. They were so pleased that they gave me a pearl-encrusted pen, which they said was for my wife. I felt so badly about losing my temper that I gave the pen to Ruth.

Ordinarily, I can keep my temper under control. There are only a few things that set me off; chief among them is when an actor is late for work. It seems to me to be simple professionalism for an actor to be on time, with his lines memorized. I have found that real pros do it; it's only the ones who think they are pros, but aren't, who don't.

I have often said that one facet of a director's job is that he must be a good psychologist to work with actors. They are really children. When you think about it, it is perfectly understandable. They are, first, usually people who are exhibitionistic, which is something of a juvenile attitude. Secondly, they are involved daily in the childish game of make-believe.

A director must realize this and treat them accordingly. They are adults, physically, but underneath that glamorous, grown-up exterior they are youthful and must be treated that way. They are inclined to be petulant, moody, immature. They have temperament, but I feel that goes with talent. Without temperament, they would be dull. Since I have explosions on the set myself, I can forgive them theirs.

You have to handle them carefully. Too strong a hand, and they rebel. Too weak, and they take advantage of you. I try to hire proficient, capable, experienced actors, men and women who know what they are doing, and then let them find their own way. I guide them, of course, but I don't force them to do things my way when they are acting.

If they have confidence in me, I can win them over. If they don't have confidence in me, I don't want them on my picture. It's easy enough to tell before you start shooting. During the wardrobe and makeup tests and the readings, you get a pretty good idea of what type of person they are and how best to work with them.

I understand actors. I realize that they must have the opportunity to express themselves. Often, I will direct a scene my way and, afterward, an actor will suggest a different approach. I may feel that the actor's idea is totally wrong, but I know it would be foolhardy to squelch him.

"May I try it my way?" he'll say.

"Sure," I'll answer. "We'll print both of them and see which looks better in the rushes."

Most often, my way turns out better—and the actor will admit it—but, occasionally, his way is superior, and I will gladly admit that, too. After all, we are both seeking the same goal, a fine motion picture.

Before every scene, I tell them, "Let's have a nice scene with a lot of feeling." Those aren't mere words, they express my philosophy about movies. What a film should have, scene after scene, is "a lot of feeling."

After every scene, I usually say to my cast, "How did it feel to you? Did you believe it?" If they don't believe it, the audience won't believe it, either. If they did believe it, then it will hit the audience in the heart.

I consider myself a typical member of the audience. When I watch a scene being shot, I change from a director to one of the folks in the balcony the instant I call for action. I forget what's gone before and don't think about what will be coming later. I look at the scene unfolding before me and, if it moves me, if I believe it, I will print it.

No matter what kind of film it is—from something as tough as *Little Caesar* to something as gossamer as *The Wizard of Oz*, the key to success is believability. Without that, there is nothing.

When I left MGM, I did so with considerable regret. In my twelve years at that studio, I had produced and/or directed nineteen films, and some of them would become classics of the screen. I had weathered a war, gotten married, lived through tragedy. It had been a dozen exciting and productive years.

I was tired. The fatigue was not only physical; I was also tired of the bickering and the infighting. I wanted a rest before I went back to my old home at Warner Brothers.

10

JACK BENNY:
I MAY AS WELL
GO HOME

It was a time for family and friends. All my life, since I was a lonely boy—possibly because I was a lonely boy—I have liked to be around people I love. If I can possibly help it, I avoid being alone. Now, with a few months of not working, I indulged my gregariousness. It was a time to relax, to unwind, and for that I require my family and those few friends who are almost family.

Warner, my son, was at Stanford and he was active in the university's dramatic society. He called to say he was producing a play, so we had to go to see our boy's maiden effort as a producer and director. The only problem was that Hollywood Park was opening the day after his play, and I had to be there, too.

That might not seem to be a problem—after all, the flight from San Francisco to Los Angeles is only about fifty-five minutes—but I had always been afraid of flying. I had flown just once, up to that time, and that was a very brief flight while I was shooting *Thirty Seconds Over Tokyo*. I didn't particularly enjoy it.

Kitty had been trying, for a long time, to get me up in a plane. She not only enjoyed flying, but she was a licensed pilot herself. Her late husband, Sidney Spiegel, had had his own private plane. When he developed leukemia, Kitty decided she should learn to fly, so she would be capable of landing their plane in the event of an emergency. So she had flown very often and she believed that flying was the best way to travel.

187

Until that weekend, however, I had cleverly avoided any necessity of flying. I managed to convince Kitty to take trains or boats or automobiles—anything but airplanes. That weekend, however, there was a time factor. If we went up to Stanford to see Warner's play, we couldn't drive back in time to get to Hollywood Park for the opening.

"We'll have to fly, dear," Kitty said, with what I can only define as a smirk.

I compromised. We would take the train north and fly back—but only if the weather was good. I made round-trip train reservations, just in case. The fates were against me. San Francisco, the fog capital of the world, came up with a bright and sunny morning on that day we had to get back to Los Angeles. I searched the sky from our hotel room window, but wasn't able to find even the tiniest cloud, or excuse.

"Okay," I said. "We'll fly back."

MGM's man in San Francisco picked us up in his car to take us to the airport. En route, a big black cloud suddenly appeared. Now I was really worried. We were committed. I had canceled our train reservations.

"Look at that cloud," I said. "Do you think maybe we should take the bus?"

"Oh, don't worry, dear," Kitty said. "We can climb above that cloud without any trouble."

We got on the plane. Kitty, without a worry in the world, pulled out a book and started reading even before the door was closed. I just sat there, worrying to myself. Then we began taxiing out. We waited at the end of the runway until there came an announcement. Something was wrong, there was an adjustment needed on the plane's front wheel. We would have to go back to the terminal. They took us back, had us get off, and eventually said they were getting another plane. By this time, of course, I was a walking case of nerves.

The MGM man was still there and I made him call the president of the airline, to check and find out if the new plane was airworthy. I don't know if he really made that call, but he came back and said he had, and that everything was fine.

Needless to say, the trip was quick, uneventful, and, I had to admit, very pleasant. Kitty congratulated me for landing the plane so smoothly and called me "Orville Wright." Since that first time, I have come to love flying.

Later, we went to Brazil for a film festival. We took the boat down and flew home. The return flight was delayed a day when the plane failed to arrive in Rio on time. The flight pattern was over the Andes and I was looking forward to it. This time, it was Kitty who was worried. I guess she knew enough to realize that it was a tricky flight. In my ignorance, all I could think of was the spectacular scenery I was going to see, and it was thrilling.

We both love to travel and, fortunately, we are in a position to indulge that passion. We made a tour of the Orient once, with Mary and Jack Benny, and visited such places as Japan, Thailand, and Hong Kong. One of the advantages of being a celebrity is that the red carpet is usually out, which makes it pleasant. In Bangkok, the Thais put on a special show for us, with a fascinating exhibition of Thai dancing that none of us will ever forget. In Hong Kong, however, nobody knew Jack at all. He is unaccustomed to being unrecognized. Not that he wants the attention, but he's so used to it that it feels strange when he doesn't get it. So I tipped all the hotel employees and the next morning everybody came up to him and called him by name. He felt at home.

Jack had to fly back from Hong Kong on short notice, and he was unable to get a first-class booking on the plane. He was very unhappy at the prospect of flying tourist class.

"My God, Mervyn," he said. "Mary and I can't fly tourist. The public thinks I'm cheap now. What will they say if they see me in the tourist section?"

He did manage to get first class from Honolulu to Los Angeles, but he was in the tourist section—trying to sink down low in his seat so nobody would notice him—from Hong Kong to Honolulu.

Jack is, as I have mentioned, one of my two closest and dearest friends, the other being Buddy Fogelson. Our friendship antedates either of us being in Hollywood, so we can remember back to the days before we made it. Like most performers, Jack has long harbored a dream of becoming a director himself. I have tried to encourage him in that, because I think he has the sensitivity and creativity to become a fine director.

During the days when I was directing *Johnny Eager*, I finally persuaded him to visit me on the set. I felt that if Jack sat with me for a few weeks, he could learn much of the directorial business. I knew that already he could direct dialogue, because he does that on his radio and television shows as a matter of course. So he sat beside me for a few days, as I directed *Johnny Eager*, and he asked a few questions and he observed.

After a week or so, I reached a point in the script where there was a large crowd scene. I looked the set over, placed the people, positioned the camera where I thought it would best capture the scene. I was getting everything ready when I felt a tap on my shoulder. It was Jack.

"Mervyn," he said, "I may as well go home."

"What for? We're just starting this scene."

"I know, but I have decided that I'll never be a director."

"Why not?"

"Well, you just placed your camera for this scene. Now, I don't think I would have put the camera where you put it."

I looked at him for a moment, and he was serious.

"Jack," I said, "tell me where you would have put it."

He showed me the spot where he thought he would have placed the camera, if he had been the director.

"Okay," I said. "Now let me tell you something. Where you would have put the camera may be better than where I put it. How do you know your spot isn't better?"

I explained to him my feelings about directing. It isn't anything that comes from heaven. There is no divine right of directing. There is no such thing as an automatic I'm-right-and-everybody-else-is-wrong about camera placement, for example. I had placed the camera where it looked, to me, like it would make for the best composition. But somebody else—Wyler or Wilder or Zinnemann or Lean or Jack Benny—might have put it someplace else and his results could easily have been superior.

Directing is simply going by your hunches, your experience, your best-educated guesses, your intuition. It isn't magic. It isn't superhuman. It isn't mysterious. It is merely using your native eye for composition, and all of us have that eye, to some extent.

Jack listened as I explained that theory and then he sat down again and stayed with me for another week or so. He never did direct, however, and I think he's always regretted that he didn't, and so have I. Chances are he would have been an excellent director.

Jack and I are on the same humor wavelength. We can sit and laugh over silly things. I have a feeling some of our favorite funny incidents don't translate well to the printed page, but I'm going to tell a couple of them anyhow. To us, at the time, they were hysterically funny.

There was one occasion when we drove to Palm Springs together. Our wives met us there, and we all had adjoining suites. Since Jack and I like to sit up late and amuse ourselves with our own brand of humor, we decided to share one room and let the girls share the other. As we were driving down, the subject of writers came up. Jack had a couple of men writing for him that he had teamed up, and they had become excellent comedy writers.

"How did you happen to decide to team up those two writers?" I asked him.

"We're driving now," Jack said, "and it's too long a story to tell in the car. I'll tell you when we get to the Springs."

When I get curious about something, however, I can't wait for the answer, so every few miles I'd press him—"How did you team them up?" He kept putting off the answer—"I can't tell you how now, I'll tell you later." It got to be one of our silly jokes and pretty soon we were laughing our fool heads off.

"How?" (Laughter.)

"I'll tell you how later." (More laughter.)

When we reached the hotel, I kept on asking and he kept on avoiding the answer, and we both kept on giggling. Finally, we went to bed. Somewhere around three o'clock in the morning, I felt someone shaking me. It was Jack.

"Mervyn," he said, "do you want to know how?"

I opened one eye.

"How?" I said.

He still hasn't gotten over the fact that even though I was fast asleep, I went along with his gag so quickly.

There was another time, also in Palm Springs. Jack went to bed early that evening, and I sat up in the living room with Mary and her brother, Hilliard (Hickey) Marks. Something Hickey said struck us as very funny and we both burst out into uproarious laughter. We evidently woke Jack up, because he came into the living room, in his pajamas and bathrobe.

"A laugh that big," he said, "I've got to hear about."

I've always considered something Jack said as one of the finest tributes I've received. He once told me that he would work for me, without even reading a script, if I said I had a part that was right for him. He did that with Ernst Lubitsch in *To Be or Not to Be*, which was probably the best film Jack ever made.

Lubitsch, incidentally, was another close friend. He lived next door to us, on Saint Cloud, and we would read each other's scripts. We would discuss scenes and comedy values. I, for one, valued his advice highly and I think it was mutual.

Regularly, on Sunday mornings, Lubitsch would be at home for his famous brunches. We went very often. I was standing next to him one Sunday morning when a tall Englishman approached him.

"Mr. Lubitsch," the Englishman said, "I want to tell you how much I admire you."

"Thank you."

"And I want to say, too, how much I like your pictures—they're wonderful."

"Why, thank you very much," Lubitsch said, wondering which films the man had seen.

"By the way," the man said, pointing to a painting on the wall, "who painted that one?"

I think poor Ernst was taken down a few pegs by that exchange, but he laughed it off. I considered him to be one of our truly great directors, and a great man, but he had one weakness—he married the wrong women.

The night before Lubitsch died, Kitty was awakened by a voice from his house. He was calling, "Mervyn, Mervyn," over and over. Kitty woke me up and we listened in the darkness to that strange and tragic voice. I got dressed and went over and sat by his bedside, and he kept repeating my name endlessly.

Poor Ernst. I've always believed he died of a broken heart, because his wife had left him.

We had many other friends. The Hollywood social set is still a relatively small one, but it is close. It is also a party-happy crowd, and, if we wanted to, Kitty and I could be out every night.

You get to know everybody in Hollywood, especially if you work in the picture business. In one picture I directed, there was a young actress I became very fond of. Her name was Nancy Davis and she is the daughter of a noted Chicago brain surgeon, Dr. Loyal Davis. She called me one evening, very agitated.

"Mervyn," she said, "you have to help me. Somebody is shoving Communist literature under my door and I don't know what to do about it."

She drove over that evening to show me some of the propaganda that was being slipped under her door. We are both anti-Communist, and strongly so, so the whole business was annoying. I didn't know what to tell her to do about it, but suggested she talk to Ronald Reagan, who was then the president of the Screen Actors Guild.

I called Ronnie and explained the problem. I said he ought to talk to the girl, because the whole thing had her so upset.

"Besides," I said, "you're single and she's kind of cute and you should meet her."

So Ronnie said, okay, send her down. Nancy went to the SAG office and met Ronnie. I never found out if they solved the problem of the Communist literature under her door, but they solved some other problems. They got married, and today the governor of California and his first lady credit me for their meeting. I always say that's the one and only thing we can thank the Communists for—if it hadn't been for their propaganda material, Nancy and Ronnie Reagan might never have met.

That wasn't the first time I played Cupid, either. I introduced Jack Dempsey to his wife, Estelle Taylor. I had known Jack a long time and he had once told me that he admired Estelle Taylor and wanted to meet her. I happened to be at a party when both of them were guests, and so I took Jack by the hand and brought him over to where Estelle was standing talking to some other people. It didn't take them long to fall in love and get married, just like Nancy and Ronnie later on.

Hollywood parties are more than just drinks and dinner. Romances begin and end, deals are consummated, feuds start and stop. I used a party at my home once as a device to bring together two people who had been feuding for a long time. One was Harry Cohn, the grand curmudgeon himself, the hot-tempered head of Columbia studio. The other was Loretta Young, the actress I had found and named.

For several years, they had been on nonspeaking terms, because of an argument over clothes she had used in a picture and billed him for. It was a matter of a few hundred dollars which was peanuts to both of them, but the principle kept them apart and angry. I felt it was foolish, and if I could get them in the same room at the same time they could work it out. So I invited both of them to a party we were giving, without telling either the other would be there.

Harry arrived first and was chatting with some guests when Loretta walked in. She recognized him immediately, even though his back was toward her. As I had hoped, she decided that this was the time to put an end to the feud. She walked over to him and addressed his broad back.

"Harry," she said, "don't turn around. You know who this is. I just want to tell you that I was wrong about the dresses and you were right. I'm very sorry about the whole silly business. I hope you forgive me. If you do, turn around. If you don't, just stay where you are and I'll go home."

Harry stood in his back-turned position for a few seconds while we all held our breath. Then he slowly turned and there was a smile on his face.

"Loretta," he said, "that's the nicest thing anybody ever said to me."

The feud was over.

I spent several months, after I left MGM, just relaxing. We traveled, we entertained, we were guests at countless parties. I played golf, which is a game I enjoy, although Jack Nicklaus isn't losing any sleep over my competition. I went to the track and I did a lot of reading.

It wasn't long until I was eager to get back to work. I had worked all my life and I was not the type to loaf for very long—and I'm still not that type.

I was debating whether or not to call Jack Warner and tell him I'd like to discuss some picture ideas I had when the matter was taken out of my hands.

One Sunday morning, the phone rang. Jack Warner and Leland Hayward were calling. There was trouble, and they asked me if I could please give them a hand. The only thing was I would have to start shooting the very next morning.

11

J. EDGAR HOOVER:
I SPEAK FOR
EVERYONE HERE

John Ford had started making *Mister Roberts*, the film based on the New York stage success. After he had been working a week or so, something happened. I had heard he was ill, which was why Warner and Hayward had to make a change.

They called me that Sunday morning and then they came over to see me and brought the shooting script. They explained that Ford wouldn't be finishing the picture. Would I come in the next morning and take over? I said I would, and I stayed up all night to read both the script and the original stage play, which I had seen twice.

When I got to the studio, the next day, it was tough. Right away, there was a big scene. I looked at the rushes that Ford had shot and decided on some different approaches. The original play, as I had seen it in New York and read it the night before was far superior to the script Ford had been using. So I called the actors together and said we were throwing away the screenplay and going back to the Broadway play. Leland Hayward and Jack Warner went along with me.

The character William Powell was playing—"Doc"—had been changed by Ford. He had made him a drunk. I made him sober, as he had been in the original play.

There was a fine cast already assembled—Henry Fonda, James Cagney, Jack Lemmon, Powell, and young Nick Adams. They all pitched in to help me. It is never easy for a director to step into a

195

partially finished film, but this one was particularly tough, because of the short notice they had given me. It was tough, very tough—but it worked.

I would estimate that I shot 90 percent of the finished product. I insisted, however, that the credits read: "Directed by John Ford and Mervyn LeRoy." They told me it wasn't necessary to give Ford credit, but I felt it was a nice gesture to make.

That was the only time I ever shared directorial credit with anyone, although there was another picture that I split with someone else. In 1946, I had stepped in to reshoot much of a picture called *Desire Me*, which had been started by George Cukor. It starred Greer Garson and Robert Mitchum. They had a good cast but a rotten script, a script that made absolutely no sense. I tried my best to make something out of it, but I failed, just as Cukor had failed. Both of us insisted that our names not appear on the screen, and so the picture came out without any director listed at all. It was a botch, and Cukor and I have always been happy we were anonymous when it was released. It was the only major film ever issued without a director's credit.

Because of my stepping in for Ford, and because my actions might be misunderstood, I hired a press agent while *Mister Roberts* was shooting. I had never had a press agent before. I had always, before that, relied on the studio publicity departments to let the world know about me and my films, but in this case I wanted to be sure the record was kept straight. It is very easy for the public to get the wrong impression when one director takes over from another, and I didn't want that. So I retained the services of a bright young man named Arthur P. Jacobs, who subsequently became a producer—and a good one.

Mister Roberts was a smash hit, which made me happy. I couldn't help but feel that it was a personal triumph for me, since I had stepped into a sticky situation and had come out smelling like a gardenia.

So I went right into another film, *Strange Lady in Town*, which had a few problems. My stars were Greer Garson and Dana Andrews. In those days, Andrews had a drinking problem, which he has long since overcome. At the time, however, it made my life difficult. We were shooting in Arizona, so we were all away from home, and I guess that let down the inhibition barriers. It was a mess, but we got it done.

Possibly more serious was Greer Garson's health. She wasn't feeling well. She isn't the complaining sort, so when she said she felt poorly, I knew she must have felt rotten. We called the company doctor, and he got doctors from the Tucson Clinic for consultation. It was unanimous; she had appendicitis. The doctors agreed that she shouldn't wait, she really should have the appendectomy immediately.

"No," Greer said, with her redheaded stubbornness. "I can't do it now. There's an entire company depending on me. They'd have to shut down for a few weeks. It wouldn't be fair to them."

She's what they used to call a trouper. She told them that they had to keep her appendix in until the picture was finished. Every night, they piled ice bags on her abdomen. Every day, they fed her pills and the nurse was there, sticking a thermometer in her mouth between every scene. To make matters even rougher on her, we were shooting outside, in the hot Arizona sun, where it was always 130 degrees in the shade—but there wasn't any shade. Lesser people folded up, but Greer stuck it out, although every moment was torture.

We moved directly from the torrid zone of the Arizona desert up to the frigid climate of the Santa Susanna Pass for a few days of night-for-night shooting. We filmed for three days, and then came a Sunday, when we took a day off. Greer's husband, my pal Buddy Fogelson, was there, and he thought Greer was looking worse, so he insisted on calling a doctor. This man didn't take no for an answer; he had her in surgery within an hour and a half. The doctors told her that if she had waited another hour, her appendix would have ruptured. She and her appendix had gone as far as they could.

They give out medals for heroism, for people who rescue cats from burning buildings and push old ladies out of the way of trucks, and I think they ought to add a category for heroic performers. I'd nominate Greer Garson for the first of those awards. For the sake of a movie, she literally risked her life.

More pictures followed in staccato succession. Jack Warner had me going from one to another. That was fine with me; I had had enough of idleness.

There was *The Bad Seed*, taken from the Broadway play about the little girl who was a murderess. I had seen the play in New York, and told Jack I wanted to do it. I had him import virtually the entire New York stage cast, at a time when it was fashionable to pepper the marquee with big movie names for their box-office value. It just seemed to me that was a silly policy. I thought it made more sense, especially in this case, to use people who were ideally cast, who had had time to temper their roles, who were genuine actors and not merely screen personalities. So we had them all come out from New York—Patty McCormack, the talented little girl, and the adults, Nancy Kelly, Eileen Heckart, and Henry Jones, all standout actors.

The biggest problem I had with *The Bad Seed* was some foolishness from the Johnson Office, which had taken over as arbiters of film morals. They simply wouldn't okay the script if we stuck to the Broadway ending. On the stage, the girl got away with all her killings and, unrepentant, was playing "Claire de Lune" on the piano as the final curtain fell. Ordinarily, I go. along with their philosophical objection: In films that millions of innocents see, guilt should be punished. This time, however, we were dealing with a fable, not reality. The culprit here was not some hardened criminal, or even a soft criminal, but a child, and nobody could possibly take it seriously.

As proof of how the story didn't trouble children, I offer the following. Little Patty McCormack—and I think hers was one of the finest performances by a child actor ever put on film—was a sweet and unspoiled little girl. One day, I decided to see how the filming was affecting her.

"How do you feel," I asked her, "about playing a girl who kills people?"

"Oh, Mr. LeRoy," she said, "I'm having so much fun."

It was fun to her, and I felt it would be fun—scary fun, but fun—to the public. I couldn't budge the Johnson Office people, however. In those days, long before the rating system, there was no halfway about it. You couldn't bargain for an R or a PG. You either got a seal of approval or you didn't, and Jack Warner wasn't about to release a film without that seal. So we had to change the ending. John Lee Mahin dreamed up the idea of having the child killed by a bolt of lightning at the end. The Johnson Office gave us their official blessing when we showed them the revised script.

Then came *Toward the Unknown* with William Holden and Lloyd Nolan, and *No Time for Sergeants*, with most of the New York cast, including Andy Griffith and Myron McCormick. The one member of the Broadway company who wouldn't do it was Roddy McDowall. I begged him to be in the movie, but for some reason he said no, and he later told me he was sorry he didn't.

With McDowall out, I was able to use an actor I loved, Nick Adams. He was a fine boy, and his death was a terrible shock to me. People misunderstood Nick. Every nickel he made he sent to his brother, who was studying to be a doctor. As a result, Nick lived a Spartan life in Hollywood, where Spartan lives are exceedingly rare. So, whenever I could, I hired him. I had to fight for him on *No Time for Sergeants*, however, but I did fight and I won and he helped the picture enormously.

There was *Home Before Dark*, which I remember mostly for the weather we had to face, and for a silly accident. We shot most of it on location in and around Marblehead, Massachusetts, in the dead of winter. It was freezing cold. Rhonda Fleming was in it, and she was so cold that she actually couldn't speak—her tongue froze. She would have to go inside one of the houses on the street where we were filming and thaw out her tongue with a cup of coffee or hot chocolate before each scene. It was so cold that one night our cameras froze.

This was a film about insanity, and we shot in a real institution for the mentally ill, outside of Boston. Jean Simmons, our star and a fine actress, walked through the place to study the inmates. I couldn't do that; I tried, but I just could not stand to see those poor unfortunates.

We came back to Los Angeles and shot a scene in the Crystal Room of the Beverly Hills Hotel. The heat of our lights was so intense that it set off the room's sprinkler system and we all got soaked.

About this time I made another film that I'm extremely proud of: *The FBI Story* is one of my own favorites.

It was all authentic, down to the smallest detail. It had to be. In the first place, J. Edgar Hoover was a personal friend and I didn't want to jeopardize that friendship by doing anything that wasn't accurate—and, anyway, he wouldn't let me. He assigned two agents to be with us at all times, to make sure of the technical details.

We shot for five weeks in the FBI Building in Washington. It was an education for all of us; we learned the amazing things the bureau's laboratory technicians are capable of doing. Given the smallest, most insignificant clues. they can build an airtight case. I think that, in the FBI, we have the finest law enforcement agency in the world. Too many of us don't appreciate what we have. Hoover, who built the bureau almost singlehandedly, was one of our greatest men. If the real history of the FBI is ever written, it will show that J. Edgar Hoover did much to save the things about America we all hold most dear.

I was thinking about that one day, after the shooting was over.

Hoover hosted a small dinner party for us in his home, and I stood up and proposed a toast. I said that I thought he should run for the presidency. He shook his head vehemently.

"Mervyn," he said, "I'll run for nothing where you have to make a deal."

Sometime later, when Eric Johnston died, I was asked by someone on the Motion Picture Producers Association Board to approach Hoover on whether he would accept the presidency of the association. The offer was fabulous—two hundred thousand dollars per year, a lovely home in Washington, and many fringe benefits.

"No thanks," Hoover said without hesitation. "I'm dedicated to the FBI."

The actual filming of *The FBI Story* went smoothly. In our two stars, Vera Miles and James Stewart, a great American in his own right, we had two extremely able and cooperative actors, and they were both excellent.

When it was done, I was certain that I had a film that was not only commercially promising, but one that would bring credit to the FBI. I wanted to be sure about that, to be sure there was nothing in it that could possibly be embarrassing or damaging to the bureau. Hoover, his men, and their work were too important to my country to risk hurting them for the sake of profit. (Besides, he had insisted on okaying it before it was released.) So I arranged to screen it for Hoover and his top aides prior to its release to the public.

Jack Warner had me take a print to Washington, and they arranged a screening in the FBI's own little theater. I had shown many films to many tough audiences, but I was more nervous that night than at any other preview. The agents and Hoover filed in, and it seemed to me they looked pretty grim. I had made no compromises with the truth, but I worried as I watched them watch my picture. As it unfolded on the screen, I tried to eavesdrop but they weren't talking. It seemed to me that they didn't laugh where they were supposed to. When the lights came on again, the whole group turned and stared at me, and I thought I read condemnation on those tough and unsmiling faces.

Then Hoover stood up. I was certain I was about to be blasted.

"I think," he said, "that I speak for everyone here. Mervyn, we are all proud of you. It's a great film."

Then all those faces, which seconds before had seemed brutal, began smiling and they now appeared positively angelic. I laughed, in pure relief. They all came up to me and shook my hand. It was one of the happiest few minutes of my entire professional life. I was very proud when I was given a Distinguished Service Award plaque by the FBI, one of the few such honors the bureau has bestowed.

I was proud, too, of a letter I received from Don Whitehead, who had written the book the movie was based on.

Dear Mervyn—

You did a magnificent job on "The FBI Story." As the author, I'm very happy with the interpretation of the book and the picture's honesty, imagination and humor. I salute you.

Sincerely,
Don Whitehead

It hadn't been an easy picture to make. There were many changes in the script, made for security reasons. Everybody on the set, down to and including the carpenters, had to be passed on by the bureau. They made me shoot one sequence over, a crowd shot, because one man in the crowd had to be removed. They never did tell me what they had against the man, who was just an extra, but we had to do it all over again.

There is a curious postscript to the making of *The FBI Story*, which involves Jimmy Stewart. After he had finished shooting, he and his wife Gloria and their four children left for Europe. It was their first such trip. Hoover told them that he had arranged for his agents overseas to keep an eye on them. Wherever the Stewarts went, FBI men were there, to meet them at the plane and to help them. Jimmy got so experienced that he could spot the agent, even before the agent introduced himself. Eventually, the trip was over and they flew back to New York. There, as they deplaned, Jimmy spotted yet another agent, and went up to him.

"You must be with the FBI," he said.

"Yes, I am, Mr. Stewart," the agent said.

"Well, thanks for meeting us, but I think we can take care of things here ourselves," Jimmy said.

"Oh, I'm not here to meet you," the agent said. "I'm just here to keep an eye on a jewel thief we've been following. I want to make sure he stays on the plane until it gets to Los Angeles, where we'll pick him up."

The agent went on to say that Stewart might be interested in seeing a real-life jewel thief. He told him how to identify the crook.

"You can recognize him easily. He wears the biggest diamond stickpin you've ever seen."

When the Stewarts got back on board, Jimmy walked through the plane and there was the biggest diamond stickpin he had ever seen. It was being worn by a man Jimmy would have never cast as a thief, a very meek-looking fellow. When the plane landed in Los Angeles, the jewel thief was arrested very quietly by two FBI men.

The FBI Story was a huge success, both with the public and generally with the critics. I like good reviews as well as anybody else—it is always pleasant to read nice things about yourself—but I do not feel that they are vital to a picture's box-office success or failure. I have always felt that word of mouth is infinitely more important than reviews. When the man in the street wants to go out of an evening to see a movie, he is much more influenced by what he's heard at the office, or across the backyard fence, or in the corner bar, than he is by what he's read in his hometown newspaper. He knows that Joe or Peggy or Herman said that *The FBI Story* is a helluva movie, so he'll go to see it, no matter what the critics have written. If Joe or Peggy or Herman told him *The FBI Story* was a lousy movie, he wouldn't pay a dime to see it, no matter how highly the critics had praised it. For most people, going to the movies, especially in these days of such high prices, is a strain on the family budget. They want advice from their own kind of people, people they know have similar tastes, not from some critic who gets into all the movies free.

My own experience has been that reviews can't help a bad picture and can't hurt a good one. I have also found that there are certain films that critics appreciate much more than the public, and vice versa. The critics raved about films like *Another Part of the Forest* and John Cassavetes' *Husbands*, but the public found them unpalatable. Similarly, the critics generally disliked the old *Francis* series and, more recently, pictures like *Airport* and *The Poseidon Adventure*, but the public thoroughly enjoyed them.

I enjoy reading reviews, and I like good, honest criticism. Too many times, however, reviewers pick on some little detail that really has nothing to do with the film itself and base their entire review on that. I was incensed, for example, at a review of my film, *Gypsy*, by one New York writer. The review devoted most of its space to a comparison between Ethel Merman, who had done the musical on Broadway, and Rosalind Russell, who starred in our film version. The reviewer criticized Warner Brothers and me for using Miss Russell instead of Miss Merman, and said very little about the picture itself. Just for the record, Ethel Merman is a great talent and I love her and I've told her so many times, but I've also told her that the company used Roz instead because she meant more at the movie box office. I think she understands, but that's not the point. The point is that the reviewer didn't really review the picture, he (or I think it was a she) simply reviewed the decision to use Rosalind Russell instead of Ethel Merman. I do not believe that was the reviewer's function and, hence, the review was not an honest one.

As well as considering reviews relatively unimportant, I also feel that previews have their bad side, too. When we preview a film—sneak it to get an audience's reaction before releasing it—the stated goal is to find out a film's weak points and, if possible, correct them. The problem with this is that often the producer panics when he hears a few harsh words or adverse criticism. I have mentioned how we almost lost "Over the Rainbow" from *The Wizard of Oz* after a preview, and that kind of thing happens often.

Time after time, I've come out of a preview and listened while the studio brass has discussed chopping up a picture because of some bad remarks by the audience.

I've developed an expression to use at a time like that: "Let's not improve this into a flop."

How this works in practice is best illustrated by the story of *Mutiny on the Bounty*. This was produced by my friend Irving Thalberg, possibly one of the greatest producers who ever lived, even though he wouldn't allow his name to be on anything. One evening, Irving called me and asked me to come with him. They were sneaking *Mutiny* at Grauman's Chinese Theater in Hollywood, and he wanted my reactions to the film. There had been a lot of trouble with it during the shooting, and some of the earlier previews had resulted in changes in the film.

As we all gathered in the lobby after the preview, many of the MGM executives expressed reservations and said they thought there should be further changes. I waited for Thalberg to ask my opinion, but the question never came. I stood there like a fool.

We drove home together—at the time, we lived close together—and Irving invited me to drop over for breakfast the next morning. I said I would come, though I was upset that he hadn't asked me what I thought about his picture.

I went over to his house in the morning.

"Were you surprised that I didn't ask you what you thought about the picture last night?" Thalberg said.

"Damn right I was surprised. I couldn't sleep I was so surprised."

"Okay. I'm asking you now. If it was your picture, what would you do?"

"I'd ship it, just the way it is."

"That's what I thought you'd say," Thalberg said. "I'm going to do just that. I'm going to exhibit it just the way it played last night. I knew you agreed with me, and that's why I didn't ask you."

You have to be careful when you fool around with a finished film. To me, picture-making is a lot like watchmaking. Some brilliant mind has designed it to function well, to do its job. There are dozens of little parts, and each one of them fits in with the others, all the cogs and gears and springs and screws working together to make the watch do its job. Finally, there are the case and the strap, which compare to the stars in a movie—they are there for the ultimate eye appeal.

If you took a watch and previewed it, and somebody said that Scene 62 had to be changed, the whole thing wouldn't operate as smoothly. In movies, that's what happens. The brass decides that Scene 62 must be changed. The scene may be improved, but the total concept of the film is harmed.

We all work hard to make the picture the best we can possibly produce. From the time I started directing, I tried new techniques, experimented with new devices, tested new methods. When I began, long dissolves were the fashion. I speeded them up and, I think, helped the pace of motion pictures as a result.

I devised a style of shooting that has been copied by many directors since. I forget which picture I first used it in, but it worked well and I've been doing it ever since. It's a mechanical thing that may be difficult to understand for those who have never seen a movie being shot.

Generally, directors shoot what is called a master scene first. This is a long shot of all the action in a particular scene. They will then move in for close-ups of the actors as required. After they have finished all those close-ups, they will move on to the next master scene. What I do is shoot the master scene, then the close-ups, and then use one of those close-ups as the beginning of my next master scene. It improves the flow of the film, I believe, as well as making the mechanics of the shooting simpler.

A film has to have the stamp of one man, and that man should be the director. You cannot have art by committee. I will listen to suggestions from anybody, from the head of the studio down to the janitor, but the picture is my responsibility. My father used to say, "A fish smells from the head," and a picture takes it flavor from its director. The director who doesn't assert himself is finished. He must be the boss. If you start to let the actors direct, you are done for.

The director is the mainspring of the watch. The script is the hands; without them, there would be nothing. To me, the script is all-important. I could never begin a film unless the script was totally finished and as good as it could be. I often helped with the script writing, although I am not a writer. I felt, however, that I had good judgment of what was and wasn't a workable script. I'd often consult with other people, but I always made the ultimate decision myself, and relied on my own judgment.

It's such a team enterprise that everything is equally important. Art directors and set dressers, for example, have never gotten the credit they deserve. Without a believable set, the greatest words and the greatest acting talent cannot make a believable picture. Conversely, the most believable set cannot help if the acting is poor and the words shoddy. Nothing will help if the whole isn't photographed well with careful lighting. Every piece must fit together. That's what makes the art of the cinema so thrilling.

There are no rules in movie-making. I would frequently rehearse the next day's shooting before I left the set at night and then, as I drove to work the next morning, revise the whole concept in my head.

Thinking in visual terms is a natural talent. It can't be taught. I've done some teaching of cinema classes at the University of Southern California, and I've tried to explain that, but it's something someone either has or hasn't. If you cannot see what a scene should look like in your mind's eye, you can never get it to look right on the screen.

Education is important for everyone, obviously. A director, though, needs more than you can learn in books. I have often wished that I had had the opportunity for more formal education. I studied hard, but I know where I am still weak, and I envy my children their command of the language.

I've heard myself described often as "a self-made man." I'm not sure I know what that means. It's true that nobody ever gave me anything, but we are not alone on this planet. The man I've become is a product of what I've learned from observing, from watching, from listening, from the day-to-day experience of living. I must have learned something, otherwise people wouldn't have given me millions of dollars to make movies for them.

Self-made? Nobody is. I'm not. There were many who helped me along the way. Without them, I might still be selling newspapers in San Francisco.

As I grew older, I came to realize more and more the debt I owed to all those who gave me a hand. Like everybody else, I also came to appreciate the one gift that is the most significant of any God can bestow—health. There came a night when that was brought home to me forcefully.

12

FRANK SINATRA:
I'M COOKING A
SPAGHETTI DINNER

On January 28, 1962, the B'nai B'rith was giving a testimonial dinner to honor Walter O'Malley, the president of the Los Angeles Dodgers. Since O'Malley is a good friend, I was asked to be the master of ceremonies and I gladly accepted the assignment. It turned out to be a memorable and frightening evening.

At the time, I was shooting *Gypsy*, and I was very tired. The prospect of going out that night didn't seem too inviting. I have never liked getting up to speak—I suppose it's the haunting fear of my childhood stutter—and that, coupled with my exhaustion, made it all appear to be insurmountable. I took a tranquilizer for my nerves and a drink for my fear and then Kitty and I left for the Biltmore Bowl and the dinner. Once we arrived, I had another tranquilizer and another drink. Nobody had ever told me that alcohol and tranquilizers work against each other.

I was sitting next to Rosalind Wyman, who was then a Los Angeles city councilwoman.

"My legs feel a little funny," I said to her.

Afterward, Ruth Bridges, my secretary, told me she thought I looked a little gray as I sat on the dais. I felt a little gray, too, but I had a job to do. I introduced O'Malley, but I kept the introduction very short. Standing up, my legs felt rubbery, and I just wanted to sit down.

That's the last thing I remember. When I came around again, I was in an ambulance.

I had passed out cold, after I had made my introduction, and
I've always regretted spoiling O'Malley's big night. There were
more than a thousand people in the Bowl that night, and I'm told
they all screamed when I collapsed. Kitty and Tony Martin and
Edward G. Robinson were the first to reach me, and Ruth Bridges
and Dr. Robert C. Woods, who was a Dodger team physician, were
close behind. Woods gave me emergency treatment and Kitty
called for an ambulance.

They took me to Cedars of Lebanon Hospital. As the ambulance
sped through the streets, I opened my eyes. I smiled at Kitty and
O'Malley, who were riding with me.

"Don't tell anybody I fainted," I said. "I have to be on the set in
the morning."

It was only a faint, an old-fashioned swoon, brought about by
overexhaustion, coupled with the foolish intake of two drinks and
two tranquilizers. It made headlines in all the papers. The next day,
the Los Angeles *Herald-Examiner* printed a banner head:

MERVYN LEROY COLLAPSES
AT DINNER FOR O'MALLEY

At three o'clock in the morning, from my hospital bed, I issued
orders to Ruth about changing the next day's shooting schedule on
Gypsy. They wouldn't let me go to work that day, although I
wanted to. Dr. Elliot Corday checked me out thoroughly before I
was discharged. I missed that one day of filming—the only day I
ever took off from a picture because of illness.

I've always been careful about my health. Because of that, there
are those who accuse me of hypochondria. I guess it's hard to draw
the line: Where does being careful end and hypochondria begin? I
vehemently deny the charge that I am a hypochondriac. I just take
extremely good care of myself. Of course, my doctor, Robert C.
Wood, says he comes to my house if the drugstore is closed, because
I keep such a full supply of medicines.

My family and my friends like to tease me about my careful
health habits. They kid me because I soak my hand in hot water
when I get a hangnail—but I've never gotten an infection from
that, and I know of people who have had hangnails mushroom into
infections. Health is so important and, if you invest a little time in
taking care of your body, you can save a lot of trouble.

The day I was in the hospital, I was given a thorough examina-
tion. It turned out to be a good thing they did, because they discov-

ered that I had some polyps. At first, I didn't want to do anything about it, although the doctors felt I should have an operation.

Kitty accuses me of liking to see doctors, but only wanting to hear good news about myself. I suppose that's true of all of us. I had reached my sixties and I had never had any serious illness. I had never been under a surgeon's knife, so the prospect didn't thrill me. I went to many doctors, trying for a clean bill of health, but they all saw those same polyps and prescribed the same thing—surgery.

I imagine I would have continued to procrastinate about it, but Kitty and the O'Malleys tricked me, with the connivance of my son-in-law, Dr. Herbert Roedling. Walter and Kay O'Malley invited us to go to a ball game in Milwaukee, and then said, "Well, as long as we're so close, why don't we all go over to the Mayo Clinic for a checkup?" I wasn't one to poop out on a party, so I went along. The Mayo men confirmed the polyps diagnosis and said I should have the operation as soon as I lost twenty pounds. They gave me thirty days to lose that weight. I managed to drop seventeen pounds. It wasn't easy, because I never was very heavy.

By the time the month had rolled around, I looked like skin and bones. My clothes hung loosely. My face was drawn. I hadn't been sleeping too well, and that compounded the haggard appearance.

Bravely, I marched forward to the Mayo Clinic with Roedling at my side and presented myself to the surgeon. The operation was a success. When I came out of the anesthetic, O'Malley was sitting at my bedside.

While I convalesced, I noted that every morning a man would come into my room, look at me for a moment, and then walk out. I could tell he wasn't a medical man, but I had no idea what he was doing there. On the fourth day, I stopped him.

"Excuse me, sir," I said, "but I've been curious who you are, why you come in every morning to look at me, and yet never say anything."

"I'm from the FBI, Mr. LeRoy," he said. "Mr. Hoover has asked me to keep an eye on you and advise him of your condition."

When it was all over and I was back home, the operation took on a new light. Now it was something to brag about, and my surgical scar became a badge of courage, to be exhibited. Until it faded, I enjoyed showing it off to my close friends. It was very pretty.

Kitty enjoys telling the story about the time I was attacked by a mouse. It happened at our home in Palm Springs. We had gone down to open the house and I went into the kitchen to get a match, opened a drawer, and this mouse jumped out. I don't like mice, especially in my house. It was too late that day to call the exterminator. We went to bed and I woke up, early in the morning, with the distinct impression that a mouse was nibbling on my forehead. I opened my eyes and, sure enough, I caught sight of that same miserable mouse leaping down from the bed. I felt my forehead and there was something there, a scratch or a bite or something. I ran into the bathroom and daubed Mercurochrome over the wound.

"I've just been bitten by a mouse," I said, and thereby woke Kitty up.

She took one look at me and laughed.

"You look like an Indian," she said.

I called a doctor as soon as it was late enough. I didn't know what dangers might be inherent in a mouse bite. He said we had better catch the mouse and check it, to see if it was rabid. Kitty and I closed all the doors and windows and, with the help of our dog, cornered the mouse in a closet. We called an exterminator, who captured the varmint, put him in a cigar box, and took him to a veterinarian. He had to keep it and examine it daily, to look for signs of rabies.

Every morning, I'd call him.

"How's the mouse today?" I'd say, while Kitty chuckled.

Things went along nicely, with no signs of rabies, and then one morning the vet told me that the mouse had gotten out of its cage and escaped. For a few days, I was worried sick. What if the mouse was gone forever? I'd have to take that painful series of rabies shots. Then the vet said he'd recaptured the mouse.

"Are you sure it's the same mouse?" I asked.

"Oh, yes, sir, Mr. LeRoy," he said. "I know my mice. It's the same mouse all right. And I'm happy to report he's feeling fine."

The dangerous period went by, and the mouse stayed well, so I didn't have to take the rabies shots.

Being careful earns a person the reputation of being a worrier, and that's the tag some people apply to me. Once, William Powell sent me a gift. It was a cocktail shaker, and on it Bill had engraved: "FROM THE CHAMPION WORRIER OF ALL TIMES TO THE RUNNER-UP."

Worrying or, as I prefer to call it, being careful, is important when you're making a movie. Everything should be thought out and planned carefully—worried over—before you begin shooting. In 1961, I was called to Columbia to make a film called *The Devil at Four O'Clock*. That was the kind of movie that a nonworrier could have gotten into big trouble with. I worried it into a hit.

The film had been in the planning stage at the studio for several years. Spencer Tracy and Frank Sinatra were the stars, but they had problems getting a director to do it because it was terribly involved. A lot of money had already been invested, and both Tracy and Sinatra wanted me to come over and bail them out. I wasn't too anxious to do it, because the story wasn't anything special. I worked with Freddy Kollmar on the script, and we did what we could to whip it into some semblance of shape.

What made it a problem was that the climactic scene involved a volcano, and that's the kind of thing you have to worry about and plan for with extreme care. The effects turned out to be remarkable, because of that preplanning. It was done partly on a Hollywood sound stage, partly in the Hawaiian Islands. And we also used miniatures extensively. We built a mountain near La Jolla, on Gil Hodges' farm.

Mostly, though, we shot in Lahaina, on the Hawaiian island of Maui. We built a lovely set there—an entire village, complete with a street, a church, and even a jail. Even though we were shooting in one of the most beautiful places on earth, it was a tough picture. Of course, anything good is tough to do, and *The Devil at Four O'Clock* turned out well despite my initial reservations.

Tracy, at the time, was in good health. Katharine Hepburn was there constantly, and she kept a wary eye on him. She is a wonderful person. She never interfered with us in any way and never tried to offer any suggestions. She just watched Spence.

Tracy and Sinatra were two complete opposites. Frank wanted everything done in one take. Spence wanted to do every scene over and over and over again. I had to keep them both happy.

I had one brief flare-up with Sinatra. It happened one day when I told the cameraman I wanted another close-up of Frank.

"Do you really need a close-up?" Frank asked.

"Yes, I do."

"Well, I don't think we need it."

"I do," I said.

He did it, but you could tell his heart wasn't in it. We were scheduled to shoot until about seven that evening but, around five, he came to me and asked if he could go back to his hotel. I knew that it would be adding fuel to the fire if I insisted on him staying, so I said, "Sure, Frank, you can go."

When I got back to my room at the hotel, I found a note stuck under my door.

"I'm sorry," the note read, and it was in Sinatra's handwriting. "I was wrong. I'm cooking a spaghetti dinner for all of us."

So I went down to the dining room and the whole cast was there and we had a big time.

For me, one of the most delightful moments during the filming of *The Devil at Four O'Clock* came when Kitty planned a sixtieth birthday party for me. There were more than seventy people who got together in the Kula Lodge, high up on Haleakala, a Maui mountain. Sammy Cahn had done his parody thing, and Frank sang the lyrics Sammy had written. Then Tracy took over the microphone.

"Tonight," he said, "I welcome my good friend Mervyn LeRoy to a very exclusive club—the Sixty Club. I am a member. My friends Clark Gable, Jimmy Cagney, and Pat O'Brien are members, or will be very soon."

Then Spence looked over at Sinatra.

"And, Frank, let me tell you this. To get into the Sixty Club, it isn't enough that you look sixty, you have to be sixty."

It was a great night, climaxed when Frank sat on the piano bench, a drink in one hand and a cigarette in the other, and sang for almost an hour. What a great guy!

After *Devil*, I did a series of films based on Broadway hits—*A Majority of One*, with Rosalind Russell and Alec Guinness; *Gypsy*, with Rosalind Russell and Natalie Wood and Karl Malden; and *Mary, Mary*, with Debbie Reynolds, Barry Nelson, and Michael Rennie.

There was a big legal hassle with June Havoc over *Gypsy*. I had picked two young girls to play the two sisters—June and Gypsy Rose Lee—when they were young. What I didn't know was that June's contract gave her the right of approval of the actress who was to play Baby June. I had never seen that contract. She came on the set during rehearsals and raised hell. She said the girl we had was too old. In the script, she was supposed to be five and June wanted the girl to be exactly five years old, too.

I told her it would be impossible to get a five-year-old to play it right. We do that in pictures all the time, by using children of eight or nine who are small for their age and look younger. It's standard procedure. June wouldn't go for it. She screamed, she yelled, she said it was a breach of contract and threatened a lawsuit. The studio tried to settle with her for $25,000, but eventually paid her $125,000. I always thought it was a tempest in a teapot.

Gypsy Rose Lee was on the set very often, and she cried a few times as she watched her own life unfolding. She was a nice woman and never caused any trouble. When the picture opened, I got a letter from Gypsy thanking me profusely.

Natalie Wood was my first and only choice for the mature Gypsy, and she was excellent. At the time, she was going with Warren Beatty and he was on the set almost every day. Natalie's striptease was done in the days before Hollywood went on its "freedom" binge, so the strip was very decorous—Natalie never even took her bra off. Still, it was exciting and it raised the blood pressure of the male cinemagoer a few points when the film came out.

For me, making *Gypsy* was like going home again, since it dealt mostly with the old vaudeville days. I don't think that I was ever so emotionally involved in any movie I ever made.

One thing about the *Gypsy* cast I had forgotten until recently was the actor I hired for a two-day bit as a press agent. The actor we had picked originally took sick and we had to replace him under the gun. An agent sent over a young man, fresh from New York, and I had him read in my trailer-office on the set. He was fine and I hired him on the spot. He worked for two days, at $250 a day, and it was his first Hollywood job. That was Harvey Korman, who matured into a top television comic on *The Carol Burnett Show*.

There was one element of *Gypsy* I devised that I was very proud of. It was the first movie ever to open like a Broadway show, with the orchestra visible as it played the overture under the main titles. Jule Styne, who had written the music, conducted the orchestra.

And one thing about *Gypsy* amused me. In films, whenever you use a real product, the manufacturer is very happy. There's no advertising as effective as the use of a brand name in a motion picture. In one scene in *Gypsy*, my characters were eating candy bars. The prop man bought a bunch of Baby Ruth bars, since they were authentic to the period. The company sent me cartons of Baby Ruth bars from then on, until my office and my house were buried under candy bars. I had to write to them and plead with them to stop sending them.

Mary, Mary was based on Jean Kerr's big Broadway hit. We

worked hard on the script, to retain as much of the flavor of the original as we could. Miss Kerr, to whom we submitted the script, was grateful. She wrote me a long letter, containing some minor suggestions and expressing her appreciation for all the energy I had put into the script, and particularly my strenuous effort to keep it as close to the play as possible. I'm sorry that after all the blood, sweat, and tears, it didn't turn out as well as it should have.

I wanted to keep it that close because I felt that the play was a well-constructed gem. I wanted to use the Broadway star, too. That was Barbara Bel Geddes, who was just right for the character. But the Warner Brothers brass talked me into using Debbie Reynolds, and that was a mistake. I don't blame Debbie, I blame myself. Debbie was okay, but nowhere near as good as Barbara would have been. After all, Barbara had created the part. Although the finished film did well and was reasonably well received, I think it would have been immeasurably better if I could have used Barbara Bel Geddes.

If there was one criticism leveled against *Mary, Mary*, it was that it was a photographed stage play and, therefore, too static. In a sense, I agree. I wanted to open it up more, but that proved to be impossible. It was the kind of piece that had to be played in one room.

Then came *Moment to Moment*. My daughter, Linda, thought up that title. We shot it mostly in the south of France, and that made it very pleasant. My stars were that wonderful actress, Jean Seberg, with Honor Blackman, Arthur Hill, and a young man named Sean Garrison. Here again the casting hurt the film. Garrison wasn't strong enough for the part; it cried out for somebody like Paul Newman.

For some reason, *Moment to Moment* aroused the ire of an actor who was then very hot. Elliott Gould was quoted as saying he hoped he would never have to make a picture with me. I don't understand his anger—I have never even met the man, and I never want to work with him either. When his attack was printed, I kept my peace. It's foolish and childish to enter into a war of words in the public press, especially with actors. I did have a champion, however. Jean Seberg went to bat for me, and sent a letter to the editor of *Time* magazine, which had printed Gould's attack.

In her letter, Jean listed some of the pictures I had made and concluded: ". . . he is one of the gentlest, most civilized human beings around."

That made me very proud, because nice words from someone I

had worked with, who knew me, meant more than unkind words from someone I had never met could hurt.

With the conclusion of *Moment to Moment*, I still looked ahead. I was, as always, full of plans. I looked forward to the next few pictures I would direct. In fact, I had some properties picked out.

But I ran headfirst into a stone wall called "The New Hollywood."

13

JOHN WAYNE:
YOU'RE A PAL—
COME ON DOWN

If I ever wrote a book about Hollywood and its inner workings, I know what I could call it—*Insincere City*.

I like making movies, but I don't like the business end of the movie business. The cornerstone of the industry is jealousy, and the other ingredients are envy, mistrust, and greed. As you are making your way up the Hollywood ladder, most of the people are trying to hold you back. After you get to the top, they are hanging on, trying to make you fall. As you begin to drop down, they take infinite delight in giving you a helping push.

Everybody is out strictly for himself, and it matters little who he hurts in the process. I remember a fine director at Warner Brothers, who was making two thousand dollars a week and doing very respectably. He met an agent who told him that if he quit Warners, he would get him thirty-five hundred dollars at another studio. So the director quit. The agent could never deliver. Eventually, the director killed himself.

He had been conned, because of the greedy ambition of a worthless agent.

Walt Disney has never been honored by the motion picture industry since his death. I think he did more for children than any man who ever lived, and the industry he helped has not seen fit to pay him tribute.

Promises are made and not kept. Deals are made and then casually broken. A word, a handshake, a signature—none of them mean a thing. Try to help somebody, and they'll turn around to-morrow and give you a kick in the rear. People give you a pat on the back—trying to find a place to stab you.

I knew all this, of course, because over the years since I started in the business I had seen it all, seen all the sordid and sorry goings-on. Still, with my bright eyes shining naïvely, I fell into the trap.

I had left Warner Brothers after *Gypsy* and *Mary, Mary*, and I'd done *Moment to Moment* for MCA and Universal. I would have stayed at Universal, except for something that happened one day. Edward Muhl, then the studio's production head, called me in and said he had found a book he wanted me to do. He handed me a copy. It was called *The History of Los Angeles*.

"You want me to make a movie out of this?" I asked him. "Has it got a story?"

"Did that picture about San Francisco, with Spencer Tracy and Clark Gable, have a story?"

"You bet it had a story. That was about real people with a real love story and a great drama. Remember, that was set against the background of the San Francisco earthquake and fire. What's this about?"

He mumbled something about how it was all about Los Angeles and all the historical places, such as Olvera Street. Obviously, it wasn't a story at all; it was strictly nonfiction.

I went down to see Lew Wasserman, the head of the studio, and told him I was very unhappy. Muhl and I didn't think alike. I said I couldn't work with Muhl, that I just didn't belong at Universal. If they wanted a travelogue about Los Angeles, find somebody else to direct it.

Wasserman reluctantly let me go, but he said something very nice as we parted: "I won't say good-bye, Mervyn, because I know you'll be back."

I hated to leave Wasserman, but I knew I had to get away, so I left. I called Jack Warner and said, "Have you got room for me?" and he said, "Any time, Mervyn, any time," so I went back to Warners again.

At just about the same time I returned, however, Jack sold out. He was bought out by Seven Arts and Elliot Hyman. Hyman's son, Kenny, took over the operation of the studio. They were both fine men, and our association was a pleasant one. We were full of plans and projects. Helen Strauss, a literary agent, had brought a book, *Downstairs at Ramsey's*, to Kenny Hyman. I liked it, so they bought it, and we were working on the script. Kenny also wanted me to make a story he had always loved, James Thurber's *Thirteen Clocks*. I was very excited about it, feeling that in *Thirteen Clocks* I had the makings of another *Wizard of Oz*. We had a score written by Richard and Robert Sherman, the brothers who did *Mary Poppins* and *Tom Sawyer*, and a fine script by A. J. Carothers. The sets and costumes were in the works.

Something came up first, however. I had to help a friend. Duke Wayne was starring in and directing his own film, *The Green Berets*, at Fort Benning, Georgia. The studio called me in and told me they were worried that the two hats Duke was wearing were too many for him. They were afraid that being both star and director was too taxing on a film as big as *The Green Berets*.

They asked me if I would go down to Georgia and give Duke a hand for a few weeks.

"Well, okay, if it's only for a few weeks," I said. "And then only on one condition. That condition is that Duke asks me himself. He's a dear friend of mine, and I'll go only if he tells me he wants me."

I didn't want to be in the position of going down there and then finding that Wayne, good friend though he was, had been pressured into taking me, and really didn't want me. A few days later, I got a call from Duke.

"Mervyn," he said, "as a favor to me, please come on down and let's have a talk. You're a pal—come on down."

Elliot Hyman told me, before I left for Georgia, that I had a free hand with the picture. I could do anything with it I wanted—even close it down if I felt it should be closed down. I never even considered doing that, certainly not with such an important star and good friend as John Wayne. Besides, I wasn't even sure, before I left Hollywood, whether Duke really needed help.

When I got to Fort Benning, Duke and I had a long talk and straightened out the question of how I could help him. Then I took over and assisted Duke with the directing whenever he felt he needed me. Those few weeks turned out to be a lot more, however. I was on the picture, as it turned out, for five and a half months. I did it primarily to help Duke—after all, every director needs some assistance once in a while. I didn't do it for nothing, of course, but I wouldn't let them put my name on it, as I didn't think that would be fair to Duke.

When it was over, I went back to the Burbank Studio and resumed my work on *Thirteen Clocks*. Then I was planning on doing

Downstairs at Ramsey's, and maybe follow that with a project I had long wanted to do, a fantasy western called *Cowboys and Indians.* I was looking forward to all three films.

Then Seven Arts and Elliot Hyman sold the studio again. The old place was bought by a conglomerate—the Kinney Company—and a bunch of pinstripe suits took over. I met Ted Ashley and John Calley and all of them, and they gave me the class A treatment. They told me how much they were going to do for me. It was a time of hearty handshakes and toothy smiles and big fat promises.

"Of course, Merv, baby," they said (I should have known by that "Merv, baby" nonsense. Goldwyn, Thalberg, Mayer—the giants never talked like that). "Of course, Merv, baby. You keep working on those films. We're behind you one thousand percent."

So I kept working. Gradually, however, I sensed that something was wrong. It was almost impossible for me to get in to see Calley —he always seemed to be tied up with his personal friends. Ashley would see me, but still things weren't right. I could feel it, I could sense it. For many weeks, I kept working, but I began to get that horrible, sinking sensation.

At last, I insisted on an appointment with Calley. He was as hearty and as smiling as ever. I was right, though. There had been "a change in corporate thinking" or some such double-talk. They were just afraid that this wasn't the time for a fairy story. Sorry, but *Thirteen Clocks* was being canceled.

"What about your promises?" I said.

"We'll have to wait and see," Calley said.

I could tell that this was the end for me at that studio. I didn't have to wait and see. As quickly as I could, I packed up my things and moved out. The day I left, I made a date to see Ashley, who was always a gentleman. He stuck out his hand.

"I'm sorry you're leaving and I want to wish you luck, Merv," he said. "And I want you to know that there's nothing here at Warner Brothers you can't have. Just name it."

I turned away, quickly. It was sad, leaving the studio where I had done so much happy work. I'm not ashamed to say there was a tear in my eye.

The Green Berets was an old-fashioned picture, which means that the public liked it, even though the critics did not. Today, the motion picture scene has changed drastically. I think the decline in motion picture quality coincides directly with the decline in the major studios. Nowadays, movies aren't made by great creative minds, but by a cartel of businessmen on the one hand and a haphazard group of young and undisciplined rookies on the other. Today's films are made too fast and too dirty and cost either too much or too little.

There's nothing easier than writing a filthy story. It's a cinch. But try and write something like *Waterloo Bridge, Random Harvest, Gone with the Wind,* or *The Best Years of Our Lives,* and it's a lot tougher. There are some fine young writers on the scene today, but not nearly enough.

I admire directors like William Friedkin, who did *The French Connection,* and Norman Jewison, who made *The Russians Are Coming, the Russians Are Coming* and *Fiddler on the Roof.* But, as with writers, there just are not enough good young directors around.

Today, you'll find many of the best writers are in television, not motion pictures. It's understandable. They can make a better and steadier living in TV. Movies, today, are a great gamble. Television has some good directors, although here the story is somewhat different. Directors can work regularly in TV, but it's not a director's medium. TV directors are basically traffic cops, telling actors to go here or go there, and they have little time to be creative. Still, a family man often prefers a regular salary to creative opportunities, and hence many good directors work in the TV mines rather than wait for that one golden opportunity to make a movie.

As for producers, I don't think there are many today. Shortly before I left Warner Brothers, I was standing outside the studio's projection room one day. A young studio producer came over to me.

"Mr. LeRoy," he said, "will you do me a favor?"

"Sure, what's your problem?"

"Please tell me why they have two projectors in the projection booth."

I thought he must be kidding. I thought everybody—certainly everybody in the picture business—must know that all booths have two projectors so there will be no pause when they have to change over between reels. This fellow, a full-fledged producer, didn't know that basic movie fact.

"Well, I'll tell you," I said. "They have two because there's been a lot of thievery on the lot lately."

I kidded him for a few minutes and he believed me, but I finally told him the truth. I walked away from that encounter stunned to realize how naïve and ignorant he was—and he was a studio producer. To me, that was positive proof that many segments of the industry had fallen into the hands of incompetents.

Even actors have changed. Stars are different. The old crop— Rosalind Russell, Gloria Swanson, Greer Garson, Irene Dunne, Joan Crawford, Lana Turner—are still stars. They know how to dress and how to walk and how to project an image of magic. The big studios taught them. When they come into a room, it's as if a light were turned on. You don't have that kind of young star on the scene today. There are some very capable young actors and actresses, but they have as much magic about them as a package of bacon.

As soon as today's movie companies realize that you don't photograph the money, you photograph the story, maybe the business will have a renaissance.

I'll always be in the movie business. I still read everything I can, looking for a property worth doing. At one point, my old press agent-turned-producer, Arthur P. Jacobs, showed me a copy of a book he had bought. He had shown it to several others and nobody thought it would make a good film. I liked it and realized at once that it had tremendous possibilities. I became very enthusiastic, and we even had some sketches made of how it should look. I would have been happy to direct it, but I was expected to put up my own money, and these days that's too risky. The property was *Planet of the Apes*, and Jacobs says I was the first director to give him any encouragement. I wish he would have encouraged me back a little, because the *Apes* pictures have been huge successes.

So I still keep looking. Meanwhile, of course, I keep busy. There are always demands on my time, which is the way I like it. Once a year, I run a picture for the people at the Motion Picture Country Home, the old, retired movie folks. I go out there and talk to them, and it's a joy.

They have asked me to produce one of the Oscar shows again. That's a thankless job. The actors never show up for the rehearsals, for one thing. I know—I did five or six Oscar shows years ago, when they held them at the Cocoanut Grove.

Kitty and I are always going somewhere, doing something. Between our friends and our family, there don't seem to be enough days in the week to do everything we'd like to do.

I enjoy living. I enjoy my family. I enjoy my home. I enjoy California. I've been everywhere, and this is the place I love best. I enjoy my days at the track. I even enjoy my clothes. I remember back to my youth, when a pair of shoes had to last a couple of years, and then I look in my closet and I realize that I have more shoes than I have socks.

Of all the things I enjoy, however, working is the most pleasurable. I have never given even a passing thought to retirement. When a man has led as full and exciting a life as I have, the idea of quitting and doing nothing is anathema. I wouldn't know what to do with myself if I retired. Age is no barrier to the quality of a man's work—George Bernard Shaw turned out some great things when he was in his eighties, and many directors older than I am are still turning out good films. Work is my joy, and I'm still at it. You're as old as you think, and I've never thought, or felt, over thirty-five.

Writing this book has forced me to take stock of myself. It's been a long life and a full one. I believe I am able to make a few statements with positive pride:

I have made some motion pictures that have brought pleasure to millions.

I've never hurt anybody in my life.

Being born with a wooden spoon in my mouth was a great break; kids who have it too easy don't have the incentive and the drive to prove that they have something to offer, that they are as good as, or maybe better than, the next guy.

Vaudeville was a wonderful place to learn.

Starting with silent films was another great break, because it enabled me to experiment.

The most important thing in life is to have love in your life—the love of a good wife, of fine children, of good friends.

All things considered, I think it's been a great life. I wouldn't change places with anybody. My feeling is that I was blessed in so many ways that, when I finally reach Saint Peter's office, I'll have to spend my first few centuries just thanking him.

Of all my blessings, however, I believe the choicest—outside of having a wonderful family—was the chance to make motion pictures. Has there ever been such a challenging, exciting, daring career as that of a movie director? You take some words on paper, a camera loaded with strips of celluloid, a group of actors, some lights and props and sets and costumes, and from all that you create—what? Just some shadows that dance on a screen and hold millions of people enthralled.

I think movies are the most complete art form the world has ever known. I use the word "complete" purposely. Movies, when they are well done, combine the literary quality of a fine novel, the visual artistry of a great painting, the drama inherent in a wonderful play, often the majesty of lovely music. Nothing the world has ever seen comes close to motion pictures in combining so many different skills into one entirely new entity.

I love motion pictures, and I always will. I am sure they will survive the recent rash of less-than-perfect films. It is understandable that young film-makers experiment; they are artists, and artists, in whatever medium, should try new things. I did my share of experimenting, and I hope to do more. The tragedy, to me, is that most of today's young film-makers are experimenting in the area of content, rather than form. They are playing around with stories that are pornographic and violent and, in my opinion, do not advance the art of motion pictures one iota. I'd like to see more new things tried in the *method* of filming, not in the *content*. To my way of thinking, a motion picture has one primary purpose: to entertain. If it doesn't entertain, it has failed. Within that guideline, experiments are valuable, but the trouble is too many directors today ignore that guideline. They make movies that puzzle and offend and confuse the audience, but do not entertain them.

I hope they will eventually come back to the basics, to solid entertainment. Let them experiment to their heart's content—new camera angles, new lighting techniques, new types of sets or makeup or whatever—but let them stick to telling a comprehensible story with warmth and feeling, in a straightforward and simple manner. That, after all, is what it is all about.

If that happens—and I'm sure it will—the movie industry will go on to greater glories. Building on yesterday's accomplishments with today's technological improvements should make tomorrow's movies greater than ever.

That bright and shining tomorrow cannot happen, however, unless we get some fresh, clean, new blood in the business. I am shocked and offended by some of today's directors and, even more, by most of today's producers. To be blunt about it, they haven't the foggiest concept of what their jobs entail. They apparently think that they make movies to impress their friends, or a small group of artsy-craftsy New York critics, or a minority of moviegoers who seem to equate bafflement with art. Just because a movie makes no sense, these in-groups consider it masterful. Many of today's films are that sort—nobody understands them but the men who made them, and I'm not too sure about them. They get raves from a few critics who are, I think, afraid to admit they don't understand them. And a few thousand followers dutifully profess to see wonders in them. The vast majority of the public, however, naturally stays away. To me, that's not what movie-making is all about.

We in the motion picture industry have an obligation to make films that the public enjoys—maybe they cry, maybe they laugh, maybe they gasp, maybe they sing. We are not here to play with ourselves, to see how obscure we can get, to try to confuse the people. We are here to entertain as many people as we can. Anything less, and we have failed.

But this business of entertaining is a narrow line between the obscure on the one hand and the prurient, ultraviolent on the other. Porno films make millions, but I would be ashamed to take the money if I had made them. Our obligation to entertain encompasses a real responsibility not to pander to the lowest instincts in man.

Happily, there is a vast middle ground and that is where we should make films. I think we are gradually getting back there. The public is tiring of the storyless, senseless films on the one hand, and getting disgusted with the sex-oriented, violence-oriented films on the other. When good entertainment films—like *Love Story, Cabaret, Airport, The Poseidon Adventure*—are released, the box-office figures indicate how the public is hungry for them.

In all this current talk about how bad things are for movies, one factor is frequently overlooked. That is that the audience is there, waiting, eager, anxious to be entertained with something more than television can provide. If we in the industry give them something they want to see, they will get off their sofas and go out to buy tickets.

This has nothing to do with the cost of a film. There are many excellent low-budget movies. Don't be impressed by reports of how costly a film is. You don't photograph the money, you photograph the story.

We're getting there, getting back to good, solid entertainment on film. The future could be brilliant, beyond our fondest dreams. It only takes the desire and the people to implement that desire.

I plan to be part of that exciting future. I'm still doing what I have always done—looking for good properties, for stories worth filming. They're pretty scarce these days, but I'll find one. I'm a patient man, and I'll keep on looking, searching for the right property.

I'm sure I'll find one tomorrow.

FILMOGRAPHY
OF MERVYN LEROY

1928

No Place to Go
First National. Director. With Lloyd Hughes and Mary Astor.
Harold Teen
First National. Director. With Arthur Lake and Alice White.
Flying Romeos
First National. Director. With George Sidney and Charlie Murray.
Oh, Kay
First National. Director. With Colleen Moore and Lawrence Gray.

1929

Naughty Baby
First National. Director. With Alice White.
Hot Stuff
First National. Director. With Louise Fazenda and James Cagney.
Broadway Babies
First National. Director. With Alice White and Charles Delaney.

1930

Little Johnny Jones
First National. Director. With Eddie Buzzell.

Playing Around
First National. Director. With Alice White.
Numbered Men
First National. Director. With Conrad Nagel and Bernice Claire.
Too Young to Marry
First National. Adapted from *Broken Dishes*. Director. With Loretta
　　Young and Grant Withers.
Top Speed
First National. Director. With Joe E. Brown and Bernice Claire.
Showgirl in Hollywood
First National. Director. With Alice White and John Drie.
Little Caesar
First National. Director. With Edward G. Robinson, Douglas Fair-
　　banks, Jr., and Glenda Farrell.

1931

Gentlemen's Fate
MGM. Director. With Alice White, John Gilbert, and Louis
　　Wolheim.
Tonight or Never
United Artists. Director. With Gloria Swanson and Melvyn Douglas.
Local Boy Makes Good
First National. Director. With Joe E. Brown.
Five Star Final
First National. Director. With Edward G. Robinson and Aline
　　MacMahon.
I Am a Fugitive from a Chain Gang
Warner Brothers. Director. With Paul Muni, Edward Ellis, and
　　Helen Vincent.

1932

Heart of New York
Warner Brothers. Director. With Smith & Dale, George Sidney, and
　　Aline MacMahon.
Elmer the Great
First National. Director. With Joe E. Brown, Mike Frankovitch,
　　Eleanor Holm, and Jane Wyman.
Three on a Match
First National. Director. With Bette Davis, Ann Dvorak, Joan
　　Blondell, and Warren William.

The World Changes
First National. Director. With Paul Muni and Aline MacMahon.
High Pressure
Warner Brothers. Director. With William Powell, Ann Dvorak, and
 George Sidney.
Big City Blues
Warner Brothers. Director. With Humphrey Bogart.
Two Seconds
First National. Director. With Edward G. Robinson and Preston
 Foster.

1933

Hard to Handle
Warner Brothers. Director. With James Cagney and Helen Winsor.
Golddiggers of 1933
Warner Brothers. Director. With Ginger Rogers, Warren William,
 Joan Blondell, and Ruby Keeler.
Tugboat Annie
MGM. Director. With Marie Dressler and Wallace Beery.

1934

Hi, Nellie
Warner Brothers. Director. With Paul Muni.
Heat Lightning
Warner Brothers. Director. With Preston Foster and Aline Mac-
 Mahon.
Happiness Ahead
First National. Director. With Dick Powell and Josephine Hutchin-
 son.

1935

Oil for the Lamps of China
First National. Director. With Pat O'Brien and Josephine Hutchin-
 son.
Sweet Adeline
Warner Brothers. Director. With Irene Dunne, Harold Woods, and
 Wini Shaw.
Page Miss Glory
Warner Brothers. Director. With Marion Davies and Dick Powell.

1936

Three Men on a Horse
Warner Brothers. Director. With Frank McHugh, Sam Levene, and Joan Blondell.
Anthony Adverse
Warner Brothers. Director. With Fredric March, Anita Louise, Olivia de Havilland, and Claude Rains.

1937

They Won't Forget
Warner Brothers. Director. With Claude Rains, Lana Turner, Gloria Dickson, and Edward Norris.
The King and the Chorus Girl
Warner Brothers. Director. With Fernand Gravet and Joan Blondell.
The Great Garrick
Warner Brothers. Producer. Directed by James Whale. With Brian Ahern and Olivia de Havilland.

1938

Fools for Scandal
Warner Brothers. Director. With Fernand Gravet and Carole Lombard.
At the Circus
MGM. Producer. Directed by Edward Buzzell. With the Marx Brothers and Margaret Dumont.
Stand Up and Fight
MGM. Producer. Directed by W. S. Van Dyke. With Robert Taylor and Wallace Beery.

1939

The Wizard of Oz
MGM. Producer. Directed by Victor Fleming. With Judy Garland, Ray Bolger, Bert Lahr, Jack Haley, and Frank Morgan.

1940

Waterloo Bridge
MGM. Director. With Vivien Leigh and Robert Taylor.

Escape
MGM. Director. With Norma Shearer, Robert Taylor, and Alla Nazimova.

1941

Blossoms in the Dust
MGM. Director. With Greer Garson and Walter Pidgeon.
Johnny Eager
MGM. Director. With Lana Turner, Robert Taylor, and Van Heflin.
Random Harvest
MGM. Director. With Greer Garson and Ronald Colman.

1943

Madame Curie
MGM. Director. With Greer Garson and Walter Pidgeon.

1945

Thirty Seconds Over Tokyo
MGM. Director. With Van Johnson and Spencer Tracy.
The House I Live In
RKO. Academy Award Winner (1945). Producer with Frank Ross. Directed by Axel Stordahl. With Frank Sinatra.

1946

Without Reservations
RKO. Director. With Claudette Colbert and John Wayne.

1947

Homecoming
MGM. Director. With Clark Gable and Lana Turner.

1948

Little Women
MGM. Producer and Director. With June Allyson, Mary Astor, Janet Leigh, Peter Lawford, Margaret O'Brien, and Elizabeth Taylor.

1949

Any Number Can Play
MGM. Director. With Clark Gable and Alexis Smith.
East Side, West Side
MGM. Director. With James Mason and Van Heflin.

1950

Quo Vadis
MGM. Director. With Robert Taylor and Deborah Kerr.

1951

Lovely to Look At
MGM. Based on Jerome Kern's musical play *Roberta*. Director.
    With Kathryn Grayson, Red Skelton, Howard Keel, and Marge
    and Gower Champion.

1952

Million Dollar Mermaid
MGM. Director. With Esther Williams and Victor Mature.
Latin Lovers
MGM. Director. With Lana Turner, Ricardo Montalban, and John
    Lund.

1953

Rose Marie
MGM. Producer and Director. With Howard Keel and Kathryn
    Grayson. Musical numbers by Busby Berkeley.

1954

Mister Roberts
Warner Brothers. Director. With Henry Fonda, Jack Lemmon,
    James Cagney, and William Powell.
Strange Lady in Town
Warner Brothers. Producer and Director. With Greer Garson, Dana
    Andrews, and Cameron Mitchell.

1955

The Bad Seed
Warner Brothers. Producer and Director. With Nancy Kelly, Patty
McCormack, Eileen Heckert, and Henry Jones.

1956

Toward the Unknown
Warner Brothers. Producer and Director. With William Holden and
Lloyd Nolan.

1957

No Time for Sergeants
Warner Brothers. Producer and Director. With Andy Griffith and
Nick Adams.

1958

Home Before Dark
Warner Brothers. Producer and Director. With Jean Simmons, Dan
O'Herlihy, Rhonda Fleming, and Efrem Zimbalist, Jr.
The FBI Story
Warner Brothers. Producer and Director. With James Stewart and
Vera Miles.

1959

Wake Me When It's Over
20th Century-Fox. Producer and Director. With Ernie Kovacs,
Margo Moore, Jack Warden, and Dick Shawn.

1960

The Devil at Four O'Clock
Columbia. Producer and Director. With Spencer Tracy and Frank
Sinatra.

1961

A Majority of One
Warner Brothers. Producer and Director. With Rosalind Russell and
Alec Guinness.

1962

Gypsy
Warner Brothers. Producer and Director. With Rosalind Russell, Natalie Wood, and Karl Malden.

1963

Mary, Mary
Warner Brothers. Producer and Director. With Debbie Reynolds, Barry Nelson, and Michael Rennie.

1965

Moment to Moment
Universal. Producer and Director. With Jean Seberg, Honor Blackman, and Sean Garrison.

INDEX